The Early Modern Town in Scotland

The Early Modern Town in Scotland

Edited by Michael Lynch

CROOM HELM

London • Sydney • Wolfeboro, New Hampshire

© 1987 (excluding chapter 2) Michael Lynch,
(chapter 2) Mary Verschuur
Croom Helm Australia, 44-50 Waterloo Road,
North Ryde, 2113, New South Wales
Croom Helm Australia Pty Ltd, Suite 4, 6th Floor,
64–76 Kippax Street, Surry Hills, NSW 2010, Australia

British Library Cataloguing in Publication Data

The Early modern town in Scotland.
  1. Cities and towns — Scotland — History
  — 16th century 2. Cities and towns —
  Scotland — History — 17th century
  I. Lynch, Michael *1946 June 15 –*
  941.1′009′732   HT133

  ISBN 0 – 7099 – 1677 – 9

Croom Helm, 27 South Main Street,
Wolfeboro, New Hampshire 03894-2069, USA

Library of Congress Cataloging-in-Publication Data

The Early modern town in Scotland.

  Includes index.
  Bibliography: p.
  1. Cities and towns — Scotland — History. I. Lynch,
Michael, 1946-
HT145.S35E27 1987   307.7′6′09411   86-24160
ISBN 0-7099-1677-9

The Publisher acknowledges subsidy from the Scottish Arts Council
towards the publication of this volume.

313903

Photoset by Pat and Anne Murphy
Highcliffe-on-Sea, Dorset, England
Printed and bound in Great Britain
by Billing & Sons Limited, Worcester.

Contents

List of Figures and Tables

Figures

Tables

Conventions and Abbreviations

With dates the year is taken to have begun on 1 January (which it did in any case in Scotland from 1600). All sums of money are given in £ Scots, worth about 3:1 sterling in 1450, 4.5:1 in 1560 and 12:1 by 1603, unless otherwise stated; a merk was two-thirds of a £. The abbreviations used for sources are those recommended in *List of Abbreviated Titles of the Printed Sources of Scottish History to 1560* (Scottish Historical Review supplement, 1963). Full details of a secondary source are normally given the first time it is cited in each chapter. The following are the abbreviations most commonly used.

Abdn. Recs.	*Extracts from the Council Registers of the Burgh of Aberdeen*, ed. J. Stuart (Spalding Club, 1844–8 and SBRS, 1871–2)
ACA	Aberdeen City Archives
ACL	*Aberdeen Council Letters*, ed. L. B. Taylor, 4 vols. (Oxford, 1942–54)
Acts of Council	*Acts of the Lords of Council in Public Affairs, 1501–1554: Selections from Acta Dominorum Concilii*, ed. R. K. Hannay (Edinburgh, 1932)
APS	*The Acts of the Parliaments of Scotland*, ed. T. Thomson and C. Innes (Edinburgh, 1814–75)
Burghs Conv. Recs.	*Records of the Convention of the Royal Burghs of Scotland*, ed. J. D. Marwick (Edinburgh, 1866–90)
CSP Scot.	*Calendar of State Papers and Manuscripts relating to Mary, Queen of Scots, 1547–1603*, eds. J. Bain *et al.* (Edinburgh, 1898–1969)
ECA	Edinburgh City Archives
Edin. Recs.	*Extracts from the Records of the Burgh of Edinburgh, 1403–1589*, 5 vols., ed. J. D. Marwick (SBRS, 1869–92), and *1589–1665*, 5 vols., ed. M. Wood (Edinburgh, 1927–40)
ER	*The Exchequer Rolls of Scotland*, eds. J. Stuart *et al.* (Edinburgh, 1878–1908)
Glasgow Recs.	*Extracts from the Records of the Royal Burgh of Glasgow*, 4 vols., ed. J. D. Marwick and

	R. Renwick (SBRS, 1876–1909)
HMC	Historical Manuscripts Commission
Peebles Recs.	*Extracts from the Records of the Burgh of Peebles, 1652–1714* (SBRS, 1910)
Pitcairn, *Criminal Trials*	*Criminal Trials in Scotland from 1488 to 1624*, ed. R. Pitcairn (Edinburgh, 1833)
RCAHMS	Royal Commission on the Ancient and Historical Monuments of Scotland
RMS	*Registrum Magni Sigilli Regum Scotorum*, ed. J. M. Thomson *et al.* (Edinburgh, 1882–1914)
RPC	*The Register of the Privy Council of Scotland*, ed. J. H. Burton *et al.* (Edinburgh, 1877–)
RSS	*Registrum Secreti Sigilli Regum Scotorum*, ed. M. Livingstone *et al.* (Edinburgh, 1908–)
SBRS	Scottish Burgh Records Society
SHR	*Scottish Historical Review*
SHS	Scottish History Society
SRO	Scottish Record Office, Edinburgh
SRS	Scottish Record Society
Stirling Recs.	*Extracts from the Records of the Royal Burgh of Stirling, 1519–1666*, ed. R. Renwick (Glasgow, 1887)
TA	*Accounts of the Lord High Treasurer of Scotland*, ed. T. Dickson and J. Balfour Paul (Edinburgh, 1877–1916)

Notes on the Contributors

James J. Brown completed his doctoral thesis at Edinburgh University in 1985 and is currently revising it for publication.

Keith M. Brown is British Academy Fellow in the Department of Scottish History, University of St Andrews. He completed his doctoral work in Glasgow University in 1983 and is the author of *Bloodfeud in Scotland, 1573–1625* (Edinburgh, 1986).

Winifred Coutts completed her research at Edinburgh University in 1982. She teaches in Edinburgh.

Michael Lynch is lecturer in the Department of Scottish History, Edinburgh University, author of *Edinburgh and the Reformation* (Edinburgh, 1981) and editor of the journal, *The Innes Review*.

Walter Makey is Edinburgh City archivist and the author of *The Church of the Covenant, 1637–1651* (Edinburgh, 1979). He is currently engaged on writing a general history of Edinburgh.

David Stevenson is the author or editor of a number of works on seventeenth-century Scotland, including *Revolution and Counter-Revolution in Scotland, 1637–1651* (London, 1977) and *Government under the Covenanters, 1637–1651* (SHS, 1982). He is reader in the Department of History, Aberdeen University and editor of the journal, *Northern Scotland*.

Mary B. Verschuur completed her doctoral thesis at Glasgow University in 1985 and is currently engaged on writing a history of sixteenth-century Perth. She teaches in Ohio.

Allan White o.p. completed his doctoral work at Edinburgh University in 1985 and is currently engaged on writing a book on Aberdeen in the sixteenth century.

Ian D. Whyte is author of *Agriculture and Society in Seventeenth Century Scotland* (Edinburgh, 1979) and numerous articles on rural society; he co-edited *An Historical Geography of Scotland* (London, 1983). He is senior lecturer in the Department of Geography, Lancaster University.

1

Introduction:
Scottish Towns 1500–1700

Michael Lynch

In the sixteenth century the sources for the study of urban history in Scotland suddenly blossom. It is normal by then to find new and substantial urban archives, with some combination of council minute books, burgh court books, accounts of town treasurers or deans of guild, burgh registers of deeds or notarial protocol books, tax rolls and even, on occasion, a muster roll. It is, however, one of the curiosities of Scottish urban history that few extra questions have been asked of the range of new evidence usually available after about 1500,[1] and fewer still have been satisfactorily answered. In contrast in the study of the early medieval burgh, where documentary evidence had long since been taken to its cultivation limits, historians have been obliged, with profit, either to turn to other disciplines — such as archaeology — for advice or to ask fresh questions of the limited evidence available. Our understanding of the twelfth-century burgh has been transformed by rigorously applying to it the notion of the market.[2] The same has yet to be done for the sixteenth or early seventeenth-century burgh. It is important from the outset to understand, however, that although a number of questions can successfully be asked of the evidence, there are others which, given the nature of the evidence available in this period for Scottish towns, are probably unanswerable. It is difficult to examine the notion of a decay of towns in the late medieval period in the virtual absence of tax rolls before 1535; the motor of immigration in increasing town populations is virtually undetectable before the 1690s, except for a few scraps of evidence such as a stray reference to 'Highland boys' in Glasgow in the winter of 1649–50 or the use of such flimsy techniques of inquiry as the appearance in the record of non-local

1

surnames; and the prospect of a detailed study of the occupational structure of towns is remote, both because of the pervading presence of the unspecialised general merchant and the scarceness, with a few exceptions,[3] of detailed tax records before the hearth and poll taxes of the 1690s.

There has recently been a great deal of research focused on a range of individual towns, especially between 1450 and 1640. Attention has drifted away from institutional urban history, which predominated the thinking of several generations of burgh historians, to the psephological, from the narrowly financial to the political in broad aspect. The institution of the merchant guildry, which long provided the common thread in much burgh history, has had its doors flung open to expose, in fifteenth-century Perth and Dumfermline and sixteenth-century Edinburgh, craftsmen inside it in numbers as well as merchants;[4] the scrutiny of burgh accounts has given way to questions about the effects on urban society itself and its relations with the outside world of much more taxation. Since much of this work has been concentrated on the habits of urban rulers in the century of the Reformation, new ambiguities have emerged to complicate and, arguably, make more plausible our knowledge of the response to the Reformation: Catholics have been found acting as elders of the new Calvinist kirk session of Aberdeen in the 1560s; a Protestant dean of guild, who numbered among his duties the upkeep of the burgh church, was in charge of the Catholic cult of Edinburgh for much of the 1550s.[5]

The impact of this kind of research on the more general history of Scotland has, however, been uneven. It has tended to cluster around the Reformation, with four recent theses on the largest towns, but has conspicuously avoided the Scottish Revolution of the 1640s. The Restoration period has been largely neglected, except for work on Glasgow. This has been crucial to our under-standing of the changing patterns of Scottish overseas trade in the period and an important shift, after 1660, in the economy,[6] but it has also probably exercised an undue influence on the thinking and approach of historians to other towns in that century. The argument that Glasgow's rise in the seventeenth century was largely due to the fact that it was, in many respects, exceptional[7] has, by its very nature, yet to be proved — by a deeper scrutiny of other towns. Different insights may result if the angle of the lens of the microscope on the early modern town is altered from the perspective of the century after 1660 to that of the century before 1640 or that before 1560. One of the propositions contained in this collection is that the early seventeenth century saw a volume of overseas trade and a concentration of wealth and credit in the hands of urban merchants which was greater than later in the century. The significance of the Restoration period thus may lie less in the abandonment of the restrictive features in the institutions and structure of the medieval burgh, as many argue, as in the notion that it was a partial recovery from the mid-century crisis of the Wars of the Covenant.

There has as yet been a natural tendency, apart from in the work based on the wide-ranging evidence which suddenly becomes available in the 1690s, for urban historians of this period to confine their researches to single towns. There has been only one recent study of a craft occupation[8] but this, because it deals with one of the smallest and humblest of the guilds, has little light to shed on general occupational patterns. More could be done to consider various groups — ranging from lawyers to metal or textile workers or the poor — within urban society as a whole. Most work has concentrated on the merchants and it has revealed that a Scottish mercantile community in a real sense did exist by 1600,[9] with wide-ranging contacts between different towns and established patterns of business practice. This, in a sense, was not surprising since it is one of the distinctive features of Scottish towns, or at least of the royal burghs, that they did collectively form an urban voice in politics. They were distinctly more integrated into the community of the realm than was the case in England and this made for an extra set of pressures working on them in this period, when the crown began to make many more demands of them. The expectations of the burghs, too, were rising in the later sixteenth century and their social structure was already becoming much more complex. The net result of all these changes was that the burghs probably had a greater impact on Scotland as a whole in the seventeenth century than in any previous one.

It is for this reason that this collection has as one of its aims an effort to integrate the history of urban Scotland into the new thinking, both about government and the other localities, which has so notably marked out the history of early modern Scotland in recent years. It numbers among its authors some who would not regard themselves as urban historians but who have much to say about the wider world with which the burghs had to deal. The volume's other two aims are simply stated. It is an attempt to draw together the threads of recent research, some of it recent indeed, in what are seen to be the most important areas of inquiry. It is also, it should be said, far from the last word on the subject but it may help set the agenda for future research.

By the middle of the fourteenth century the burghs of Edinburgh, Aberdeen, Perth and Dundee were recognised as 'the four great towns of Scotland'. The evidence of customs returns for the 1370s confirms their pre-eminence, even if Perth and Dundee were then only narrowly ahead of towns like Linlithgow and Haddington, which had also enjoyed a brief stimulus at the expense of Berwick after its loss to the English in 1334. One of the most obvious, but least recognised, facts of Scottish urban history is the length of time which these four burghs held and consolidated this position. In the 1370s they accounted for 58 per cent of the customs paid in the export trade; in the period 1460–1600, they averaged 80 per cent and their share was increasing almost throughout — despite at least three catastrophic falls in exports, in the 1320s, 1420s and 1540s, and a series of shifts in the patterns of trade.[10] In 1535 their combined share of the national taxation paid by the burghs amounted to 51.5 per cent; in 1583 it was 54.5 per cent and in 1613 53.66 per cent. It was only in 1649 that the ranking of the four top burghs was disturbed, when Glasgow finally rose from fifth place, where it had lain since 1594, to displace Perth. By the next reassessment, in 1670, Glasgow had sharply risen to overtake both Aberdeen and Dundee as well. By 1697 the overall picture had changed as markedly as the ranking of the largest burghs: 55 per cent of taxation was paid by just two burghs — Edinburgh and Glasgow — rather than four. Edinburgh, of course, still predominated — and increased its lead in the 1690s over Glasgow and all other burghs — paying no less than 40 per cent of taxation.[11] The break in the stranglehold of the four east-coast regional centres over the Scottish urban economy is as good an indicator as any of the fundamental shift — in patterns of trade and urban wealth — which took place in the second half, and especially in the last quarter, of the seventeenth century. By then, Scottish urban history had become largely a tale of two cities;[12] but for the previous three centuries, ever since the loss of Berwick until well into the seventeenth century, it had been dominated by the same four burghs.

This is a different way of looking at the evidence of the series of tax rolls, which begin only in 1535, giving the percentage paid by each royal burgh. They have often been used to demonstrate the inexorable rise of Glasgow, the 'boom town'[13] of seventeenth-century Scotland, and to chart the corresponding decline — in relative if not absolute terms — of Dundee and Perth and, to a lesser extent, of Aberdeen. The sixteenth-century rolls have been studied less closely than those of the seventeenth and tend to reveal more ambiguous patterns, especially amongst middle-ranking towns, which then included Glasgow itself. It was assessed at 2.01 per cent in 1535, rose to 2.56 per cent by 1550, fell back to a fraction over 2 per cent between 1556 and 1574, recovered to 2.225 per cent by 1579, rose quite sharply to 3.5 per cent in 1583 and 4.5 per cent in 1594 but fell back to 4 per cent in 1612. At least a dozen other towns, ranging in size from Ayr to Rothesay and in geographical location from Montrose to Wigtown, reveal a similar pattern of short-term crisis and recovery, which is to be distinguished from a pattern of minor fluctuations within a larger trend, whether of rise or fall.[14] One of the factors to bear in mind in dealing with tax roll evidence is that it was assessed by the burghs themselves, in the Convention of Royal Burghs, which usually lent a sympathetic ear to hard-luck stories. So the assessments, which fluctuate far more in the sixteenth century than the seventeenth, may well reveal, with reasonable accuracy, localised short-term urban crises which were much more characteristic of that century than the one which followed it. They may also reveal how complicated the structure of the regional market was. Rival burghs, such as Glasgow, Dumbarton and Ayr, did not always necessarily profit or lose at each other's expense. Ayr clearly did prosper at the expense of its near-neighbour, Irvine, whose harbour was progressively silting up and whose tax payments correspondingly remained virtually static throughout the century. But the assessments on Ayr and Glasgow both fluctuate up and down, with little apparent connection between them, until Glasgow took a decisive lead, which it never lost, in 1583. Dumbarton was a more modest rival but its assessments rose in 1579, fell in 1583, and peaked in 1612. The material which can be gleaned from the tax rolls underlines how little is as yet known about the web of relationships which existed between one town and another. This is the case whether they were rivals — in overseas trade or with overlapping rural hinterlands — or satellites of larger centres, which is the theme of Ian Whyte's essay on the 1690s. The evidence before then is scattered and less full, but it can be worked harder. One of the major tasks that confronts Scottish urban historians is the charting of the shifting boundaries between provincial or regional centres and the various types of smaller market towns around them.

Viewed in this perspective or over a longer time span, the rise of Glasgow seems less certain; it rose above its west-coast rivals only in the 1580s but still does not seem to have escaped the short-term cycle of rise and fall by the turn of the century, for its assessment fell in 1612 while those on the four largest burghs were maintained at their existing levels.[15] The relative fortunes of all the burghs in the early seventeenth century are masked by the continuance of the 1612 roll as the basis of taxation on the burghs until 1649. It is unlikely that there was no movement in differentials in a period marked by the increase of trade and then, after 1638, by its partial collapse. The evidence which indicates that differentials in reality were sharply increasing between Edinburgh and other burghs provides the underlying theme of James Brown's essay. The merchant princes of Edinburgh were almost certainly undertaxed, as David Stevenson indicates, because of the political influence they enjoyed, both in the Convention and the corridors of power. Edinburgh was assessed at 28.75 per cent in 1612, but was briefly reassessed at 32.7 per cent in 1639–40 until its influence re-established the 1612 basis in 1641. Yet there were persistent complaints of the capital's underassessment, which were only partly satisfied by its increase to 36 per cent in 1649; some argued it should be 50 per cent. An alternative reading of the tax rolls from 1649 onwards is possible to that which sees in them the story of the 'spectacular breakthrough' of Glasgow.[16] It might run as follows: the assessments on Edinburgh, in 1649 and 1670, show two fundamental truths about the seventeenth-century economy. The capital was continuing to consolidate its grip over all sectors of trade and credit, at the expense of all other burghs, up until the collapse of the covenanting regime in 1649–50. That grip, which had been progressively tightening over the course of the past three centuries, was decisively slackened after 1650: in 1670 Edinburgh's assessment was lowered for the first time, from 36 per cent to 33.33 per cent, where it remained until the 1690s. In fact, the real drop may have been much greater, if the capital was indeed still under-assessed in 1649. The alternative version to the rise of Glasgow is of the spectacular collapse of Edinburgh in the 1650s, which made way for a rather different Scottish economy in the later seventeenth century, in which the capital still figured largely but did not dominate in the way it had earlier in the century. There were, as James Brown argues, similarities in the techniques and mechanisms of trade used by Edinburgh merchants in the early and the closing years of the seventeenth century, but quite different patterns of investment. The Wars of the Covenant had not only broken individuals like William Dick, the doyen of the Edinburgh merchant princes; they had jeopardised and shrunk the horizons of the Edinburgh money market.

Thus the attention which until now has been placed on Glasgow's rise to prominence needs refocusing; the fact is undeniable but the context in which it took place may be more important. It has been argued that Glasgow was not unique in managing to survive the turmoils of the 1650s relatively unscathed; Aberdeen also experienced a revival of trade by the early 1650s, re-establishing the levels of the 1630s.[17] It would be difficult to establish the same case for Perth or Dundee, the only town in Scotland to be taken by storm by Cromwell's army, although there is merit in the point that the crises of the 1640s and 1650s only exaggerated difficulties both were already experiencing. Yet at Dundee in September 1651 the victims also included refugees from Edinburgh, who were 'stripped even to the sark' and experienced losses allegedly totalling £200,000. That was only one of many losses inflicted on the capital's merchants and their experience contrasts sharply with that of Glasgow, where even Robert Baillie, one of its ministers, admitted the invading army had caused 'less displeasure nor if they had been in London'.[18] The remarkable vacuum in our knowledge of the effects on towns during the years of both the Scottish Revolution and the Cromwellian occupation, which David Stevenson points to, has had the effect of obscuring the relationship between the Scottish economy in the first and second halves of the century as well as disguising the reasons[19] behind the changing fortunes of the major burghs.

There is a danger in the eye drifting from the 6.5 per cent of tax which Glasgow paid in 1649 to the 12 per cent it was assessed at in 1670, placing it second, paying almost twice as much as Aberdeen and Dundee and three times as much as Perth, if it is viewed as part of an inevitable and steady rise, at the expense of its rivals. Parliament as late as 1667 made a series of minor adjustments to the relative assessments on the major burghs and placed Glasgow behind both Dundee and Aberdeen.[20] The evidence, which might include both customs and excise returns, is complicated but partly conflicting before the 1670s. This is hardly surprising as there is little trace in Glasgow of any growth of manufactories before 1655, and of little more than half a dozen before 1680.[21] The significant growth of Glasgow — at the expense of east-coast burghs which were experiencing a fresh and more serious crisis in the form of the collapse of part of the Dutch trade — probably belongs to the last quarter of the seventeenth century. The Aberdeen plaiding trade survived the 1650s; Dundee's decline, despite the fall-off in trade with the Baltic after the boom years of the 1620s and the traumatic effects on it of the Cromwellian occupation, was fairly gentle until the 1670s.[22] The conclusions to be drawn are multi-faceted rather than simple: Aberdeen may well have staged a recovery in the 1650s before facing a more serious threat to its livelihood in the 1670s; Dundee probably did recover from the Cromwellian occupation, if at an appreciably slower rate than Aberdeen or Glasgow, but it too faced a new crisis of trade at the end of the 1670s; the effect of the mid-century crisis may have been more severe in the already ailing case of Perth, where it is difficult to detect any sign of recovery before the very end of the century; but the greatest — and most significant — crisis was probably that in Edinburgh. If this is the case — and the matter requires research to substantiate the level of the collapse in the capital — the aftermath of the Scottish Revolution takes on a fresh twist. It had a fairly predictable effect on burghs like Dundee and Perth and it gave indirect advantages to Glasgow, but above all it dealt a telling blow to Edinburgh's growing monopoly of trade and credit, which had so characterised the first forty years of the seventeenth century.

It is difficult to be certain of the general characteristics of any Scottish town before the sixteenth century as no significant burgh archive, except for that of Aberdeen, pre-dates 1500. There are, however, indications that the four leading burghs, whose fortunes had probably all originally been based on the wool trade, had each diversified their economies since its collapse in the 1320s, but in rather different directions. As the wool trade recovered, it was increasingly monopolised by Edinburgh, which had 22 per cent of it in the 1320s but 71 per cent by the 1490s; the only other burgh to reclaim its former share was Aberdeen, which had 25 per cent of the trade in the 1320s and 18 per cent by the 1490s. Edinburgh's increasing share of overseas trade was startling by the sixteenth century, when it paid 60 per cent of all customs revenue, but it is significant that the degree of its monopoly varied markedly from one commodity to another. By the 1590s it had a complete monopoly in the export of raw wool, 83 per cent of hides, 80 per cent of woolfells and 76 per cent of woollen cloth, but it had claimed only 25 per cent of the trade in salmon and rather less in other fish and had very little stake in the marked increase in the export of coal and salt which took place from the 1570s onwards.[23] The evidence from trade leaves an impression that Edinburgh's economy rested on an exceptionally wide base by 1500, which is further confirmed by the fact that it granted letters of incorporation to no less than fourteen crafts between 1473 and 1536, whereas no other burgh had more than nine; the evidence of a muster roll of 1558 — with about 367 merchants and 400 craftsmen — also shows an unusually even balance between trading, manufacturing and service functions. The merchants had as yet a near monopoly of the wealth of the capital but Edinburgh was clearly already more than a merchants' town.[24] The annuity tax of 1635, the first to tax all householders, which is described by Walter Makey, indicates how far there had been an influx of the professions by then. The course of the sixteenth century would see, in tandem with the growing stranglehold the capital had of overseas trade, a growth of a prosperous craft aristocracy with its base in the service or luxury trades like the skinners, tailors and goldsmiths, who paid more tax and were in return granted more privileges, including that of near-automatic entry to the merchant guildry, and more power, both in representation on the town council and over their fellow craftsmen. The seventeenth century saw the consolidation of the professions and the increasing but still occasional residence of nobles and gentry, many with largely peripatetic domestic households — one of a number of factors making it increasingly difficult to calculate the capital's population with any precision.

Although there is little systematic evidence, by way of tax or muster rolls, for either Perth or Dundee throughout most of the period, the former was clearly, as Mary Verschuur establishes, a craft town. Its craftsmen paid as much tax as the merchants, had infiltrated the merchant guildry in large numbers from the point at which its records begin in the 1450s and were the first in any of the major burghs to gain direct representation on the town council, which they secured and consolidated in the 1530s and 1540s.[25] The burgh itself had been losing its share of the wool trade to its neighbour at the mouth of the Tay even before the crisis of the 1320s and seems increasingly to have fallen back on its functions as a regional and local market centre, although even those were jeopardised from time to time because of the precarious state of repair of its bridge over the river. Perth was, as a petition of 1554 pithily put it, 'a dry town far from the sea', whose overseas trade progressively dried up with the silting up of the Tay.[26] Its merchant community, as a result, was rather different from that of the other major burghs, made up largely of 'chapmen, rude, unlearned people', as the crafts witheringly termed them.[27] This was the unusual backcloth to the bitter political disputes between merchants and craftsmen in the burgh. It may well be that Perth is the best evidence for what has been called an 'economic revolution' taking place in Scotland in the three-quarters of a century or so after 1450, with overseas trade still languishing but, it is deduced, increased demand in rural society for manufactured goods which must largely have been met by urban craftsmen.[28] If so, the disputes in Perth in the second quarter of the sixteenth century may have been a reflection of a shift in general economic conditions which temporarily favoured domestic craftsmen at the expense of international traders. Yet the other serious disputes between merchants and craftsmen took place at least half a century later — in Edinburgh and Aberdeen in the 1580s, in Dundee between 1600 and 1610 and in Stirling in the decade after that — when general economic conditions were very different. Overseas trade had by then recovered but the wage levels of many urban craftsmen, especially in the manufacturing and victualling sectors, were falling.[29] The political campaign waged by Perth's craftsmen provided a precedent and a *modus operandi* for the craftsmen of other burghs. Yet their campaigns took place in burghs which had a markedly different social structure from that of Perth and in rather different economic circumstances; by then the balance had swung in favour of overseas merchants and other crafts which had specialist skills or services in demand, but against the others. There was no general craft revolt in the sixteenth century.

The campaign in Perth in the 1530s was led by the metal workers (or hammermen) and the baxters, who claimed precedence in civic ritual and were loudest in objecting to the admission into the guildry of 'litsters [dyers], hucksters, cadgers and horse hirers'.[30] They were almost certainly the crafts which were losing most ground from 1550 onwards. Even if the figure of 300 in the hammermen craft in 1533[31] is an exaggeration — and Edinburgh had 151 masters and servants in 1558 — the statistic provided by Ian Whyte of a mere 3.9 per cent of the Perth manufacturing labour being in the metal trades by the 1690s — a third of Edinburgh's percentage figure — is clear evidence of the sustained, long-term decline of Perth's foremost craft in 1500. Perth was a craft town whose leading crafts gained political power before 1550 but lost economic status thereafter.

Not surprisingly the burgh of Dundee, which had only two craftsmen on its council by the end of the sixteenth century and a third after 1604, claimed that it was more 'civilly governed' than Perth, which by then had given equal representation to merchants and craftsmen. Behind the rhetoric, Dundee's characteristics are the most difficult of the four major burghs to determine. It is likely, drawing conclusions from the gaps in an assessment on the burgh community of 1588, that the merchants met some 40 per cent of taxation, the nine incorporated crafts about 27 per cent, the dyers and maltmen, who were both unincorporated, 6.7 per cent and 8 per cent respectively and the mariners 20 per cent. Dundee was obviously pre-eminently a port but it was one which had weathered both the loss of its share in the wool trade in the fourteenth and fifteenth centuries and in the export of hides in the sixteenth by diversifying into a trade in timber with the Baltic and the export of fish. There are signs, none the less, that, along with Aberdeen, it was facing further difficulties by the 1580s or 1590s, when its tax assessments began to drop, as trade with France and the Low Countries was increasingly funnelled through Leith.[32] There may be a case for seeing the late sixteenth and early seventeenth centuries in Scotland, as in England, as a period of upheaval for a number of ports, large and small, which were forced to switch into coastal traffic to accommodate themselves to the growing monopoly of Edinburgh in many sectors of overseas trade.[33]

Aberdeen seems to have survived the sixteenth and seventeenth centuries on a more even keel than most other burghs because it was able to remain in contact both with the rural craftsmen in its hinterland and its traditional overseas markets. It had relatively few craftsmen — a tax roll of 1637 lists 127 — in contrast to the 361 craftsmen in the smaller burgh of Glasgow in 1604.[34] The proportion in Aberdeen is close enough to Ian Whyte's figure for 1691 of 28.7 per cent to indicate that the manufacturing sector within the town did not increase during the century. The burgh had its close-knit group of overseas merchants — which in 1600, it has been estimated, numbered no more than seventy-five — but they were not prominent in burgh politics, as in Edinburgh or Dundee, and tended to specialise in one commodity, particularly cloth, unlike most overseas merchants elsewhere. The bulk of merchants were smaller men, most probably drawing in different ways on the network of market centres and smaller towns in the shire. The ruling patriciate was largely made up of a rather different species of merchant — merchant lairds — who had also connections with the rural hinterland, but in the form of investments in estates and through intermarriage with gentry.[35] These links drawing town and country together had existed in the fourteenth century, if not before,[36] and they had a number of consequences: the bulk of urban capital was — rather unusually in early modern Scotland — invested in rural landholding; most issues in burgh politics either directly revolved around the relationship between landed and urban interests — as when local lairds unsuccessfully demanded a vote in burgh elections in 1525[37] — or were sucked into it, or complicated by it. That applied to the nature of a Protestant settlement in the town after 1560, when, as Allan White shows, however Catholic its sympathies were, it saw the issue at stake as the integrity of the burgh community, caught between the competing claims of a Protestant regime in Edinburgh and an ambitious Catholic noble patron in the locality. The issue of town and country also shaped the nature of the craftsmen's campaign in the 1580s for political representation; they chose, in alliance with other interests, to focus on the undue amount of rural influence in burgh politics exercised by the Menzies family who, they alleged, had not only monopolised the provostship but had acted like a 'landward baron'. They found, in this line of argument, common cause with both the lawyers and overseas traders, who by 1590 had begun to spend most of their time in Leith and Dundee, leaving Aberdeen, as the guild court complained, 'a dry pond'.[38]

The major burghs thus showed marked variations in their social and economic structure and it is likely that the same can be said of other towns. There were, so far as one can see from the available evidence, no one-industry towns although it is possible that the fastest growing towns in the sixteenth century were those, like Dysart, Crail and Pittenweem, which were associated with a specialist function — in their case the export of salt, coal or fish. But these also seem to have been the most vulnerable to decay in the first half of the following century and outright slump in the second.[39] But it is difficult to find in Scotland before the eighteenth century examples of towns — outside Edinburgh or Glasgow — which grew because of specialisms in manufactures, as Ian Whyte's fourth table demonstrates.[40] It is a good deal easier to find towns — like Perth, or Linlithgow and Stirling, which both complained in 1692 of the collapse of their inland trade[41] — whose staple industries, usually in metal or cloth, had fallen into long-term decay.

Aberdeen's prosperity depended to a large degree on its plaiding industry, but it was in the control of merchants who sub-contracted the work to rural craftsmen; there were twenty-three weavers in the town in 1637, but more than half of them lived in the poorest quarter of the burgh. What seems striking about Glasgow's social structure while it remained a middle-ranking burgh is the unusually large ratio of craftsmen to merchants; there were 213 merchants and 361 craftsmen in 1604. The only two towns of consequence for which a similar breakdown is available are Edinburgh and Aberdeen. The capital, probably two or three times the size of Glasgow, had about 500 merchants and 500 craftsmen in 1583; Aberdeen had 114 craftsmen and approximately 350 merchants in 1623. So Glasgow, which has come to be thought of as a merchants' town in the seventeenth century had, in fact, an unusually large manufacturing sector, especially in the leather, clothing and malting sectors. It had also — like Edinburgh — a comparatively small merchant community, with power, wealth and overseas trade concentrated in an inner circle which contained no more than a quarter of the burgh's merchants.[42]

Two important related questions — about the nature of burgh government and how open urban society was — which have attracted a good deal of attention from Scottish historians take on a different light if the assumption is grafted on to them that there were significant variations from one burgh to another in the social or economic make-up of the burgh community. It is clear enough that in larger towns, most of which underwent a significant increase in their populations in the course of the sixteenth century, there was a steady drift towards a consolidation of an urban oligarchy. But different routes could be taken towards oligarchy, and burgh government was as varied in the seventeenth century as it was in the sixteenth, when the Convention of Royal Burghs admitted the 'great variance standing in diverse and sundry burghs'[43] in office-holding and electoral practices. In Edinburgh the doors of the guildry, which had never been closed to craftsmen, were opened wider in the second half of the sixteenth century to accommodate a new craft aristocracy who did not soil their hands but employed others to do so. Drawn from only six or seven of the fourteen incorporated crafts, they were the beneficiaries of the redrafted burgh constitution of 1583, the decreet arbitral, which gave them automatic seats on the town council. The grip of the Edinburgh merchant oligarchy over the government of the burgh was tightened by selective recruitment from outside; the decreet admitted a select range of craft employers and, equally importantly, it debarred the lawyers.[44] The common indenture, which remodelled Aberdeen's constitution in 1587, bore distinct similarities to the Edinburgh decreet — both were drafted by commissions set up by the privy council to impose a solution on troublesome burghs — but it had rather different effects; its proposal to put two craftsmen on the town council was accepted in principle but not implemented for a number of years.[45] In Aberdeen craftsmen and lawyers allied rather than competed for place in the 1580s. It was the lawyers, however, who gained promotion to a new, and more formidable governing coalition, composed of the 'old blood' of the town and the rising legal establishment. So the similarity of burgh constitutions is in some respects an illusion, fostered by the widespread government intervention in burgh affairs between 1580 and 1625, when a number of commissions drew up revised constitutions which, with mixed success, sought to solve local disputes by imposing a uniform solution — usually the 'example of Edinburgh' — upon them. Glasgow's constitution of 1604, which is often held up by historians of the city as a model of open government, needs to be placed in this context. Glasgow was certainly not immune to trouble between merchants and crafts, both before and after 1604; it is significant that when its laird provost visited the burgh to settle such a dispute in 1583, he took with him a copy of the Edinburgh decreet.[46]

There were different patterns of challenge to the established order and reaction in different towns. In burghs like Stirling, where the staple industries were in decline, the greatest resistance to change came, not from the merchants, but from the older, established crafts. There the skinners and hammermen tried to resist the representation on the council of both unincorporated crafts and the food-producing trades.[47] In Perth, as Mary Verschuur points out, the same two crafts, along with the baxters, once they themselves had gained a place on the council, tried to fend off the claims of the other guilds. It has to be remembered that many of the pressures of the sixteenth century bore most heavily on the established craft guilds: the Reformation removed not only the cult of saints, which gave a focus to each craft, but also their customary — and highly visible — place in the Corpus Christi procession, the symbol and guarantee of their place in the ordered hierarchy of the burgh community; the older crafts were often those in which real wages were falling most sharply in the second half of the sixteenth century; and the food-producing crafts were those which suffered most from the deliberate policy of town councils — usually themselves under pressure from government — to hold down food prices, at times to artificially low levels. It was not therefore surprising that these crafts, faced with a genuine crisis of identity, would be anxious to conserve what privileges and status they had.

There is, therefore, at times some unreality about the question of how open burgh society was to incomers. It could vary from one part of the community to another. The most dedicated mono-polists were often the craft masters; in Perth it was comparatively easy to enter the guildry, but not through the skinner and baxter crafts, which were virtual closed shops; and in Edinburgh the recurrence over generations of the same names in crafts — like the wrights, fleshers and baxters — suggests the same exclusiveness. The measuring-sticks which are conventionally applied to the problem — the proportions of those who entered either burgess-ship or the guildry other than by right of heredity — have serious deficiencies once they are used to compare one burgh with another. In Aberdeen, for instance, admission to the guildry was far more common than simple burgess-ship, so much so that in 1590 the guild court complained that the town had been reduced to poverty by the admission of too many ordinary retail merchants to the guildry.[48] Aberdeen, in a sense, was too open for its own good. It is unrealistic to expect that any comparison of Glasgow and Aberdeen — when one had three times as many craftsmen as the other — will reveal anything but a disparity in the proportions of craftsmen entered into the guildry.[49] There were more craftsmen to become apprenticed to, more craftsmen's daughters and widows to marry in Glasgow. The real difference between the two towns lay, not in their openness or flexibility, but in their underlying occupational structure. Edinburgh may be something of a special case, in this as in many other respects, because the wide-flung activities of its merchants, whether in trade or credit, may have encouraged an unusually wide pattern of recruitment into it. Approximately 8,000 apprentices were registered between 1583 and 1699; the bulk of them — some 87 per cent — came from within a fifty-mile radius of the capital, but towns like Dumfries, which had established patterns of contact with Edinburgh, as Winifred Coutts points out, often put sons into apprenticeships with both merchants and craftsmen. Yet again it is significant that the pattern varied appreciably from craft to craft: outside recruit-ment was at its highest in flourishing crafts like the tailors and at its lowest in smaller and humbler crafts like the wrights. There is a serious flaw in the evidence, however, for less than a quarter of these apprentices ever became burgesses.[50] The case for Edinburgh, rather than Glasgow, being the most open urban society in seventeenth-century Scotland is seductive but as yet remains not proven. Yet the two merchant princes chosen by James Brown to symbolise the wealth and pre-eminence of the Edinburgh merchant elite themselves make the point: William Dick was the son of an established merchant family but Patrick Wood gained entry via the marriage bed.

There is a more general point to bear in mind about the nature of urban society and government in the early modern period. The social order was shifting, to some degree, in many towns and burgh government was also shifting, albeit more slowly, to accommodate the groups which were emerging to claim a status which befitted their new-found prosperity. But the changes were usually justified, as changes often are by governments, as a return to the old order and were camouflaged by the use of conventional language: the Edinburgh decreet claimed that it had 'reunited' merchants and craftsmen in 'one society' by promoting the 'best and worthiest' of the crafts to the council — a deliberate use of the phraseology of fifteenth-century craft legislation.[51] Yet, on the face of it, the changes, cosmetic as they usually were, seem to have worked. The middling ranks of the community were found new, but minor responsibilities in civic government — as elders or, more probably, as deacons in kirk sessions, as constables acting on behalf of the new justice of the peace courts,[52] or as muster masters. Yet power remained — and was consolidated — within the inner circles of the urban elite. As Allan White shows, the kirk session in Aberdeen offered a further instrument through which the ruling elite could increase its grip over burgh society, even if both for the moment were overwhelmingly Catholic in sympathies. And sessions were under far more explicit secular control in the seventeenth century than before. The justice of the peace courts were presided over by the normal burgh magistrates, who were given new and wider-ranging authority, which was sometimes used to displace the jurisdiction of the session in morals cases. Civic government was becoming more authoritarian but there was, if anything, even less social disorder in urban society in the seventeenth century than in the sixteenth, despite the fact that there was a good deal more political upheaval after 1600 than before.

One of the most important factors in bringing to an end the distinctively medieval burgh community was, so it will be argued in Chapter 3 of this volume, the pressure exerted upon it by the crown, especially in the reign of James VI, whether in the form of direct interference in its government or by more indirect means, including the growing burden of taxation. Both forms of pressure increased markedly over the rest of the century up to the Revolution of 1689 – 90. Initially, the government of Charles I intervened rather less in burgh government than that of his father and it is unclear how seriously he intended his demand made in 1637 that 'a constant council' be set up in every burgh. Yet, as David Stevenson emphasises, it was finance that lay at the root of the burghs' grievances with the Caroline regime. As an illustration of the new dimension of the crown's demands, the capital was in the first two and a half years of Charles' reign faced with a larger tax bill — some £85,000 — than in the whole of the last twenty-five years of James VI's reign.[53] The effects on the structure of society were nothing less than dramatic. The constituency of tax-payers in Edinburgh was widened by over 40 per cent in the 1630s to meet the series of tax demands from the crown — lawyers, money-lenders, occasional residents, whether landed or merchants from other burghs, were all taxed for the first time.[54] It was because of the unpopularity of the new taxation that the payment of the burgh's ministers was diverted into a separate tax on valued rent — the annuity tax, which Walter Makey analyses; the town council would collect the money but the kirk session the opprobium. Edinburgh was in a sense fortunate that it had within it large untapped reserves of residents who could bear part of the new burden of taxation. It is likely that there was elsewhere nothing like the same number of inhabitants who lived within the burgh's physical limits but outside the recognised catchment of burgess-ship or neighbourhood, even in a provincial capital like Aberdeen; its tax roll of 1637 reveals a number of novel criteria for tax — 'for land' or housing within the burgh, even 'for his pupil' — but there are 569 entries on it, only twenty-one more than on that of 1608.

The demands of the covenanting regime and the Cromwellian regime which followed it both made the exactions of the 1630s pale into insignificance. The strains — and opportunities — which the Scottish Revolution brought with it have yet to be examined in their detailed effects on any burgh. Did the revolutionary years bring new opportunities and, if so, did they go to new groups within burgh society? The evidence for Glasgow, where, it has been argued, a radical regime gained power in 1645 but lost it by 1652, seems inconclusive; the boundaries between the 'new men' and those they displaced often seem elusive and in policy there appears to have been more in common between them than at dispute.[55] It is striking, however, that of the nine Edinburgh burgesses who were at the centre of the administration and supply of the covenanting armies, only three had figured in the merchant elite in 1637.[56] The unique feature of the 1640s lay in the combined effects of war and plague, for the outbreak of 1645 was the most severe in that century or the one preceding it. If, as has been estimated, a fifth of the population of the capital and its suburbs died in the mid-1640s,[57] what effect did that have on the structure of investment and credit, whether for housing or trade? Investment in urban property in a town which had at least doubled in population over the previous half century had become one of the ways by which Edinburgh merchants seem to have extended the length of their active careers; the effects of the demographic crisis in the 1640s and the enforced reduction of rents in the capital by a third in 1651[58] may have had serious longer-term consequences for the Edinburgh merchants whose careers James Brown highlights.

Urban politics in the Restoration period is known only in out- line. The reaction in favour of the aristocracy took a number of forms: they were allowed, as has already been said, to extend or defray their accumulated debts, which were mostly to burgh merchants; interest rates were brought down, from 8 per cent to 6 per cent; burgesses with rural holdings were debarred from shire elections; and the nobles returned to urban politics, often as the agents of a regime far more arbitrary than that of James VI. Inter- ference with town councils spotted the Restoration period and reached new heights, as in England, after 1685. It was serious enough to have become one of the main grievances encapsulated in the Claim of Right in 1690.[59] The scale of religious dissent in the burghs remains unquantified; the treatment of dissenters, par- ticularly in Perth and perhaps also in Glasgow, was more dogmatic than that inflicted on Presbyterian radicals either in the 1580s or the early 1620s,[60] but seems modest if compared to the regime's reactions to rural dissent. Its effect on burgh politics is virtually unknown. Rather more difficult to evaluate, but also largely untested, is the impression made on urban society by the other face of the Restoration regime — in the form of a deliberate appeal to the values implicit in gentility, patronage and heredity. It certainly made an impression, particularly during the years of the duke of York's residence in Edinburgh, on the professional classes in the capital. Aberdeen went so far as to have a coat of arms designed for it by no less a figure than Sir George Mackenzie of Rosehaugh to emphasise its long — and largely mythical — history and one of its provosts in a pamphlet written in 1685 gloried in the 'fatherly care and protection' which came to the burghs with absolute monarchy.[61] It is so curious a reading of the Restoration period as we know it as to demand serious attention.

There were two obvious and fundamental principles which lay at the core of the thinking of towns and townsmen and both were in process of adjustment in the early modern period: the status of the burgh community rested on a long-established network of economic and social privilege, which also involved a special relationship with the crown; but towns, as market places, regional or provincial centres or as seats of sheriffdoms, had to live and prosper in the localities in which they found themselves. Burghs were set apart from the surrounding countryside by their charters but were part of it too, through ties of kinship as much as the tentacles of trade. Burghs were tenants-in-chief of the king but also potential clients of local nobles or lairds. Major issues — whether national, like the Reformation settlement, or local, such as the disputes between merchants and craftsmen — were liable to affect both of the worlds in which townsmen lived and to be recast by them. The Reformation, which for most burghs — outside Dundee and Perth — took the form of a minority movement imposed, with varying degrees of co-operation, from outside, posed a stark threat to the fabric of the burgh community; it also — as Allan White emphasises in his study of the most determinedly Catholic of the major burghs — raised, not for the first time in the sixteenth century, the question of the relationship between town and country, Aberdeen and its noble patron, the even more resolute Catholic earl of Huntly. The burgh of Perth took a rather different path in the Reformation period, even if little evidence has emerged, despite close scrutiny by Mary Verschuur, that its Protestant populism was anything more than, as John Knox himself admitted, 'young and rude in Christ' in 1559. There is no trace of a privy kirk or organised Protestant worship in Perth before the Reformation, as had emerged in Edinburgh by the mid-1550s.[62] The capital was still overwhelmingly Catholic in its loyalties but, unlike Perth, it was an intellectual centre in which books and ideas could readily be exchanged.

It is noticeable that the internal disputes in Perth between crafts-men and merchants, which had been going on since at least the early 1530s, did not take on a religious dimension, either before or at the Reformation — and seem not to have done so in other towns either. They did, however, become involved with the struggle for control of Perth between rival nobles in the early 1540s and came to be complicated, as Mary Verschuur shows, by the authority of Lord Ruthven as provost of the burgh once he came into an undis-puted monopoly of the office after 1546. So the Perth dispute, which proved incapable of resolution within the normal framework of the town council, guildry or head courts, was next referred to the nearest outside agency — the noble patron. It was only when he was found wanting that it was passed for resolution to the various agencies of central government and Perth, as a result, found itself entangled in a web of conflicting jurisdictions. It is a revealing episode which goes some way towards demonstrating that the relationship of patron and client involved more than one set of expectations. Perth asked for more than security or protec-tion as part of good lordship. Burghs could make demanding clients.

What were these mutual expectations of burghs and their landed patrons? For nobles and lairds burghs were market places for food, credit and wives; they had schools to attend, tailors to frequent, and collegiate churches with shrines to patronise and be buried in. They also had status to impart. Burghs, in their turn, had various expectations. A simple but fairly typical example of the benefits a smaller burgh might accrue is that of Peebles, which had a long-standing relationship with the Hays of Yester, a noble family of middling rank, which held the office of provost for over fifty years from the point at which the burgh's surviving regular records begin, in 1555. The reassuring presence of Yester's seat, Neidpath Castle, barely a mile to the west of the burgh, was the visible seal on the relationship. But Peebles was also the seat of the sheriffdom and its burgesses could expect a certain partiality from the sheriff court so long as the office was held by Yester. Time and time again in the sixteenth century Yesters interceded in Edinburgh, both in the central law courts and the royal court, on the burgh's behalf in cases of encroachment by local lairds on burgh lands. A noble provost could arrange for a burgh to be taken under royal protec-tion, as Peebles was in 1563, or for its trading privileges to be confirmed or extended by royal charter, as they were in 1554, when it was granted two new fairs. Yet the relationship was a delicate one that had within it a delicately balanced mechanism: Yester was duly elected, year after year, as provost but the burgh refused to grant him the office in liferent, just as Perth refused Lord Ruthven. None the less, there can hardly be a better measure of the trust Peebles put in the Hays of Yester than the habit, in times of danger, of entrusting the burgh's charters and records to them. It was equally characteristic of the relationship that Yester was prone to mislay them; the mile between burgh and castle was not a fixed distance.[63]

The obviously close relationship between certain towns and nobles falls into the general reappraisal of the relationships between nobles and their kindred or clients on the one hand, and between them and the crown on the other. This is the context of Keith Brown's reassessment of the spilling of the noble feud into burgh society. Burghs were not simply natural victims of feudal violence; they could mete out violence too, when needed, as Perth did to a particularly troublesome laird, Robert Bruce of Clackmannan in 1594. Nobles might find out their differences in town streets, as in the infamous 'cleansing of the causeway' in Edinburgh in 1520, but so could burghs themselves, as when the rivalry of Perth and Dundee spilled on to the streets of the capital during a session of parliament in 1568.[64] There were many condemnations, both by parliament and the crown, of leagues between nobles and burghs. Some probably arose from a particular objection raised by a burgh, like the act of 1458 which, it has been suggested, was the product of pressure from Aberdeen; yet that burgh entered into a bond of manrent with the earl of Huntly five years later.[65] Such legislation also noticeably clustered in the personal reigns of James IV and James V, strong kings who knew their own minds and thought they knew what was best for their subjects. It is doubtful, however, that burghs always welcomed solutions imposed by the crown. The privy council blamed disturbances in Renfrew in 1576 on the appointment of 'outland men' as provosts and tried to effect a settlement by balancing the rival factions on the town council. It did not work, for the burgh in 1580 voluntarily entered into a bond with the earl of Argyll, which gave him the right to nominate one of the bailies.[66] What had happened in Renfrew was that the burgh had chosen the wrong patron — a client of Lord Ross who had managed to lose the town's charter chest — rather than the wrong arrangement. A close understanding with a noble was usually preferable to the heavy-handed intervention of the crown.

Burghs tended to prefer the protection of a great rather than a lesser lord but nobles, too, were attracted to the fatter regional centres, like Perth and Aberdeen, rather than the minnows. But the bigger the town the less absolute was the lord's voice in it. The influence of the earls of Huntly was far from total over the burgh of Aberdeen and it was regularly disputed. A string of other nobles, including the earls of Buchan and Erroll, tried to plant their clients on the town council in the early sixteenth century and the burgh encouraged a climate of good will which extended beyond the Gordons of Huntly, either by distributing largesse in the form of small but regular gifts of wine or meat or by annual pensions, which in the 1490s accounted for almost half the burgh's income. Should it be thought that these were in reality blackmail payments, it is interesting to note that the earl of Crawford, who had long abandoned any direct interest in the burgh, was still being paid a pension in 1559–60.[67] Problems arose either where one noble enjoyed an excess of power in the locality — like the earl of Huntly did in the north-east — or where there were competing noble patrons — as in Perth in the 1540s, Jedburgh in the 1580s and 1590s, or Stirling in the 1550s and 1560s, when it was caught up in a feud between the Erskines and Livingstons. The Erskines won, but sought to protect their position by packing the town council with client lairds; there were no less than six of them on the council in 1563.[68] That degree of active involvement in burgh politics by landed interests was unusual but, as the studies of Perth and Aberdeen in this collection show, there was no one set form of *modus vivendi* between burghs and their lords. Aberdeen tried, for the most part successfully, to keep Huntly at arm's length; Ruthven's relationship with Perth was closer, but he seems to have attended only the three head courts held each year; if closer supervision of council business was necessary, he drafted in a client laird as a bailie, as he did in 1556.[69] Edinburgh, as the capital, had an assortment of noble provosts thrust on it in the sixteenth century but those who, like Lord Seton, were local do seem to have regularly attended council meetings. It was Seton's very absence from the council chamber in the deepening crisis of 1558–9, culminating in his threat to revisit the burgh with his 'kin friends' which signalled the breakdown in the relationship.[70] The final twist in relations between burghs and nobles came with the novel attempt by the crown to plant noble placemen in a chain of major burghs in 1584; it was then that the burghs involved were brought hard up against the competing claims, which Aberdeen spent much of the sixteenth century trying to resolve, of local lordship and royal authoritarianism.

The relationships between the burghs and their landed neighbours is only one aspect of a wider subject which demands closer attention from Scottish urban historians — that of town and country. That link has until now usually been discussed only in the most obvious of terms, such as the fact that, as both property records and the series of seventeenth-century views of various Scottish towns indicate, agricultural land ran directly up to burgh boundaries and often was to be found inside them. The number of gardeners in burghs like Aberdeen and the Canongate makes much the same point. Yet, in Dumfries, which was large enough to be ranked twelfth on the tax roll of 1649, as Winifred Coutts points out, burgesses reared animals and grew both vegetables and grain inside the town but also leased farming land outside or made arrangements with farmers to graze their animals on a regular basis, thus establishing a systematic link between the agricultural hinterland and the market. Here burgesses were neither buying rural estates nor migrating to cheaper suburbs or nearby burghs of barony, as was alleged to have happened around Aberdeen, particularly after the act of parliament of 1672 which formally broke the monopoly of the royal burghs in retailing and export.[71] The Dumfries model is probably a typical one of middle-ranking towns which were regional centres. It is an example that might prompt urban historians to think more about the middling and smaller towns, as Ian Whyte has demonstrated so convincingly of agricultural society,[72] in terms of the ability of the old system to stretch, improve and maximise profit, yet stop short of fundamental change.

It seems apparent, although much work remains to be done on the subject, that there were marked variations in the relationships each of the major burghs had with their rural hinterlands. A brief analysis of the land transactions recorded in the *Register of the Great Seal* between 1593 and 1660 revealed that the 600 which involved burgesses showed a disproportionately large interest by merchants from Edinburgh, Aberdeen and Stirling, more or less what might be expected from Perth or Dumfries, if judged by their size alone, but disproportionately little interest by merchants from Dundee and, strikingly so, those from Glasgow.[73] The prominence of Aberdeen is not surprising. The direct investment of urban capital in rural estates, which had been a feature of Aberdeen's history since the fourteenth century, was unusual elsewhere before the eighteenth century.[74] Merchants were not generally attracted to gentrification or the purchase of rural property, although there are a number of well-known examples, particularly of seventeenth-century Edinburgh merchants who did so. It was the lawyers, the most under-studied group in early modern Scottish society, who led the movement into the rural estate in the seventeenth century. There were, however, hidden patterns of investment and indirect links between town and country. The systematic study of the private papers of Edinburgh merchants by James Brown has revealed rather more investment by them in the early seventeenth century in coal and salt, which were previously thought to be the preserves of rural landowners.[75] The bulk of Edinburgh merchant capital which went into the countryside in this period, however, went neither on satellite industries nor on outright purchase of estates; it went on wadsetting, loans to a very large number of nobles and greater lairds ranging from the north of Scotland to the Borders, although there was a certain concentration in Lothian and Fife, all secured on the estate.[76] William Dick, who is often used in this volume as a symbol of the Edinburgh mercantile community, held the whole of Orkney as a mortgagee. This was almost certainly the reason which lay behind the burghs' determined opposition in the parliament of 1621 to the new tax on annual rents; the tax would have to be paid by the wadsetter, not the nominal owner of the estate. The burghs managed to secure individual arrangements with the crown to commute the tax by making a fixed payment over a period of years, which would be collected as part of ordinary taxation; in effect, the ordinary burgh taxpayer was forced to pay the wadsetters' tax bills. It was therefore the credit system rather than the desire to ape the gentry which brought Edinburgh merchants and rural estates together in the early seventeenth century but it was an arrangement which did not survive the Wars of the Covenant. This is an important point because it contrasts markedly with studies of the period after 1660, which have concluded that merchants made only a limited impact on the land market before 1740.[77] This may be a further indicator that the Restoration period, which is usually described in terms of a recovery from two decades of crisis, was also a sea-change in patterns of investment and credit. The Edinburgh money market, after having had its fingers badly burned both by the successive regimes of the 1640s and 1650s and by the settlement of debts forced on it by parliament in 1661, turned to manufactories as a safer form of investment.

The burgh of Edinburgh itself invested considerable sums in the seventeenth century, as Walter Makey points out, to buy up the various suburbs and burghs, both of regality and barony, which lay around it. The capital was able to compensate for the eccentricities of its site by investing in the control of its immediate hinterland, allowing the setting up of a series of manufactories at or near a supply of water. It is also apparent, from the evidence of the households recorded in the annuity tax of 1635, both from their numbers and the range of wealth they reflect, that large numbers of labourers, as distinct from apprentices, must have lived outside its walls. Aberdeen was able to establish interests in a network of smaller towns around it to find cheap labour for its plaiding industry. As Ian Whyte points out, the occupational structure of the rural labour force around certain of the larger urban centres may indicate co-operation rather than cut-throat competition between some rural burghs of barony and royal burghs. It is as yet unclear on what basis, if any, this was arranged. Yet other burghs plainly suffered from the proliferation of market centres around them; Perth mournfully listed twenty-four in its report of 1692.[78] Again, the impression is that the situation varied from one major burgh to another — a further reason for their varied fortunes in this period. One of the most striking pieces of evidence for later seventeenth-century Scottish history is the dramatic increase in the number of burghs of barony and licensed market centres, especially after 1660.[79] Yet the counting of Scottish burghs of barony is probably as inexact a science and as unsatisfactory a methodology as the counting of English manors. More knowledge is needed of the markets they supplied as well as of the lairds who ran them, their contacts and their provenance.

The relationship between town and country was a factor which, outside of the rarified atmosphere of the capital, affected almost every aspect of urban life, including its politics. In Aberdeen the attempted influx of local lairds into burgh politics in 1525 marked no more than the sharpening of a pattern which had been taking shape for over a century; the fall of the Menzies oligarchy in the early 1590s also marked, so it has been argued, the retreat of the lairds from Aberdeen politics, leaving a vacuum into which the craftsmen and lawyers could aspire to move.[80] In Stirling the retreat of the lairds from burgh government also seems to have taken place in the 1590s, and it again left room for a tussle between merchants and craftsmen for position on the council which lasted into the 1620s. If there was a fundamental pattern which lay behind the crisis of identity which the burgh community went through in the course of the sixteenth century it probably lay in the shifting relationship between town and country.

The explanation of an urban crisis which has been offered until now — of an alleged wholesale friction between merchants and craftsmen — falls down on the particulars. There was craft agitation in sixteenth-century Scottish towns but the craft riot has been used as a convenient shorthand to impose meaning on disparate scraps of information which are otherwise difficult to evaluate. The evidence, when tested, is often suspect. Purely political demonstrations — such as those that took place in Edinburgh against Arran's pro-Protestant policy in 1543 — have been mistaken for craft riots; the craftsmen carried the blue banner, the symbol of craft privilege, because it was also the banner of the Holy Ghost. Usually a craft riot involved only one craft and very often that craft was either the baxters or the fleshers, the crafts most directly affected by the deliberate policy of town councils to hold down the prices of basic foodstuffs. There were no bread riots in sixteenth-century Scotland, either in the towns or elsewhere. There were instead fairly frequent minor riots involving the producers of bread and other basic commodities against town councils which ruthlessly implemented a cheap food policy at their expense. There was no compulsory poor rate in Scottish towns and the victims were the food producers. The typical revolting craftsman was a baxter apprentice — in a trade with a low level of technical skill, a high proportion of apprentices and journeymen and sharply falling wage levels.[81] Perth, as Mary Verschuur makes clear, saw a particularly bitter confrontation between its merchants and craftsmen, but its crafts took to the courts rather than the streets. The craftsmen of Edinburgh and Aberdeen followed their example. It is difficult to think of an image which better illustrates the changing habits of the burgh community in the sixteenth century than the resort made by sections of it to outside agencies to settle its disputes.

The group in Scottish urban society which has been most scrutinised is the merchants. The poor remain unexplored territory, largely because there was no compulsory poor rate which would have left behind it adequate records. There were some experiments in establishing charitable workhouses in Edinburgh and Glasgow for the manufacture of cloth, in 1619 and 1638, but they failed to take root. There is, however, some material stemming from voluntary arrangements or the deliberate registration of the town's poor; this is particularly true of Aberdeen, which listed the burgh's 'pensioners' on a quarterly basis.[82] The only recent study of a craft occupation concentrated on the bonnet-makers, the humblest and least influential of all the craft guilds. It would be useful for closer attention to be paid across a range of burghs to certain occupations, particularly those which, it has been suggested here, were in steepest decline — the metal workers and the textile trades. It was certainly the hammermen, often the acknowledged senior guild in the hierarchy of crafts, who most resisted the rise to influence of a craft aristocracy, both within their own ranks, in the form of goldsmiths, armourers or saddlers, and outside. There are also some indications, in Edinburgh and even in supposedly Protestant Perth a generation after the Reformation, that it was crafts like this that clung most to the old cult of saints, which underpinned their autonomy as a guild.[83] The numbers and status of lawyers in towns varied considerably: in Aberdeen they joined the merchant guildry in numbers but in Edinburgh their influence was covert, as non-elected assessors who advised the town council, until they were removed by the revised constitution of 1583. In Perth an exasperated town council banned procurators from representing clients in smaller cases in 1561.[84] There is, however, some substance in the notion of a surplus of notaries, clerical and lay, thronging the corridors of government, both central and local, by the middle years of the sixteenth century. The rise of the lawyers accentuated the drift towards more oligarchical town government and underpinned the more formal relations which characterised its dealings with central government. Conversation between burghs and the crown was increasingly conducted, on both sides, by lawyers.

The closer links which were being forged, often under duress, between the burghs and the community of the realm, especially in the last quarter of the sixteenth century, were, Chapter 3 will argue, a key factor in the break-up of the medieval burgh community. The break was not total for it was cushioned by the survival of many of the customary institutions of burgh society, or at least the semblance of them, and by the fact that the appearance of towns changed little over the course of the two centuries. More domestic housing was built of stone but few, if any, burghs spilled out of their medieval ground plans.[85] Head courts continued to be called three times a year, but they had by 1560 usually become a forum only for the rubber-stamping of routine regulations fixing prices of food and drink. Access to the council chamber was being restricted and the council itself usually met in closed session; the kirk session, although it made a show of accountability to the congregation once a year, followed the same practice. The institutions of the burgh were being stretched to accommodate and camouflage a new authoritarianism and remoteness in burgh government. The factor which lay at the root of most of the changes was the substantial increase in the population of most of the major burghs in the course of the sixteenth century. The precise proportions of the increase are usually difficult to quantify but the effects are clear enough. The most obvious symbol of the burgh community was the large burgh church, built or extended in the hundred years before the Reformation and raised to collegiate status. It was designed to accommodate all the burgh's population but also to give each of the separate communities within the burgh its own identity and focus, with its own craft altar, chaplain and saint. The Reformation swept away the altars and, rather more slowly, it eroded the cult of saints; it was not surprising that the craft guild was one of the main incubators of Catholic survivalism. The single parish burgh — which had existed since the Scottish burghs' first foundations in the twelfth or thirteenth centuries — survived the Reformation, but only just. By the 1590s it became a canon of ultra-Presbyterian thought to carve out model parishes of a manageable size in the larger towns. At a time when in England steps were being taken to rationalise their medieval heritage of multi-parish boroughs by reducing the number of parishes, precisely the reverse process was happening in Scotland. In Edinburgh, the presbytery planned eight model parishes, each of a thousand adult communicants, but settled for four in 1598; Aberdeen was divided into two parishes in 1596 and its ministers drew lots as to which charge each would take.[86] The historic link between medieval burgh and parish was disappearing.

This was the most obvious of a series of changes which were by 1600 taking grip both of the burgh community and its relations with the outside world. A shift had taken place within most urban establishments, although its nature varied from one burgh to another. New groups, such as lawyers, the other professions and perhaps also in places a resident gentry, who did not belong within the traditional framework of the burgh community or owe it the same loyalty, had become more prominent in society but in many respects stood apart from it. There was, almost certainly, a larger work force, made up of labourers and domestic servants, who were wholly unrepresented in burgh government. Many of the conventions which had held burgh society together — including the notion of the just price, a strict limitation on the number of apprentices and journeymen a master might have, and the link between burgage tenure and burgess-ship, which all went back to the *Leges Burgorum* and *Statuta Gilde* of the twelfth and thirteenth centuries — were in process of being abandoned. Just as kinship, the cement which held rural society together, was beginning to evaporate by 1600, so in the burghs many of the habits and values implicit within the bond of neighbourliness were beginning to dissolve. The burgh communities which faced the various storms of the seventeenth century were very different from those which had weathered the squalls of the sixteenth.

Notes

1. A significant exception is Aberdeen, which has burgh court books extant from 1398 onwards in a near-continuous sequence. The first (and in many ways least interesting of the early books) has been published in full, as *Early Records of the Burgh of Aberdeen, 1317, 1398–1407*, ed. W. C. Dickinson (SHS, 1957). Otherwise the printed extracts, *Extracts from the Council Register of the Burgh of Aberdeen, 1398–1570* and *1570–1625* (Spalding Club, 1844–8), are the poorest printed burgh source in this period and gave little indication of the riches which lie hidden in the archive.

2. See esp. A. A. M. Duncan, *Scotland: The Making of the Kingdom* (Edinburgh, 1975), 465–501.

3. The two significant exceptions are Aberdeen, which has a number of tax rolls surviving between 1448 and 1472 but none after that until 1596, and Edinburgh, which has a continuous set of tax rolls starting in 1581. It has also a unique annuity tax roll of 1635, which resembles an eighteenth-century valuation roll; see Makey, Chapter 9, this volume.

4. Less than half the royal burghs had a merchant guildry before 1560; see the corrected list (which itself is flawed), with dates, in *Scottish Review*, 32 (1898), 61–81; Dumfries, e.g., had not an incorporated guildry until 1621. The records of the guildries of Perth and Dunfermline, which both begin in the second half of the fifteenth century, are due to be published by SRS. See E. P. D. Torrie, 'The Gild of Dunfermline in the Fifteenth Century' (Edinburgh Univ. Ph.D., 1984) and M. Lynch, *Edinburgh and the Reformation* (Edinburgh, 1981), 29, 51–3.

5. White, Chapter 4, this volume; Lynch, *Edinburgh*, 29, 277. See M. Lynch, 'Scottish Calvinism, 1559–1638' in M. Prestwich (ed.), *International Calvinism, 1541–1715* (Oxford, 1985), 239–41, for a general discussion of the reaction of towns to Protestantism.

6. See T. C. Smout, *Scottish Trade on the Eve of Union, 1660–1707* (Edinburgh, 1963) and R. Mitchison, *Lordship to Patronage: Scotland, 1603–1745* (London, 1983), 93ff.

7. T. C. Smout, 'The Glasgow merchant community in the seventeenth century', *SHR*, 47 (1968), 53, 70; see also his 'The development and enterprise of Glasgow, 1556–1707', *Scot. J. of Pol. Economy*, 7 (1960).

8. Helen M. Bennett, 'The Origins and development of the hand-knitting industry in Scotland' (Edinburgh Univ. Ph.D., 1982).

9. See Brown, Chapter 6, this volume. This should be compared with a series of articles by T. M. Devine, concentrating on the last quarter of the seventeenth century and later; see his 'The Scottish merchant community, 1680–1740' in R. H. Campbell and A. S. Skinner (eds.), *The Origins and Nature of the Scottish Enlightenment* (Edinburgh, 1982), 26–41, and 'The merchant class of the larger Scottish towns in the seventeenth and early eighteenth centuries' in G. Gordon and B. Dicks (eds.), *Scottish Urban History* (Aberdeen, 1983), 92–111.

10. The quartet were recognised as such by Bruges; cited by A. W. K. Stevenson, 'Trade between Scotland and the Low Countries in the Later Middle Ages' (Aberdeen Univ. Ph.D., 1982), 141. See ibid., 39, 208–9, 249, 258, 262–3, 283, and I. Guy, 'The Scottish Export Trade, 1460–1599' (St Andrews Univ. M. Phil., 1982), 20, 79, 92, 166–7, 170, on which all these figures are based.

11. The figures for national taxation of the royal burghs are contained in vols. i–iv of *Burghs Conv. Recs.* A representative sample of those between 1612 and 1705 is conveniently printed in Smout, *Scottish Trade*, 282–3. The Edinburgh figure for 1583 has been reduced by 2 per cent to take account of Kinghorn and Inverkeithing, which were taxed jointly with it. See Smout, 'Development and enterprise', 194–5, for Glasgow's rise in the table.

12. M. Lynch, 'The Scottish early modern burgh', *History Today*, 35 (Feb. 1985), 10–15.

13. Smout, 'Merchant community', 53.

14. These dozen towns do not include obvious cases, such as Haddington, Peebles or Dumfries, which suffered severe disruption from the English invasions of the 1540s.

15. Perth's assessment fell a fraction in 1612, from 6.33 per cent to 6.16 per cent, but rather less so than Glasgow's, which dropped from 4.5 per cent to 4 per cent.

16. Smout, 'Development and enterprise', 195.

17. T. M. Devine, 'The Cromwellian union and the Scottish burghs: the case of Aberdeen and Glasgow, 1652–60' in J. Butt (ed.), *Scottish Themes* (Edinburgh, 1976), 1–16.

18. L. M. Smith, 'Scotland and Cromwell' (Oxford Univ. D. Phil., 1980), 36–7, 42.

19. Many of these reasons are still obscure. One of the most important, but as yet unexplored, may be the rather different usages of credit by merchants of Edinburgh and of those based elsewhere in the years leading up to the crisis of the 1640s. A recent thesis on Glasgow could find only three significant, unpaid sets of debts owed by nobles to its merchants, while another on Edinburgh found a procession of its merchants with capital tied up in substantial debts owed by nobles and greater lairds; cf. W. S. Shepherd, 'The Politics and Society of Glasgow, 1648–74' (Glasgow Univ. Ph.D., 1978), 195, 207–8, 332–3, and J. Brown, 'The Social, Political and Economic Influences of the Edinburgh Merchant

Elite, 1600–38' (Edinburgh Univ. Ph.D., 1985), 313–54. The Restoration brought little compensation for one of the most important, but least recognised, of its aspects was the decision of parliament in 1661 to allow debts of over £1,000 contracted before 1658 to be repaid by instalments over a further six years. It also reduced the interest rate to 6 per cent (*APS*, vii, 317).

20. *APS*, vii, 540. It is possible that Glasgow was being compensated for its military garrison; see Shepherd, 'Thesis', 332.

21. Smout, 'Development and enterprise', 199. A list of manufactories is given in G. Marshall, *Presbyteries and Profits* (Oxford, 1982), 284ff.

22. Smout, *Scottish Trade*, 142, 159, 243; S. G. E. Lythe, *The Economy of Scotland in its European Setting, 1550–1625* (Edinburgh, 1960), 160, 164.

23. Stevenson, 'Thesis', 258; Guy, 'Thesis', 77, 93–4, 116, 168, 170.

24. The regulations pertaining to Edinburgh crafts are conveniently printed in J. D. Marwick (ed.), *Edinburgh Guilds and Crafts* (SBRS, 1909). The totals of craft masters and servants, but an undifferentiated total for merchants and their servants, are given in *Edin. Recs., 1558–1571*, 24–5; see Lynch, *Edinburgh*, 10, for corrected totals. Thirty-one lawyers are given in a voluntary tax roll of 1565 (Lynch, *Edinburgh*, 317). The shape of Edinburgh's pyramid of wealth is analysed, on the basis of tax rolls, in Lynch, 'Whatever happened to the medieval burgh?', *Scot. Econ. and Soc. Hist.*, 4 (1984), 11.

25. See Verschuur, Chapter 2, this volume. 44 per cent of admissions to the Perth guildry 1565–8 were comprised of craftsmen; Verschuur, 'Perth and the Reformation: society and reform, 1540–1560' (Glasgow Univ. Ph.D., 1985), 567. Edinburgh did, however, have craftsmen on its council by the 1530s, although the decision was not recorded; one of the councillors of 1534–5 was specifically called a mason (*Edin. Recs.*, iii, 292).

26. Stevenson, 'Thesis', 249; Pitcairn, *Criminal Trials*, i, 418.

27. In Craftman's Book, no. 34; see Verschuur, 'Thesis', 610–16.

28. See Stevenson, 'Thesis', pp. iv, 262–3, and Grant, *Scotland*, 85–6, who pushes the reasoning further. But cf. J. Wormald, *Court, Kirk and Community: Scotland, 1470–1625* (London, 1981), 48–9.

29. Lythe, *Economy*, 30.

30. Craftsman's Book, no. 34; Verschuur, 'Thesis', 614.

31. As Given in *Acta Dom. Concilii et Sessionis, 1532–3* (Stair Soc., 1951), 78–9.

32. A. Maxwell, *The History of Old Dundee* (Edinburgh and Dundee, 1884), 287–9; Stevenson, 'Thesis', 172, 228n, 258; Guy, 'Thesis', 90. The general development of Dundee is discussed in I. Flett, 'The Conflict of Reformation and Democracy in the Geneva of Scotland, 1443–1610' (St Andrews Univ. M.Phil., 1981).

33. Cf. P. Clark (ed.), *Country Towns in pre-industrial England* (Leicester, 1981), 8, in which much the same development is outlined in English ports.

34. ACA, MSS Stent Roll Bundles (1596–). There are a total of 569 entries on the 1637 roll; an earlier, less explicit roll of 1608, which lists only eighty craftsmen, is printed in *ACL*, i, 392–406. The Glasgow numbers, broken down by craft, are conveniently printed in D. Murray, *Early Burgh Organization in Scotland* (Glasgow, 1924), i, 484n. It should be

noted that in Glasgow the fifty-five maltsters were recorded amongst the trades, unlike Edinburgh or Aberdeen.

35. D. MacNiven, 'Merchant and trader in early seventeenth-century Aberdeen' (Aberdeen Univ. M.Litt., 1977), 104–6, 134, 145, 231, 236; cf. Brown, 'Thesis', 34, on specialisation in Edinburgh.

36. E. L. Ewan, 'Aberdeen in the fourteenth century' in J. S. Smith (ed.), *New Light on Medieval Aberdeen* (Aberdeen, 1985), 40–1, See also ch. 3 of her 'The Burgesses of Fourteenth-Century Scotland: a Social History' (Edinburgh Univ. Ph.D., 1985).

37. *Abdn. Recs., 1398–1570*, p. xxxiv; A. White, 'Religion, Politics and Society in Aberdeen, 1543–1593' (Edinburgh Univ. Ph.D., 1985), 19–20.

38. These issues are all analysed in White, 'Thesis', 309, 319, 321–4, 329–32. See *Burghs Conv. Recs.*, i, 313–15, for the allegations. The guild court ordinance is contained in the council register; ACA, MS Town Co. Recs., xxxii, fos. 622, 637, 640. I am grateful to Allan White for supplying me with this reference.

39. The tax rolls show a sharp increase in assessments for Dysart by 1574 and Crail by 1579; Pittenweem appeared for the first time in 1579. Their decline in the seventeenth century is charted by Smout, *Scottish Trade*, 136–7, 282–3.

40. Cf. N. Goose, 'English pre-industrial urban economies', *Urban History Yearbook* (1982), 28.

41. See 'Register containing the state and condition of every burgh within the kingdom of Scotland in the year 1692', *SBRS Miscellany* (1881), 166–70. The occupational structure of Stirling is briefly outlined in R. C. Fox, 'Stirling, 1550–1700: the morphology and functions of a pre-industrial Scottish burgh' in Gordon and Dicks (eds.), *Scottish Urban History*, 67–9.

42. Lynch, *Edinburgh*, 378; Smout, 'Merchant community', 61–3. The Aberdeen figures are based on a tax roll of 1623, analysed in MacNiven, 'Thesis', 101; it is easier to try to count the number of merchants before the influx of new taxpayers in the 1630s, although account has still to be taken of resident heritors.

43. At its meeting in Edinburgh in April 1552; the only record of this and another meeting at Perth in August 1555 is in Scottish Catholic Archives, Fort Augustus MS A1; see fo. 330r.

44. Lynch, *Edinburgh*, 63. The effect on lawyers was stressed by Sir John Lauder of Fountainhall, *Historical Notices of Scottish Affairs* (Bannatyne Club, 1848), i, 75.

45. See White, 'Thesis', 329, and E. Bain, *Merchant and Craft Guilds: a History of the Aberdeen Incorporated Trades* (Aberdeen, 1887), 334.

46. *Glasgow Recs., 1573–1642*, 471.

47. *Stirling Recs., 1519–1666*, 112, 137.

48. No ordinary burgesses were admitted in Aberdeen 1590–1613 and only eleven 1613–24; MacNiven, 'Thesis', 262n.

49. The ratios of Aberdeen entrants to the guildry 1623–6 are analysed by MacNiven, 'Thesis', 120–1, 256–7, and are very similar to those of the fifteenth century, as tabulated by H. Booton, 'Economic and social change in later medieval Aberdeen' in Smith (ed.), *Medieval Aberdeen*, 49;

in both 64 per cent were sons of fathers who had been in the guildry. The Glasgow ratios, which relate to entrance to burgess-ship rather than guildry, are set out in Smout, 'Merchant community', 69. There are a number of differences in the method of sampling and the constituency drawn upon, too many to make safe comparisons.

50. The Edinburgh apprentice records are analysed in J. McMillan, 'A Study of the Edinburgh Burgess Community and its Economic Activities, 1600–1680' (Edinburgh Univ. Ph.D., 1984), 58–84. The social mobility detected by Devine, 'Scottish merchant community', 29–31, based on apprentice records 1666–1700 — showing 34 per cent as sons of lairds, 9 per cent from professional families and 7 per cent sons of craftsmen — clearly existed before that, but not in the same proportions.

51. Lynch, 'Medieval burgh', 14–15.

52. A justice of the peace court was set up in Edinburgh in 1611 and town constables took over the traditional responsibilities of all burgesses to watch and ward. Records of the Glasgow and Aberdeen courts survive for the Restoration period. The virtues of the Aberdeen court are extolled by Alexander Skene in his *Succinct Survey of the famous City of Aberdeen* (1685; reprinted 1833), 160ff, where he commends its use, rather than the kirk session, as a morals court. I am grateful to Mr Gordon Desbrisay for information on this subject.

53. Brown, 'Thesis', 381.

54. There were 1,152 taxpayers in 1605 and 1,548 in 1637 (ibid., 16–18). Yet there were, by the evidence of the 1635 annuity tax, over 4,000 households. The effects on Aberdeen are seen in *ACL*, i, 198.

55. Shepherd, 'Thesis', 49, 51, 90.

56. This is drawn from a comparison of the lists in D. Stevenson (ed.), *The Government of Scotland under the Covenanters, 1637–1651* (SHS, 1982), 189–98, and the appendix detailing the Edinburgh elite in Brown, 'Thesis'.

57. M. Flinn *et al.*, *Scottish Population History* (Cambridge, 1977), 137–40.

58. Smith, 'Thesis', 26–7.

59. T. Pagan, *The Convention of the Royal Burghs of Scotland* (Glasgow, 1926), 82–9; *Burghs Conv. Recs.*, iii, 502; Mitchison, *Scotland*, 95; cf. J. R. Jones, *Country and Court: England, 1658–1714* (London, 1978), 34, 242–3, and G. C. F. Forster, 'Government in provincial England under the later Stuarts', *Trans. Royal Hist. Soc.*, 33 (1983), 44–8.

60. Shepherd, 'Thesis', 260, 287, 291–2. Perth has yet to be analysed although there is much material, e.g., in Lauder of Fountainhall, *Historical Notices* (Bannatyne Club, 1848).

61. H. Ouston, 'York in Edinburgh: James VII and the patronage of learning in Scotland, 1679–1688', in J. Dwyer *et al.*, *New Perspectives on the Politics and Culture of Early Modern Scotland* (Edinburgh, 1981), 133–55; Skene, *Survey of Aberdeen*, 38–9.

62. John Knox, *History of the Reformation in Scotland*, ed. W. C. Dickinson (Edinburgh, 1949), i, 163; Lynch, *Edinburgh*, 38–9, 83–5.

63. *Peebles Recs.*, *1165–1710*, 66–9, 71–2, 205, 217; R. Renwick, *Peebles during the Reign of Queen Mary* (Peebles, 1903), 39–44, 51, 64–5, 68–9, 123–6; J. W. Buchan, *A History of Peeblesshire* (Glasgow, 1925), ii,

23, 25, 36, 221–6, 257–9; *Acts of Council*, 595.

   64. *RPC*, i, 604–5.

   65. J. Wormald, *Lords and Men* (Edinburgh, 1985), 138, 408.

   66. *RPC*, ii, 556–7, 559, 573, 733; Wormald, *Lords and Men*, 138.

   67. The ambivalent relationship between Aberdeen and the earls of Huntly forms a major theme in Allan White's thesis. See Booton, 'Economic and social change in Aberdeen', 51–2, for noble patronage of the burgh in the fifteenth century. ACA, MS Town Treasury Accts., I(i), has the 1559–60 accounts, but none are extant between then and 1595.

   68. Perth and Jedburgh are discussed by Verschuur and Brown respectively, below; see *Stirling Recs., 1519–1666*, 213; *RPC*, i, 11–12, 116, 470, and Chapter 3, below, for Stirling.

   69. Verschuur, 'Thesis', 191, 498.

   70. Lynch, *Edinburgh*, 74–7; *Edin. Recs., 1557–1571*, 38.

   71. A. Skene, *Memorialls for the Government of Royall Burghs in Scotland* (Aberdeen, 1685), 108, stresses the effects of the act of 1672. Dumfries had 531 households and 952 paid hearths in 1691; see D. Adamson, 'The hearth tax', *Trans. Dumf. & Galloway Nat. Hist. & Antiq. Soc.*, 47 (1970), 147–77.

   72. I. Whyte, *Agriculture and Society in 17th Century Scotland* (Edinburgh, 1979); see also his 'Early modern Scotland: continuity and change' in G. Whittington and I. D. Whyte (eds.), *An Historical Geography of Scotland* (London, 1983), esp. 127–36.

   73. J. di Folco, 'The Hopes of Craighall and investment in land in the seventeenth century' in T. M. Devine (ed.), *Lairds and Improvement in the Scotland of the Enlightenment* (Glasgow, 1978). His figures (followed by the assessments in the tax roll of 1649) are: Edinburgh 50 per cent (36 per cent); Aberdeen 11 per cent (6.67 per cent); Perth 4 per cent (4 per cent); Dundee 3 per cent (7 per cent); Stirling 2.5 per cent (1.1 per cent); Glasgow 2.5 per cent (6.5 per cent); Dumfries 2.1 per cent (1.67 per cent).

   74. Devine, 'Merchant class', 105.

   75. Cf. Smout, *Scottish Trade*, 149–50.

   76. Brown, 'Thesis', 313–54.

   77. Devine, 'Merchant class', 104–6.

   78. *SBRS Miscellany*, 59–60.

   79. J. G. Ballard, 'The theory of the Scottish burgh', *SHR*, 13 (1916), 22, 27–9; 143 new centres were created 1550–1660, 346 1660–1707. They are detailed in G. S. Pryde (ed.), *The Burghs of Scotland: A Critical List* (Glasgow, 1965), 59ff. See Whyte, *Agriculture and Society*, 178–92.

   80. White, 'Thesis', 304, 309, 319, 350.

   81. Lynch, 'Medieval burgh', 14–16; see also Wormald, *Scotland*, 46.

   82. M. Wood, 'St Paul's Work', *Bk. Old Edin. Club.*, 17 (1930), 49–75; Shepherd, 'Thesis', 89–90, 322–3; Lynch, 'Calvinism', 234, 239; ACA, MS Kirk Session Accts. (1607–75). The best treatment of this subject is R. Mitchison, 'The making of the old Scottish poor law', *Past and Present*, 63 (1974); see esp. 62–80.

   83. Lynch, *Edinburgh*, 56–9, for the hammermen. The Perth bakers show a persistent attachment to their patron saint when the kirk session record becomes extant, in 1577; see *Spottiswoode Misc.*, ii (1845), 234.

   84. The only study of lawyers to attempt to cover the whole period is

G. Donaldson, 'The legal profession in Scottish society in the sixteenth and seventeenth centuries', *Juridical Review*, 21 (1976), 1–19. For Aberdeen, see MacNiven, 'Thesis', 101; Edinburgh, Lauder of Fountainhall, *Historical Notices*, i, 73–7; Perth, Verschuur, 'Thesis', 210.

85. I. Adams, *The Making of Urban Scotland* (London, 1978), 31–40.

86. Lynch, 'Medieval burgh', 7, 18n; Lynch, 'Early modern burgh', 12–13; H. Scott (ed.), *Fasti Ecclesiae Scoticanae* (Edinburgh, 1915–50), vi, 461, 466; cf. P. Collinson, *The Religion of Protestants* (Oxford, 1982), 209–10, and W. T. MacCaffrey, *Exeter, 1540–1650* (Cambridge, Mass., 1958), 176–7, 196–7. None of Exeter's nineteen parish churches could hold more than 200 or 300. St Giles, in Edinburgh, had, along with Trinity College which was pressed into service after 1560, to accommodate the smallest of the burgh's quarters, a congregation of 8,000 adults in the 1590s. New churches were built after 1612.

2

Merchants and Craftsmen in Sixteenth-Century Perth

Mary Verschuur

At the outset it seems important to clarify two points. Firstly, the early modern town discussed here is Perth and events which took place there did not necessarily take place in all other towns. Current research is demonstrating that Scottish burghs responded differently to the Scottish Reformation. The same principle of regional variation no doubt holds true with the other changing social and political circumstances in sixteenth-century Scotland as well. Secondly, the terms merchant and craftsmen are scattered liberally throughout this essay. In view of a recent article which pointed out the dangers of separating sixteenth century burgesses into groups of merchants and craftsmen,[1] it seems important to explain that the reason for identifying an individual as either a craftsman or a merchant is simply that these were the names by which the burgesses of Perth identified themselves. In arguing their respective cases against one another the participants in the debate, which polarised Perth society for at least a quarter of a century up to the Reformation of 1560, referred to themselves as craftsmen and merchants.[2]

Perth is situated twenty-two miles up the river Tay from Dundee and the east coast of Scotland. There was a settlement on the site that the town still occupies long before written records began to document the history of the burgh. The siting of a bridge or crossing over the Tay at Perth from a very early date had always provided a measure of prosperity to the town. Perth was raised to the status of a royal burgh in the mid-twelfth century, giving its merchants the right to trade overseas and allowing foreign ships to unload their cargoes on the shore there. By the mid-fourteenth century, Perth along with Aberdeen, Dundee and Edinburgh was

36

recognised as one of the 'four great towns of Scotland'.[3] The assassination of James I at Perth in 1437 led, however, to the court's withdrawal from the town as a place of residence. With the departure of the court a period of economic decline set in, which was probably made worse by outbreaks of plague in the town in the first half of the sixteenth century.[4] By 1550 Perth was the smallest and least important of the four largest burghs.

Sixteenth-century Perth was not unlike most other Scottish burghs of the period. It was governed by a provost, four bailies and a council of twelve, all wealthy and prosperous merchants who formed an elite and self-perpetuating oligarchy. Elections were held annually at Michaelmas at which time the retiring council convened to choose a new one. The old and new councils, together with the deacons of the incorporated crafts, elected a provost and four bailies to serve as magistrates for the coming year. Four to eight sergeands were appointed by the magistrates to serve a police function in carrying out the decreets of the burgh court. A minor variation in electoral practice was that in Perth the dean of guild and burgh treasurer were not chosen until Martinmas. All of these officers normally served for one year although the retiring provost, bailies, dean and treasurer automatically sat on the council in the year following their year in office.

The merchant guild, which had been authorised by charter of King William the Lion in 1209,[5] was experiencing repeated incursions into its independence and authority by the mid-sixteenth century. The provost and magistrates assumed the regulation of trade disputes and the setting of prices with increasing regularity. The guild at Perth reached its nadir in 1544, for from that year onwards the town council and magistrates of Perth appointed the dean of guild, thus depriving the merchants of any say in the choice of their leader.[6]

In addition to the guild, there were nine officially incorporated craft organisations in sixteenth-century Perth, each with its annually appointed deacon and officers. No craft possesses an extant seal of cause but it seems likely that Perth's craftsmen, like their counterparts in Edinburgh, had acquired some legal identity by the mid-sixteenth century. In most towns the craft organisations had organised themselves into a hierarchical order which placed certain occupations above others in importance, status and wealth. This relative importance of one craft to another varied from town to town depending on the natural resources and needs of the burgesses. To be a tailor in Edinburgh, for example, was to belong to a wealthy and important craft, but tailors in Perth had fewer demands for their services and were ranked sixth of the nine official incorporations. Goldsmiths in some towns had their own incorporation and in others were even considered to be merchants, but in Perth they were members of the hammermen incorporation. This was the most important as well as the largest of Perth's crafts, with members drawn from a variety of trades including saddlers and iron smiths as well as goldsmiths.[7] Behind the hammermen, in descending order of rank and importance, came the baxters, skinners, cordiners, fleshers, tailors, wrights, weavers and fullers. Several of the other incorporations also encompassed more than one art: wrights and coopers were the most prominent members of the wright incorporation but it included bowers, masons and barber surgeons as well. Hatmakers and bonnetmakers belonged to the fullers' incorporation and glovers to the skinner craft. In addition to the nine official craft guilds there were substantial numbers of maltmen and litsters in Perth and the usual assortment of carters, horse hirers, stablers and porters engaged in the most menial occupations. Collectively all these workers were known as the unincorporated trades and although politically of little consequence, since they could not participate in elections either by voting or as candidates, the maltmen and litsters, at least, could be counted amongst the town's most wealthy residents.

Wealth was spread unusually widely in sixteenth-century Perth. It was not the exclusive preserve of the merchants but extended to the trades, both incorporated and unincorporated. A comparative survey of twenty craftsmen's testaments and twenty merchants' revealed that the average net assets of the craftsmen amounted to only £60 less than the merchant average.[8] There is also direct evidence to indicate that Perth was viewed as predominantly a 'craftis toun', unlike any other of its size in Scotland.[9] A royal charter acknowledged that the craftsmen far outnumbered all the rest of the inhabitants and that the economy of the burgh was based upon their productivity, rather than on the revenues from overseas trade.[10] The craftsmen of Perth claimed that they paid more than half the taxes levied on the town, which was considerably more than their peers in other, merchant-dominated towns paid.[11] A variety of contemporary evidence makes it abundantly clear that the prosperity of Perth was largely dependent upon her craftsmen.

Social and political unrest was a familiar if variable phenomenon of urban life in sixteenth-century Scotland. It existed to a high and intense degree in Perth. This fact is corroborated by a collection of documents, letters, extracts of court proceedings and decreets, and a series of well reasoned, but sometimes emotional arguments, which were gathered together by the craftsmen of Perth around 1561 for the defence of their privileges. These miscellaneous documents are unique to Perth and they demonstrate that the town and its citizens had been subjected to several violent outbursts over the previous forty years when the craftsmen burgesses demanded political concessions of the merchant burgesses. The tension was so extreme at times that the merchants of Perth described themselves as living in fear of war.[12]

In addition to the internal pressure brought to bear on the burgh by the craftsmen burgesses seeking to improve their political power and influence, most sixteenth-century Scottish burghs (and here again Perth was a prime example) were also subjected to interference by locally influential magnates or lairds who sought to control their neighbouring towns either for power, wealth or both. Royal intervention into the affairs of burghs also increased as the sixteenth century progressed. As the national government became more centralised burghs were increasingly courted or coerced into supporting a ruler or a policy in exchange for some favour.[13] Neither the issue of increased political rights for craftsmen burgesses nor that of lordly influence in burgh affairs was new to the times or unique to Perth. Craftsmen burgesses had been seeking some say in burgh elections since the middle of the fifteenth century but at the heart of the sixteenth-century argument between the merchants and craftsmen of Perth was not merely the issue of voting rights but the question of political representation. The pattern which unfolded in the second quarter of the sixteenth century in Perth was that the craftsmen's campaign against the merchants became enmeshed with the attempts of the local nobility to gain influence in the town

The principal noble contestants for control of Perth were Lord Gray and Lord Ruthven. The burgh itself was probably not the *casus belli* but it was a significant and strategically placed prize in a long-standing noble feud between the Ruthvens, heritable sheriffs of Perthshire, and the family which, it was said, controlled 'the Tay north'.[14] In the 1520s the family of minor lairds, Charteris of Cuthilgurdy, normally held offices in the burgh as representatives of Lord Gray. The interests of William, 2nd Lord Ruthven were initially represented by a merchant burgess but he later assumed the provostship himself, as did his successors. The feud between the families was over by 1550 but the Ruthvens' control of the burgh, first attempted in 1528 and confirmed in 1544, passed through three generations of the family.

Two other patterns would recur with increasing frequency in the mounting tension between Perth's merchants and craftsmen which marked the forty years up to the Reformation of 1559–60. One was the recourse made by both parties to the central agencies of law and government, the Court of Session or the privy council. The second was the intervention which was from time to time forced on the central government to diffuse a local crisis in the burgh, which particularly between 1555 and 1557 amounted to a virtual breakdown of authority.

The untimely death of James IV at Flodden in 1513 and the demise of most of the nobility in that same battle left Scotland leaderless and floundering. As the long period of James V's minority wore on an unsettled state prevailed causing the English ambassador in Scotland to write to his master that 'the Scottish realm is so divided, it is hard to say whom to trust. There is no justice, but continual murders, theft and robbery'.[15] It was during this period, in 1520 to be precise, that Perth chose its first known laird provost, Patrick Charteris of Cuthilgurdy. One of the bailies elected that year and the following year was Constantine Arthur, a goldsmith by trade and a member of the hammerman incorporation.[16] Arthur was a burgess and guild brother who had probably abjured his craft in order to hold the office of bailie, but he was still a craftsman and his appointment to a bailie's seat at that juncture was an unprecedented innovation.

In June 1522 Charteris, who was still provost of Perth, appears to have obtained a precept from the regent John, duke of Albany, granting the craftsmen of Perth the right to four seats on the town council.[17] The council roster for 1523 fails to reveal whether or not the precept was implemented that year, but the coincidence of Charteris' tenure as provost of Perth and the improved political outlook for the craftsmen seems to suggest something more than mere coincidence. Charteris probably needed popular or numerical support to retain the provost's office. He may have sought that support by proffering political offices to the largest social group within the burgh, the craftsmen. They in turn could ensure the support of all the members of their incorporations since obedience to the deacon, who was almost always a burgess, was required practice. It is also possible that the craftsmen burgesses brought pressure to bear on Charteris to grant political concessions in exchange for support.

Although the innovation of a craftsman bailie does not appear to have persisted after 1522, the craftsmen of Perth obtained a second precept after the change of government brought about by the rise of the Douglases at court in 1526 to confirm their right to four seats on the town council.[18] The few extant council records for the years 1527 to 1533 make it clear that the terms of the precept were not enacted immediately. The councils of 1531 and 1532 continued to be dominated by merchants, who were pointedly listed in the election register as 'merchant councillors'.[19] The real shift in Perth's affairs came in a different form, when in 1528 Charteris was replaced as provost by William, master of Ruthven, second son and heir of William, 1st Lord Ruthven at the direction of the crown in a manoeuvre which may have coincided with the shift of power at the court brought about by James V's escape from the Douglas faction. By intervening in local politics the young king had, perhaps inadvertently, thrust a second local magnate into the arena of Perth burgh politics and in the long run had probably exacerbated rather than eased tensions.

In 1534 matters came to a head when the opposing factions within the burgh chose rival provosts. An appeal for resolution of this quandary was made to the Lords of Council, the king's justiciars, who formed the highest court in the land. The Lords not only decided which man had properly been elected as provost but also nominated a council of twelve which included two craftsmen burgesses, identified by name and occupation.[20] The fact that the Lords chose a council as well as a provost of Perth indicates that the root of the political argument in 1534 lay in the repercussions of the precepts of 1522 and 1526. Although craft representation on the council had been whittled down from four to two, it had been confirmed at law. From 1534 onwards, apart from occasional assaults on one or both of the seats, Perth always had at least two craftsmen on its town council. The practice of seeking the aid of an outside agency to resolve internal difficulties was established.

Between 1534 and 1542 the contention between merchant and craftsmen burgesses abated as the craftsmen annually took up their two seats on the council but the feud between Lord Ruthven and Lord Gray continued to affect the burgh as the office of provost see-sawed between their partisans. The national crisis produced by the death of James V in December 1542 and the succession of a week-old infant, Mary, had disruptive effects on many localities, not least Perth. The bewildering shifts of both policy and allies on the part of the governor, the earl of Arran, in the course of the next twelve months — first seeking rapprochment with England and favouring Protestantism, then abandoning both — bred both political indecision and opportunism. One such opportunist was the Perthshire laird, John Charteris of Cuthilgurdy, who between December 1542 and January 1544 supported five distinctly different causes and factions.[21] Charteris, either the brother or the son of Patrick Charteris, the provost of the 1520s, arrived in Perth in September 1543 with a letter from the governor commanding the community to accept him as its provost.[22] Equally opportune was the renewal in 1543 of the craftsmen's campaign for a place on the magistrates' bench. At Michaelmas they mounted a full-scale demonstration parading through the town with flags flying. The parade ended in the council chamber of the tolbooth where the craftsmen 'constrained and compelled' the council to choose Gilbert Rattray, a goldsmith, as one of the bailies.[23] The election register for that year does not, however, name Rattray as a bailie, which may indicate that the demonstration was unsuccessful, but in 1544 a craftsman was chosen as one of the four bailies and that year the election stood.

On the face of it there were no obvious reprisals for the riot in the Perth tolbooth in October 1543. The next outside intervention in the burgh's affairs came three months later, in the form of a visit made by Cardinal Beaton, metropolitan of the church in Scotland, and the governor, who had recently recovered from his 'godly fit', for the avowed purpose of punishing certain heretics in Perth.[24] During their brief two-day stay in the town four men and one woman were found guilty of heresy and put to death. Most historians have seen deep-rooted Protestant activism as the chief cause of the heresy trials at Perth in January 1544. However, the craftsmen of Perth claimed in a document written some twenty years later that the burgh's merchants had encouraged the governor and cardinal to come to Perth to take repressive action against the craftsmen; the change of heresy, they alleged, was a convenient veil to obscure the real reason for the persecution.[25] Certainly all five put to death were craftspeople.[26] The trials may well have been a punishment for insurrection as much as for heresy.

The governor's reconversion meant that Charteris of Cuthilgurdy was no longer useful to him as provost of Perth and before departing from the town Arran replaced him with an elderly burgess who was a close associate of the abbot of Coupar Angus.[27]

The governor's choice of a new provost had the effect of creating a vacuum in authority within the burgh into which the noble feud moved with mounting violence. The climax came in July 1544 when Lord Gray and his kin stormed the burgh with the intention of reinstalling Charteris as provost. Their attack was foiled by Patrick, master of Ruthven, son and heir of 2nd Lord Ruthven, who organised the defence of the burgh. Three months later the burgh's new noble protector accepted the offer of the office of provost.[28] The election of 1544 marked the beginning of the long domination of Perth and its affairs by the noble family of Ruthven. The second and third lords, together with their client Oliver Maxton, monopolised the office of provost of Perth from 1544 until Patrick's death in 1566.[29] The contest between the Grays and the Ruthvens for control of the burgh was largely settled in 1544, even if the official end to their feud did not come until 1546, when the governor extracted pledges of good behaviour from both parties and a promise that neither would use the burgh as a pretext for further trouble between them.[30]

The election of 1544 had another important result. Chosen to serve as one of the bailies of Perth in Ruthven's first year as provost was a goldsmith, Dennis Caveris.[31] There is nothing in the record to explain the coincidence of Patrick Ruthven's election with that of the first in a continuous succession of craftsmen bailies of Perth. In that Ruthven countenanced the election and allowed it to stand, we must conclude that he had no objections to the innovation. Like his predecessor Patrick Charteris, Ruthven may have been astute enough to realise that the strength of Perth's craft population would provide a landed outsider with a broad base of support. From then on one of Perth's four bailies was always a craftsman burgess, despite annual but ineffective protests by the dean of guild or other prominent merchant. Furthermore, since the retiring bailies always sat on the council for the year following their terms as bailies the crafts' representation on Perth town council increased to three seats after 1544.[32]

Having secured representation as magistrates and town councillors Perth's craftsmen soon began to experience internal divisions as to which crafts should benefit from the new privileges. In 1547 the hammermen, skinners and baxters, who comprised Perth's three wealthiest crafts, again resorted to the outside authority of the Lords of Council, gaining a decreet that the craftsman bailie be chosen only from these three crafts. The smaller crafts disputed the authenticity of the judgement and an impasse was reached.[33] Since Lord Ruthven was absent from the burgh it was decided to wait until his return before seeking a resolution to the dilemma. The result was that a nominee of the six smaller crafts was duly appointed craftsman bailie in 1547. The arbitration of Ruthven both prevented the escalation of an internal struggle for power within the crafts and blocked the efforts of the merchants to return to a wholly merchant-dominated council. The merchants, effectively isolated, were restricted to minor political manoeuverings: they attempted in 1549 to restrict the choice of craftsman bailie to the council itself and barred all but three of the craft deacons from the election process in 1551.[34] Neither move had a lasting effect. These episodes only served to underline the new-found dependence of the burgh on its noble provost. The confidence placed in the Ruthven provosts was one of the most striking and unusual features of the relationship between the burgesses of Perth and the dominant local magnate. In placing its trust in a noble patron the burgh community achieved a unity rarely found when the burgesses dealt with issues on their own.

It was not only in Perth that urban craftsmen were finding themselves in conflict with other segments of society or were asserting their independence in some way. During the summer of 1554 the craftsmen of Cupar in Fife staged a violent demonstration in which they threatened the bailies, disregarded an order of the burgh court and formulated a bond amongst themselves to defend their common interests.[35] This incident, along with mounting friction between merchants and craftsmen in other burghs, undoubtedly gave the authorities cause for concern and lay behind the passage in the parliament of May 1555 of an Act against Craftsmen in Burghs.[36] The likelihood that influential Edinburgh merchants instigated this act is borne out by the allegation by the craftsmen of Perth that the act was passed by way of merchants in other burghs who were 'great in court' at the time.[37] The act abolished the office of craft deacon, prohibited all craft meetings and placed all craftsmen in burghs 'under the provost, bailies and council'.[38] All of these provisions threatened to undermine the progress made by Perth's craftsmen over the previous quarter of a century.

Reaction to this statute can be documented in many Scottish burghs during the year which followed[39] but the reaction in Perth was complicated by the existence of the precept of 1526, which specifically allowed craftsmen representation on the burgh council. While the merchants of Perth found ample justification in the act for excluding the craftsmen from offices, the position was further complicated by the craftsmen's familiar device of seeking a specific remission from the crown. Walter Piper, a flesher burgess, obtained an exemption from the act on the eve of the Michaelmas election of 1555.[40] The merchants refused to honour the exemption and anarchy resulted: from October until December 1555 the town of Perth was without either a council or bailies. No candidates other than the provost — Ruthven — were acceptable to all parties.

The scale of the political crisis in Perth in 1555 can be judged by the flurry of appeals it provoked from different sources to seek a resolution. Early in November certain bailies and councillors of Perth wrote to the burgh of Stirling inviting representatives of that burgh to attend a public discussion of the contention between merchants and craftsmen in burghs which was scheduled to take place later that month in Perth.[41] There is no record of the meeting but another letter, of December 1555, indicates that the provost of Aberdeen had been called upon by the regent, Mary of Guise, to help settle the turmoil in Perth.[42] The regent had herself been drawn into the affair by the provost of Perth as a mediatrix. It seems clear that no internal resolution of the problem was possible and once again the burgh sought the aid of outside authorities to mediate in its internal problems. The affair was settled only by the regent dictating the names of the twelve councillors and four bailies,[43] but tension persisted. The council nominated by the regent broke with custom; it included a craftsman bailie but the craftsmen were given only one other seat on the council. In mid-December the regent noted in a personal letter to Lord Ruthven that it had come to her attention that discord and threatened violence continued to persist between the merchants and craftsmen of Perth,[44] which suggests that the resolution which had been worked out was unsatisfactory to some, if not all, of the parties involved in the conflict.

By that time however, the problem was no longer confined to Perth and a Convention of Burghs was called to meet in Edinburgh on 15 January 1556 to consider the question of the reconciliation of merchants and craftsmen in all burghs of the realm.[45] The minutes of this meeting are not extant but the fact that it was felt necessary to call it indicates that strife between merchants and craftsmen in burghs had become so widespread as to pose a threat to established authority. The outcome was the revocation of the Act of Parliament against Craftsmen in April

1556.[46] Although the craftsmen of Perth already possessed an exemption granted the previous September, and despite the general revocation, they sought a particular revocation of the act and obtained it on 28 May 1556.[47] This revocation clearly stated that the craftsmen of Perth were to have 'equal privileges, offices and liberties with merchants' and the charter was granted on the basis that the town was upheld by the prosperity of the crafts and that craftsmen outnumbered the rest of the population.[48]

The issuance of this specific exemption precipitated a full-blown crisis of authority in Perth and threatened a complete breakdown of its government. Throughout the spring and summer of 1556 the dean of guild waged an active campaign against the craftsmen which led him into a direct conflict with the provost. Besides depriving certain craftsmen of their freedom and closing up their booths for alleged misappropriation of burgh privilege, the dean of guild categorically refused to admit any craftsmen's sons or sons-in-law into the guild. When charged by the provost to answer for his discrimination against the craftsmen, the dean of guild refused to appear in the burgh court but instead instigated a suit against the provost and certain craftsmen burgesses in the Court of Session. Fifty-seven merchants joined the dean in agreeing to raise a tax upon themselves to meet the expense of the suit.[49] The provost, in attempting to administer justice to the craftsmen burgesses, had been thrust into the role of their champion. Clear lines of demarcation were drawn between the merchant and craftsmen burgesses of Perth in the summer of 1556.

The animosity was so great that it threatened to disrupt the Michaelmas elections in 1556 and it caused the regent to order the magistrates to hold their elections despite threatened non-attendance by the participants.[50] On the day of the head court two factions appeared in the tolbooth of Perth, one headed by a skinner burgess claiming to represent 'certain of the bailies and merchants' and the other faction headed by a merchant burgess, spokesman for 'the bailies, merchants and council'.[51] The former asked Ruthven, as the provost, to conduct the election in accordance with the recent charter granted by the regent which gave full equality to craftsmen burgesses. The merchant representative urged the provost to conduct the election according to 'former practice'. The provost, caught between rival factions each citing outside authority, proposed the interim appointment of one merchant and one craftsman to act as bailies of the burgh while he consulted with the regent. No one present was willing to agree to the temporary appointments and in the ensuing clamour Ruthven left for the court.

At this juncture the town of Perth was threatened with a serious failure at law. Election day was about to pass without any officers having been chosen to serve the court and community of the burgh. Claiming that the burgh must choose its officers on the appointed day or forfeit its privilege one of the merchant bailies convened a court and ordered the sergeands to summon the councillors, magistrates and burgh clerk to return to the tolbooth for the purpose of holding an election. Some of the merchant councillors returned as did the town clerk, but the provost, the other three bailies, the dean of guild and the deacons of crafts did not. The rump, nevertheless, went ahead and elected a new council which, like that of the previous year, had Lord Ruthven as provost and only one craftsman councillor in its number. More controversially, it seized the chance to turn the clock back to the situation which had obtained before 1544: four merchant burgesses were chosen as bailies.[52]

The disputed election of October 1556 sparked off another craft riot.[53] It also forced Lord Ruthven into action. Either on his own initiative or prodded by the craftsmen, he obtained royal authority to deprive the four merchant bailies and reinstate the bailies of 1555 until such time as the regent could come in person to settle the matter.[54] Again, however, Ruthven's attempt at a compromise broke down when only one of these bailies — a saddler called John Kinloch — proved a willing participant. Perth was therefore left with a single craftsman bailie, backed by the provost and the craftsmen. The burgh's merchants, however, continued to dispute his authority, convened rival courts and appointed their own common clerk.[55] The crisis had begun with the prospect of no civic administration; it continued and worsened when competing administrations emerged.

It is impossible to say how long this situation continued and if Kinloch was ever able to act effectively as sole bailie. At this point even the documents and extracts in the Craftsmen's Collection fall silent. The regent probably passed through Perth on her way from Aberdeen to Edinburgh between 19 October and 2 November 1556.[56] The breakdown of authority was officially ended only in May 1557, when the council and deacons of crafts ratified an agreement regarding the election of bailies.[57] No names are legible on this much defaced agreement but notaries' protocols dating from about April 1557 onwards reveal that two merchants, one craftsman and a client of Lord Ruthven eventually served as bailies of Perth for part of the 1556–7 electoral year. In the end it was Lord Ruthven who increased his influence in the town by obtaining a bailie's seat for one of his tenant lairds at the expense of the merchants. The noble connection which had controlled the burgh since 1544 was forced, as a result of the severe crisis in the mid-1550s, to secure for itself a more conspicuous presence in burgh government.

Two years had passed between the passage of the Act against Craftsmen in Burghs through parliament in 1555 and the agreement over the choosing of bailies. During those two years Perth had been in turmoil. Inflammatory debates between merchants and craftsmen burgesses had led to violence on more than one occasion and the provost had felt it necessary to call upon the regent to come to the burgh at least twice, and possibly three times, to settle the controversy. During this period Lord Ruthven's position had been threatened and openly challenged by the merchants of Perth, but with the support of the craftsmen and the regent he had successfully maintained and strengthened it. The craftsmen, or at least the most political of their leaders, had also triumphed to the extent of retaining the bailie's seat, and the loss of one seat on the council was only temporary for the records show that the second seat was restored to them at Michaelmas 1557. As for the merchants, they had accomplished nothing in the way of curtailing the aspirations of the craftsmen.

The crisis which engulfed Perth in the mid-1550s concerned the workings of its political constitution rather than religion. There had been outbreaks of popular Protestant feeling in Perth since the 1530s, but the growth of heresy was not a disruptive issue in the town in the 1550s. At times the crafts did adopt explicitly Protestant language in arguing their case for increased political representation, as when they drew up certain arguments outlining the debate between merchants and craftsmen in burghs.[58] This document reveals that the craftsmen's thinking was marked by a considerable departure from the prevailing view of society. It utilises a strong reliance on biblical argument to support its radical point of view. But overall, it seems clear that in Perth the growth of Protestant ideas did not cause the disputes between the merchants and the craftsmen, not did it resolve them.

For a brief period between 1558 and 1559, the political disaffection abated. As the Reformation crisis overtook the burgh its citizens turned their attentions to forming a community of Christ and for a short time unanimity prevailed. Yet, the immediate aftermath of the Reformation of 1559 – 60 saw no resolution of the basic dispute between the burgesses of Perth. The merchants persisted in their attempts to exclude the craftsmen from the affairs of the burgh while the craftsmen continued to fight for increased political participation. By July 1560, just over one year after Knox's famous sermon in the parish kirk at Perth which had ignited the Scottish Reformation, it had become apparent that the merchants were excluding the craftsmen burgesses, even those on the town council, from participation in the common affairs of the burgh. At issue was the selection of the burgh's representatives to the Reformation parliament of August 1560. When the burgh court failed to provide the craftsmen with a satisfactory explanation as to why they had been excluded from the choosing of representatives to the parliament, the craftsmen wrote to the Lords of the Congregation, leaders of the Reformation movement and the undisputed provisional government since Mary of Guise's death in the previous June. This appeal to an outside authority was made too late to have any effect on the selection of commissioners to the parliament, but it demonstrates yet again the pattern of faith in leaders above and beyond the confines of the burgh.

A few months later the craftsmen of Perth decided that the best way to ensure against further exclusion from the common affairs of the burgh was for their representatives to attend council meetings, even if uninvited. To this end they put an extra table in the revestry of the parish church where the council was meeting for the nine deacons of the crafts.[59] The evidence suggests that the manoeuvre was inconclusive. Yet by late December 1560 it was clear that no internal resolution of the conflict was possible and the merchants and craftsmen of Perth sought outside arbitration of their quarrel. The craftsmen received a letter from the leaders of the Congregation dated at Edinburgh 28 December 1560, which ordered them to appear in Edinburgh on 15 January next with all titles and evidence which would support their claims against the merchants so that the controversy might be resolved once and for all.[60] The letter did not say who was to hear the arguments, but it seems likely that a convention of burghs had been called to arbitrate in the dispute between Perth's merchants and craftsmen.

On 11 January 1561, 257 citizens of Perth subscribed a commission to two of the bailies — Ruthven's client, Patrick Murray of Tibbermuir, and the craftsman bailie, George Johnson — to represent the burgh at a forthcoming convention to be held in Edinburgh on 15 January. The subscribers included two crafts-men councillors, nine craft deacons, the master of work and 245 others whose names appear on the document without occupational designation. The commission, endorsed by the whole community because 'we could not obtain godlie our seal hereto', appears to be conspicuously devoid of the signatures of any other members of the council or any names associated with the more wealthy merchant families.[61]

There are no extant records of a convention of burghs having taken place in January 1561, but a convention of nobles was held in Edinburgh on 17 January to approve *The First Book of Discipline*. The Perth evidence indicates that a convention of burghs was called at about the same time possibly, but not necessarily, for the same purpose and that in addition the debate between Perth's merchants and craftsmen was to be publicly aired and mediated.

Either in preparation for this meeting, or as a result of the first hearing, the craftsmen were advised to gather all the laws of the realm, burgh statutes, election results or anything else which might prove their right and title to office-holding in Perth.[62] It would appear that the documents in the Craftsmen's Collection at Perth, which deal with issues and events covering a period from October 1526 to January 1561, were gathered for this purpose. They end abruptly with the selection of the commissioners to the convention of January 1561 and thereafter fall silent.

The documents do reveal, even in their inconclusive state, that the crisis which dominated the affairs of Perth in the mid-sixteenth century was politically motivated and although it pitted merchants against craftsmen it was not a conflict between rich and poor. Rather it was a quarrel between men of approximately equal wealth: men whose wealth allowed them a degree of social mobility and the opportunity to seek influential positions of authority within the government of the burgh. The Reformation was inci-dental to the craftsmen's drive for political equality although its message fitted in with their political aspirations. The craftsmen gained most of their political concessions long before the onset of the Reformation and, although they were able to withstand the pressure brought to bear on their position in 1555–7, they failed to make any political gains as a result of the Reformation itself.

The scanty burgh records for the entire decade of the 1560s reveal no apparent change in the ratio of craftsmen to merchants in burgh offices. It would appear that somehow the crisis of 1561 was resolved and the *status quo* maintained. However, the paucity of extant records for the 1560s precludes clarification of the issue with any degree of certainty. After 1570 burgh records became more prolific, and judging from their content, the conflict between the merchants and craftsmen of Perth was far from ended. In 1572 the regent, James Douglas, earl of Morton, was persuaded to grant Perth's craftsmen an equal share of the council seats with the merchants and in the same grant he proposed that the office of treasurer of the burgh be alternated between a merchant and a craftsman.[63] Once again the burgh was torn by internal conflict as the forces favouring and opposing equal representation on the council fought the issue with one another. As had been the case with the precept of 1526, the proposed increase in the number of council seats for the craftsmen was only partially implemented. In the wake of all the polemic which followed upon the grant, the craftsmen obtained not six, but four seats which, with the seating of the retiring bailie, gave them a total of five craft seats on the town council. They also ultimately served as treasurers of the burgh, alternating the office with a merchant burgess.

The heads of the noble family of Ruthven continued to secure election to the provostship of Perth into the 1580s. Their position, even if at times made virtually untenable, had nevertheless provided Perth with three generations of stable leadership of a sort. However, as their influence at court increased the Ruthvens became less active in the daily affairs of the burgh even if they continued to exercise hegemony. When they fell from power, convicted of treason, in 1584 the pattern of a nobleman as provost and protector of the burgh was so well established in the minds of the burgesses that they chose another nobleman, John, earl of Montrose, as their provost[64] rather than go back to the former practice of choosing a merchant burgess as provost.

The first tentative steps at altering the make-up of town government in Perth had been taken in the 1520s. Each proposed change had met with opposition, thereby creating an atmosphere of near-continuous tension throughout most of the middle decades of the century. By the 1580s most of the changes had become established practice. Influential rural landowners held provostships and their client lairds had infiltrated the magistrates' bench; craftsmen sat on town councils and participated in burgh government, while merchants continued to fight to retain some vestige of their old monopoly of power but without any great success. The competition of merchants and craftsmen was further complicated by the interweaving of rural interests with urban; both contributed, in Perth at least, to the struggles which were a common feature of many burghs in sixteenth-century Scotland.

Notes

1. M. Lynch, 'Whatever happened to the medieval burgh? Some guidelines for sixteenth and seventeenth-century historians', *Scottish Econ. and Social History*, 4 (1984), esp. 12–17.

2. See S. Reynolds, *An Introduction to the History of English Medieval Towns* (Oxford, 1977), 75–6, where much the same point is made.

3. Cited in A. W. K. Stevenson, 'Trade between Scotland and the Low Countries in the later Middle Ages' (Aberdeen Univ. Ph.D., 1982), 141.

4. *Acts of Council*, 522–3.

5. *Regesta Regum Scottorum* [hereafter *RRS*], ii, no. 467.

6. Perth, Sandeman Library, MS Perth Burgh Court Book, B59/12/2, fo.3v and following.

7. In a case brought in 1533 it was claimed that there were more than 300 hammermen in the burgh (*Acta Dom. Concilii et Sessionis, 1532–33* (Stair Soc., 1951), 78–9). That number, however, seems exaggerated when compared to the known approximate numbers in other guilds; fifty-one masters of the baxter craft were named in an action brought against the council in 1550 (SRO, MS Acts and Decreets, CS7/3, fo.520r).

8. This study formed part of the author's Ph.D. thesis, 'Perth and the Reformation: society and reform, 1540–1560' (Univ. of Glasgow, 1985).

9. Perth Museum and Art Gallery, MS Convener Court Book of Perth: Original papers and letters produced by the craftsmen of Perth in defence of their ancient rights and privileges, 1365–1717 [hereafter CB], no. 34, 'Representation by the craftsmen of Perth to parliament of their grievances against the merchants'.

10. *RMS*, iv, 1076; Pitcairn, *Criminal Trials*, i, 418.

11. CB, no. 7, 'Order by the queen regent to the magistrates of Perth to continue electing craftsmen to office as formerly'; *RMS*, iv, 1076.

12. CB, no. 23, 'Matters of complaint by the merchants of Perth against the craftsmen, represented to a Convention of Burghs'.

13. See Lynch, Chapter 3, this volume.

14. J. Wormald, *Lords and Men in Scotland* (Edinburgh, 1985), 149.

15. R. G. Eaves, *Henry VIII's Scottish Diplomacy, 1513–1524* (New York, 1971), 163.

16. MS Burgh Court Bk., B59/12/1, fo.42v.

17. Perth, Sandeman Library, Perth Burgh Records, Documents Collection Royal Charters, 1365–1777, 'Inventory of all material writs relating to the trades of the burgh of Perth found in the convener's chest by Patrick Reoch, deacon convener and other members of that court and John Mercer their clerk, 1710'; the item is the only reference to the privilege having first been granted in 1522.

18. CB, no. 2, 'Precept by King James V for causing the magistrates to

secure the common good of the burgh, 6 October 1526'.

19. MS Burgh Court Bk., B59/12/1, fos. 72r, 76v.

20. *Acts of Council*, 429–30; CB, no. 4, 'Decreet by the Lords of Council appointing the magistrates of Perth, because of the dissension among the inhabitants of Perth at their elections, 20 November 1534'.

21. J. Bain (ed.), *The Hamilton Papers* (Edinburgh, 1890–92), i, p. xcviii, no. 414; ii, nos. 138, 149.

22. MS Burgh Court Bk., B59/12/2, fo. 2r.

23. CB, no. 23.

24. *TA*, viii, 252.

25. CB, no. 34.

26. The occupations of the five have been variously given by Knox, Calderwood and others who have written about these trials. The conclusion that all five had connections with crafts is based on a reference to the trials in CB, no. 34; see Verschuur, 'Thesis', 349–53.

27. SRO, MS Registrum Assedatione B. Marie de Cupro, 1539–59, CH6/2/2, fos. 32v–33r.

28. MS Burgh Court Bk., B59/12/2, fo. 3v.

29. There was a one-year break in the Ruthven tenure of the provostship, in 1552, the year of the 2nd Lord Ruthven's death, when an elderly and probably neutral burgess was elected provost.

30. *Acts of Council*, 543.

31. MS Burgh Court Bk., B59/12/2, fo. 3v.

32. The craftsman bailie had to belong to the guildry and come from one of the more prestigious crafts.

33. Perth, Sandeman Library, Perth Burgh Court Records, Register of Decreets, B59/12/3, fo. 30r.

34. MS Burgh Court Bk., B59/12/2, fos. 11r, 12r.

35. Pitcairn, *Criminal Trials*, i, 367–8.

36. *APS*, ii, 497, c.26.

37. CB, no. 34.

38. *APS*, ii, 497, c.26.

39. SRO, MS Acts of Lords of Council and Session, CS26/29, fo. 7; I. F. Grant, *The Social and Economic Development of Scotland before 1603* (Edinburgh, 1930), 430–1.

40. CB, no. 7.

41. *Stirling Recs., 1519–1666*, 64–5.

42. CB, no. 9, 'Letters by Queen Mary charging the provost of Perth to receive in office such as have been chosen thereto, St Andrews, 2 December 1555'.

43. Ibid., no. 9.

44. Ibid., no. 20, 'Letter from the Queen Dowager to the provost of Perth regarding the controversy between the merchants and craftsmen of the burgh, 15 December [1555]'.

45. *Abdn. Recs., 1398–1570*, 239. On 16 Dec. 1555 Aberdeen appointed its commissioners to the convention to be held the following January.

46. *RMS*, iv, 1054.

47. Ibid., iv, 1076.

48. Ibid., iv, 1076.

49. Perth Museum and Art Gallery, MS Guildry Book of Perth, 303–4. An edition of the Book, edited by Marion Stavert, is to be published by the Scottish Record Society.

50. CB, no. 16, 'Letters by Queen Mary charging the bailies of Perth to convene for the electing of magistrates, Banff, 13 September 1556'.

51. Ibid., no. 17, 'Minutes of the election of magistrates in Perth, 5 October 1556'.

52. Ibid., no. 17.

53. Ibid., no. 23.

54. Ibid., no. 18, 'Minutes of the deprivation of the provost of Perth by royal warrant of the bailies wrongfully elected on 5 October, 19 October 1556, with protest by the craftsmen defending the provost's action'.

55. Ibid., no. 27, 'Complaint by the craftsmen of Perth to the Queen Regent especially against Archibald Blinsels, and desiring to be heard anent the act of parliament against them'.

56. *RMS*, iv, 1111 (at Aberdeen), 1112 (at Edinburgh).

57. MS Burgh Court Bk., B59/12/2, fo. 18r. This folio is very wasted and a copy of the agreement which is contained in a later transcription of the court book has to be heavily relied upon.

58. CB, no. 30, 'Grounds of the debate between the merchants and crafts of Perth in form of a petition either to the privy council or to a Convention of Burghs'.

59. Ibid., no. 23.

60. Ibid., no. 35, 'Letter from some statesmen to the craftsmen of Perth to compear with the merchants for the settlements of their disputes, Edinburgh, 28 December 1560'.

61. Ibid., no. 23A, 'Commission to Patrick Murray and George Johnson bailies of Perth to appear and represent the burgh of Perth in the ensuing Convention of Burghs, signed by the magistrates and inhabitants of Perth, 11 January 1560/61'.

62. Ibid., no. 29, 'Information for the craftsmen of Perth to support their privilege of electing and being elected as bailies and councillors'.

63. MS Burgh Court Bk., B59/12/2, fos. 23v–24r.

64. Ibid., fo. 34r.

3

The Crown and the Burghs
1500 – 1625

Michael Lynch

The relationship of the burghs with the rest of the realm of Scotland, in a period when many elements in society — nobles, lairds, burgesses and the crown — were in process of significant adjustment, one with the other, is only beginning to be examined in a systematic way. The sixteenth century, half of it taken up with royal minorities, was a volatile one, not least for Scotland's monarchs, and it induced a fundamental reappraisal of the relationship which had existed, largely unimpaired, both between centre and localities and between town and country for centuries.[1] One of the more unexpected effects of the Reformation of 1559 – 60 was to pull the nobles, more insistently than during usual minorities, into the limelight of national politics;[2] many of the burghs followed in their wake, if no less reluctantly. Although the lairds attended the Reformation parliament in large numbers only twenty-two — less than half — of the burghs were represented. Yet such was the potential impact of the parliament on the local community that some of the burghs which did attend took unusual steps to demonstrate the representative nature of their commissioners. Aberdeen took three commissioners rather than the usual one, in order to represent all shades of opinion within the burgh, including the Protestant minority one; Edinburgh doubled the usual representation and included its noble provost and a lawyer as well as two merchants, although all were drawn from the Protestant council forced on the capital by the Lords of Congregation eight months before. And in Perth, where Protestant opinion was more widespread, 255 burgesses, most of them craftsmen, witnessed a document protesting against their exclusion from the burgh's commission.[3] The sixteenth century saw the return, in a

55

number of different ways, of the royal burghs to the national stage, and, as an inevitable corollary, their closer involvement both with central government and with their landed neighbours. Each of these developments brought new strains to bear on the fabric of the burgh community.

How did the burghs fare in these shifting sands of the sixteenth century? One anonymous, undated English memorandum had little doubt:

> The boroughs and burgess towns are wholly at the devotion of some nobleman or other, few excepted: as Couper of Fife at the earl of Rothes, St Johnstoun [Perth] at the earl of Montrose, Dundee at the earl of Crawford, the northern towns at the earl of Huntly's command; whereby they have their own, and the common voices [*or* votes] in parliament; nothing can pass that may prejudice the state of the nobility, or in large the prince.[4]

This much quoted observation, which is conventionally taken to demonstrate the power the nobility exercised over many burghs, great and small,[5] does in fact, when more closely examined, reveal almost exactly the opposite. It belongs to the period after the fall of the Ruthven regime in the summer of 1583 and the ruthless royalist counter-coup, carefully orchestrated by the earl of Arran, which reached its climax in the secret sessions of the parliament of May 1584.

The conventional view of the early 1580s that they represented one of the worst examples of noble aggrandisement, at the expense of both the crown and good government, sits uneasily with the new assessments, which as yet have largely been concentrated in the fifteenth century,[6] of the relative powers and obligations of the crown and nobility, both at court and in the localities. The Ruthven regime, which took its name from the ultra-Protestant magnate, Lord Ruthven, earl of Gowrie, was in reality neither particularly radical nor ruthless: its composition was fairly broadly based and certainly went beyond the relatively small circle of ultra-Protestant enthusiasts amongst the nobility;[7] it did little for the Melvillian party in the kirk and fell into disarray after it lost the rationale of its existence, the person of the young king, in June 1583. The regime's collapse and the disastrous involvement of many of its inner circle in a second, abortive putsch, the 'Stirling raid' in April 1584, precipitated an attempt at a fundamental readjustment, not just of power at court, but in the scope of power the court exercised over the localities. Gowrie was executed, a number of nobles fled into exile in England, and others accommodated themselves to life in the atmosphere of a new 'opinion of absolute power',[8] put in the young king's head by his alternative — and more ruthless — team of advisers, which manifested itself in the reassertion by parliament of the authority of the crown over all estates, temporal as well as ecclesiastical. The real significance of the crisis of 1583–4 was that it represented the most serious crisis of aristocratic power in the sixteenth century. The burghs could not escape the consequences, which brought them again into the spotlight of national politics. Burgh government was in turn subjected to interference on an unprecedented scale — not by the nobles listed in the memorandum as such but by the Arran government which they represented. The memorandum describes, not the general relationship of nobles and towns in the sixteenth century, but the new grip taken by the crown of the burghs in the mid-1580s.[9]

Three of the four earls listed in the memorandum were not, in fact, the natural leaders of the localities in which the burghs they now headed lay. The earl of Rothes had his chief residence in Fife, but fully fifteen miles from Cupar and he had more kin and influence in the north-east; but control of Cupar was vital because of the closer proximity to it of Lord Lindsay of Byres, a Ruthven supporter.[10] The influence of Montrose, who was described in two separate contemporary analyses of the nobility as of 'small power', was also based further north, in Kincardine. None the less, he was appointed provost of Glasgow by royal fiat, in the first round of court appointments to the major burghs, at the time of the municipal elections of October 1583, some three months after the fall of the Ruthven regime. The position of the earl of Gowrie as provost of Perth, an office which his family had held almost without break for forty years, was too secure for the new regime to attack until his second and final fall from grace, in April 1584. It was only after Gowrie's execution that Montrose, who also succeeded him as treasurer of the realm, was transferred to Perth; he assumed the provostship on 5 June 1584, although he had first to be admitted as a burgess.[11] The link between the earl of Crawford and the burgh of Dundee was rather closer, even if he also had to be admitted a burgess before taking up burgh office; his family had had associations with it for almost two centuries; he lived in the centre of the burgh and many of his ancestors, including his father, were buried in the precincts of its Franciscan friary. But if Dundee had a landed family which had significant political influence in the burgh, it was not the earls of Crawford, who had held the provost-ship only twice in the previous three-quarters of a century; it was rather the Scrymgeours, heritable constables of Dundee, whose links went back a century longer, to at least 1298, and who had frequently held the office of provost. The Scrymgeours were, how-ever, too closely associated with the Ruthven regime to be trusted; in contrast, Crawford, like Montrose, had a bitter feud with a prominent Ruthven supporter to commend him.[12]

The period in power of the Arran regime saw a concerted attempt to secure by novel means, which often involved the bypassing of usual magnatial interests, seven of the twelve largest burghs of the realm — Edinburgh, Dundee, Perth, Glasgow, Stirling, Dumfries and Cupar[13] — for the crown. The provosts who were successfully planted in these burghs were not mere place-men but the key figures in the Arran administration — the earls of Crawford, Montrose, Rothes and, of course, Arran, for whom the greatest prize, the capital itself, was reserved. In October 1583 Edinburgh's town council was subjected to its most comprehensive purge since the Reformation crisis; Melvillians were excluded from the council and Melvillian and Ramist thought expunged from the curriculum of the new town college. A year later, as the second stage of the process, Arran, who had by then secured Edinburgh castle, forced himself on the town as its provost as well; under his supervision the purge was extended to the kirk session, which was, for the first time since the Reformation, directly nominated by the town council.[14] The capital was used to inter-vention by the crown in its government — a long series of courtiers had been planted upon it over the course of the previous century — but new heights of loyalty were demanded of it by the Arran regime.

The mid-1580s represented the high-water mark of Stewart authoritarian government. The burghs would not again be con-fronted with such systematic interference in their affairs for almost exactly a century — until the reign of James VII.[15] Yet this was more than an unrepresentative episode, which can be explained away as the response to fears of a Calvinist conspiracy in the midst of the tangled web of politics of the 1580s.[16] It is a significant example of the principle that the most overt encroachments by the crown on the independence of the burghs came, not in the majority of strong-minded kings like James V and VI, but in royal minorities — and especially in the 1540s, 1550s and early 1580s.

The contrasts between royal minorities and adjacent majorities are revealing. Between 1528 and 1530 James V intervened in two of the most important burghs of the realm. Both actions were probably part of the intense political manoeuvering which followed the fall of the Douglases in 1528 but they were also attempts to respond to local crises rather than a reflex effort to reimpose the royal will when the king came of age. They endorsed rather than created political settlements: in Aberdeen, where a long-running dispute with Lord Forbes over the protection of the burgh's valuable salmon fishings on the River Dee had deteriorated to the point of violence in the streets, a signet letter from the king in 1530 in effect put the burgh under royal protection, even if by then the Forbes had already given up the fight.[17] In Perth the position of the laird provosts, Charteris of Cuthilgurdy, who had virtually monopolised the office of provost since 1520, had already begun to slip before they were permanently dismissed from office at the direction of the crown in 1528. In the medium term James V's solution — the introduction of the Ruthven family to office in Perth — probably made matters worse but in 1528 its town council obeyed 'very gladly'.[18]

The earl of Arran, while governor in the early 1540s, by contrast sought to impose novel policies by still more novel means. Kings of Scotland had long held a special affinity with the north-east but Arran, as he admitted to Henry VIII, had 'all his land and living . . . on this [the southern] side of the Forth';[19] he tried to compensate by drawing the provost of Aberdeen, the regional centre of the north-east as well as seat of the sheriffdom, into his own circle of patronage. This was an unusual device for it involved the circumvention of the traditional royal agent in the north-east, the earl of Huntly, and it lasted only a little over a year.[20] In Perth, Arran tried an alternative but no more successful means of establishing a power base: he resorted to rehabilitating the discredited Charteris family but was obliged to jettison them only four months later, in January 1544. Even more disastrous was his attempt in 1546 to displace Lord Ruthven from the provostship in favour of 'a neutral unsuspect man' — presumably meaning one more amenable to Arran's influence — shortly after Ruthven had donned the mantle of noble protector of the burgh through his successful defence of it from armed attack by Lord Gray.[21] The earl of Arran's successive failures to draw these major burghs into his ambit underlined not simply the unpopularity of his pro-English stance or the bewilderment of the localities in following his shifts of policy but the failure of good lordship during his regency.

A direct relationship did exist between the crown and royal burghs, who were, as much as the nobility, its tenants-in-chief. But the relationship was more complicated than that for it usually involved — although Edinburgh, as the capital, was an obvious exception — a third party, in the form of a noble or nobles, who acted as an alternative point of contact for royal policy. A major burgh was thus enmeshed in a symbiotic, triangular relationship which worked so long as none of the parties overstepped the demands and expectations implicit within good lordship: the events of 1543–6 in Aberdeen and Perth demonstrated that a burgh would reject the role of royal client as readily as that of noble fief.[22] Two further conclusions might be drawn from these examples. Stewart monarchs had generally a surer grasp of the subtle mechanics of royal government in the regions than had the hapless regent, the earl of Arran: they, with the possible exception of Queen Mary,[23] for the most part avoided imposing a potentially embarrassing strain on the dual loyalties of regional capitals such as Aberdeen, Perth, Stirling or Ayr. Yet such burgh communities survived the royal minorities of the sixteenth century with remarkable resilience, bruised perhaps, but generally intact. What was potentially more dangerous than royal minorities were, it might be concluded, the minorities of their noble patrons. The situation in Aberdeen in the 1520s was particularly dangerous because the two happened to coincide.[24]

The government of Mary of Guise, who took over the regency from Arran, now duke of Châtelherault, in 1554, saw a conscious return to the older order, even if it was combined with a new, French-influenced, administrative efficiency. Her one parliament, of 1555, re-enacted much fifteenth-century legislation bearing on burgh government and trade, including an act, which harked back to the reign of James I, banning deacons of crafts.[25] It is likely that the regent and her parliament had been listening — as a number of fifteenth-century parliaments had done — to the advice and complaints of influential merchants, probably of Edinburgh who were 'great in court at the time'.[26] But a device which had proved less than effective in the 1420s provoked a full-blown crisis in a number of burghs — most notably in Perth — in the mid-1550s and shook the regency itself. Mary of Guise was forced into the unusual step of a series of personal visits to Perth to quell the resulting dissension amongst its craftsmen. Specific royal exemptions of Perth from the legislation did not reassure its craftsmen and indeed made matters worse by provoking its merchants to take counter-measures in the central law courts. The crisis was solved only by the outright nullification of the act fifteen months after its passage through parliament.[27] This is an instructive episode, which inflicts some damage on the notion that the extension of royal government in what up till now had been a feudal kingdom with a remarkably loose set of reins holding it in check was always conducive to law and order. The burghs were still too pluriform in both government and social structure to allow far-reaching blanket reforms of either.[28] Traditional measures, if pressed too hard or in too sweeping a manner on the burghs, could be as damaging as innovation, as Mary of Guise discovered. The solution to the crown's dilemma lay in the evolution of new and more regular forms of contact between the agencies of central government — whether parliament, privy council or the crown itself — and the royal burghs; and this was principally effected through the recasting of the old Court of the Four Burghs in a more regular role, as the Convention of Royal Burghs. In 1552 the Convention ratified the decision it had made in 1533 to meet once a year, but it met no less than four times in the space of eight months during the crisis of 1555–6.[29] By 1578 the emergency schedule had become almost routine, the response of the burghs more co-ordinated and self-regulation through the medium of the Convention was usually preferred to *diktat*, whether by crown or parliament.[30]

The second half of the sixteenth century saw an extension of royal power into the localities, including the burghs, but the results were seldom predictable. More government meant, when translated into practice, a jostling for position of the various agents and agencies of royal and local power as they came into closer contact with each other; it was often a bad-tempered process and, on occasion, it resulted in a fundamental collision between different concepts of order and authority. Yet it was no accident that the Convention of Royal Burghs became by the early seventeenth century the most highly developed of these agencies; a spirit of co-operation had existed amongst representatives of different burghs since the fourteenth century or earlier, encouraged by the crown.[31] The Convention met more frequently than either parliament or General Assembly — a total of eighty-seven times between 1600 and 1625. The burghs seldom exerted direct political power as such, but they knew their own mind better than any of the other estates and perhaps, at times, better than the crown itself.[32]

The rebukes adminstered by a number of major burghs, both to Arran in 1542-3 and to Mary of Guise in 1555-6, were a harbinger of future relations between the burghs and the crown. The essential difference was that — with a few dramatic exceptions — the relationship was usually conducted in a more discreet fashion on both sides. Neither Queen Mary nor James VI was faced with such explicit opposition, either from individual burghs or the burghs as a whole, despite their gradual formation of a single voice in the shape of the Convention. Yet it is not surprising that Mary of Guise, having experienced such an unprecedented surge of urban protest as in 1555-6, should have acted brusquely when confronted with the appearance — if not always the reality — of religious dissent in certain towns during the Reformation crisis three years later. She paid the price: one of the pretexts used by the Protestant Lords of the Congregation for deposing her was her arbitrary interference in the government of Perth, Edinburgh and Jedburgh.[33] The next time such an allegation was used was 130 years later — in the Claim of Right drawn up against James VII.[34]

There was never, in fact, a rebellion or conspiracy against the crown in this period which enjoyed significant urban support. The Reformation movement significantly failed to rouse widespread Protestant dissent in the vast bulk of the Scottish towns.[35] Where support was given to the Congregation, it was usually carefully qualified, as it was in Aberdeen and Peebles.[36] Throughout the sixteenth century rebellious nobles conspicuously failed to recruit burgesses to their cause, even in towns where they enjoyed a certain influence. The burgh of Aberdeen managed to detach itself from the earl of Huntly in 1562; the former leaders of the Congregation, the earl of Moray and duke of Châtelherault, failed to raise a fifth column in Queen Mary's capital in 1565 and, despite the support of its provost, also failed to find much support in Dundee, the most Protestant burgh in Scotland; the earl of Mar, whose family held the royal castle which dominated Stirling, had exercised power in the burgh itself through a series of client lairds as provosts since 1520, yet could raise only token support for the Gowrie conspiracy in 1584. And there is little evidence to show that the Gowrie family itself, despite its near-monopoly of the provostship of Perth, was able to persuade its burgesses into rebellion against the crown, either in 1584 or in 1600.[37]

Yet if the respect owed by individual burghs to their noble patrons was qualified, so was the obedience they were prepared to give to the crown. Even the royal *coup d'etat* of 1583-4, the most full-blooded attempt to impose the royal will on the burghs in the century, was patchy in its impact and generally short-lived in its effects. Dumfries refused outright to accept Arran's nominee, a mere laird, and displace Lord Maxwell, whose family had a long association with the burgh.[38] It is unclear precisely what happened in Dundee in 1583; the earl of Crawford seems on occasion to have exercised the authority of provost but the council registers of the burgh continued to recognise the incumbent, James Haliburton, who had held the office for all but one of the previous thirty years. Certainly by October 1584 Haliburton was restored to office unchallenged.[39] In Edinburgh it took Arran himself fully a year to secure his grip on all sections of burgh government.[40] In Perth his regime shrunk from attempting to end the forty-year reign of the Ruthven family; the earl of Gowrie in effect dismissed himself through his own remarkable capacity for political miscalculation.

The real trial of strength between the crown and the Ruthven family for control of Perth came, not in 1584, but over the remaining years of the 1580s; a succession of royal nominees, including the earl of Atholl as well as Montrose, were used by the crown to force home its advantage against the minor who succeeded the 1st earl. The burgh itself, it seems, was not so sure. It elected the 2nd earl as provost in 1588 despite the fact that he was nine years old and again in 1593, although it was known that he would spend much of his year in office furthering his education abroad; even the election of a minor could be used to reassert the burgh's proper independence of the crown.[41] There are traces in Perth in these years of the strains which might result from a vacuum in local power. The council records are fragmentary but they seem to indicate that two opposing factions had crystallised in burgh politics, which led to wholesale purges as each followed its respective master — nominal or not — in and out of power. There briefly emerged in Perth — as there had in Edinburgh a few years earlier in the reprisals which followed the fall of the Ruthven regime — a struggle between two factions in burgh politics which are perhaps best described as court and country parties.[42] Yet such an explicit confrontation of rival interests within urban politics was distinctly unusual before the troubles of the 1640s. In Perth the conflict evaporated after 1600, when the Ruthvens were again caught up in an abortive conspiracy against the crown.

It is possible to list a series of attempts in the 1590s and after by the crown to impose its nominees as provosts or magistrates of various burghs: in 1599 the burgh of Montrose was condemned by the privy council for failing to respond to royal injunctions to elect the earl of Mar, despite his local connections, and Dumfries for rejecting a local laird.[43] Yet, if the examples could be multiplied, so could the number of rebuffs to the crown. It would be a mistake to try to detect a rising tide of direct interference by the crown in burgh government from the 1590s onwards.[44] The level of interference, as distinct from the number of cases, was more modest than in either the 1560s or the 1580s, when whole town councils had been purged. It may be that the crown was intent on a gentrification of the key posts in burgh government rather than wholesale interference in it. The protest made by the Convention in 1590 against royal endorsement of 'lords, earls, barons and other gentlemen'[45] to offices in burghs fell on deaf ears but by 1609, when parliament passed an act against any landed outsiders holding burgh office,[46] this policy had been wholly discredited. The probable reason for this volte-face, which has not been given the attention it merits, was the crown's bruising experiences in Dundee where it had persisted in its support of the increasingly unpopular provost, Sir James Scrymgeour, who held the provostship between 1601 and 1609. As in Perth in the 1550s, the situation and the issues involved escalated out of royal control: by 1604 the crown found itself obliged to insist that Scrymgeour continue in office without any election and was confronted by the formidable figure of the minister, Robert Howie who, it was claimed, had said 'if they would choose a provost for greatness . . . the Devil was greatest of all'; by 1605 it was faced with determined opposition from the craft deacons whom it was obliged to throw out of office. The issues involved were complex and included the rights of patronage, both of the Scrymgeours and the town council, as well as long unresolved questions relating to the political rights of the crafts and ecclesiastical property in the town.[47] James VI's privy council found that it had in Dundee — which until then had been one of the less troublesome of the major burghs — opened Pandora's box. The act of 1609 may well have been the price the crown had to pay to shut it.

The act of 1609 was a milestone in the relationship between town and country. It effectively brought to an end — at least until the Restoration — the age of noble provosts but it would be unrealistic to imagine that it wholly curtailed noble influence in burghs. Some burghs perversely continued to prefer to elect noblemen from time to time. Perth, when it was denied a craftsman as provost, tried to elect Lord Scone in 1613 and persistently re-elected him in the years following; it no longer needed a noble protector, but a noble provost, especially one who was also a member of the privy council, was a useful status symbol, and particularly so to a 'craft town' like Perth.[48] In Peebles the Hays of Yester, who had held the provostship throughout the second half of the sixteenth century, stepped down as provosts but continued to exert much of their customary influence as 'ordinary' councillors.[49] There was still, however, no more a typical burgh in 1609 than there was in 1500 and the effects of the act varied, to an extent, from burgh to burgh. In Stirling local lairds, many of them clients of the Erskine family, earls of Mar, had long dominated burgh politics, both monopolising the provostship and forming a substantial wedge on the council; but by the 1590s it was uncommon to see more than a couple of lairds on the council. In 1615 the burgh's craftsmen claimed that the 1609 act had little application in Stirling, which was not a town where the council any longer 'consists of gentlemen', but had been used by the burgh's merchants as a pretext to consolidate their own position.[50] In Aberdeen the 1590s also marked the partial demise of the landed interest on the council, which had there become synonymous with the 'race of Menzies' provosts who, it was revealingly claimed, acted like 'a landward baron' treating the royal burgh of Aberdeen as if it were 'a burgh of barony'.[51] The topic requires further investigation but an interim conclusion might well be drawn from the available evidence that the first half of the reign of James VI had seen an intensification, encouraged by the crown, of a process of gentrification of burgh government, which had been going on since 1500, if not before. The second half of the reign, however, seems to have seen the retrenchment in burgh government of urban interests at the expense of rural. The lairds returned to their estates and left the urban elements — merchants, craftsmen and, in some cases, lawyers as well — to compete for place and influence. By the last decade of the sixteenth century the boundaries between town and country were shifting again; the crown monitored the process but did little to influence it.

The channels of communication between the crown and the burghs were changing, too, especially after James VI's removal to London in 1603. Edinburgh, which had unexpectedly benefited from the influential nobles, among them the chancellor, the earl of Dunfermline, imposed on it as retribution for the Presbyterian riot of 1596, had to seek alternative means to influence royal policy; Dunfermline was built a special seat in St Giles in 1616 in recognition of his services; Viscount Annand, keeper of the privy purse, was profusely thanked in 1623 for his 'good success in their affairs'.[52] The consultative processes between the crown and the burghs continued, as each had a good deal more to say to the other after 1603 than before, but the venues had shifted decisively from the localities to the central corridors of power, adjacent to the court and privy council. The Convention had appointed an agent in 1590 to represent its views to parliament and the privy council; by 1613 it needed one at court in London as well. Edinburgh also employed its own agent at court, Sir John Hay, with reasonable success. Aberdeen, never to be outdone in the matter of greasing of palms, scored a notable success through its agent at the parliament of 1617, which upheld the burgh's flimsy claim to pay its feu ferm to the crown in Scots money rather than sterling, which by then was worth twelve times as much. By 1621 most of the protracted negotiation, with both the court and the privy council, which produced a settlement commuting the payment of the new tax on annualrents granted by parliament, was done by burgh agents.[53]

It is easier to describe the channels of communication between the burghs and the various agencies of central government than it is to assess the instructions and expectations which passed along them, in both directions. There can be little doubt that one of the hallmarks of the period lay in the fact that the crown and the burghs increasingly expected more of each other, but that is not quite the same as saying that a natural identity of interests existed between them. A mutual concern for law and order clearly did exist[54] but it would not necessarily have been placed as the first priority of either party. One of the most awkward of the many problems which the crown and its associated institutions posed for the burghs, particularly in the middle quarters of the sixteenth century, was that it offered not too little law but too much. In 1500 burgh magistrates were concerned by the frequency of the practice of replegiation, the habit of litigants transferring cases from burgh courts to other local courts, both ecclesiastical and baronial.[55] By 1540 they may have been more worried by the practice of litigants taking their cases to the Lords of Council or the law courts in Edinburgh for resolution. Increasingly a whole range of local disputes — whether between burgh and burgh,[56] burgh and local landowner[57] or burgh and sheriff[58] — were taken to the capital.

Most worrying of all for burgh magistrates was the growing fashion for one section of the urban community to seek recourse either to the courts or the king's administration to resolve burgh disputes, usually but not always about representation on the town council.[59] The craftsmen of Perth took their political grievances to the Court of Session in the 1540s and 1550s; the merchants of the burgh were obliged to follow suit but first had to tax themselves to meet the legal costs.[60] The craftsmen of both Edinburgh and Aberdeen did the same in the 1580s. In Aberdeen the merchant guildry immediately raised a tax on itself of two shillings a week and the town council tried to call certain craftsmen to account for raising an action in the Court of Session but this only had the effect of bringing the privy council into the dispute, in defence of the authority of the king's courts.[61] Settlements were eventually arrived at, redrafting the constitutions of the two burghs — the decreet-arbitral in Edinburgh in 1583 and the common indenture of 1587 in Aberdeen[62] — but what was by then at stake was not simply a local dispute between merchants and crafts: it was a major conflict of rival jurisdictions, local and national. The mid-sixteenth century dispute in Perth, which was at one time or another referred to all the agencies of central government — the Court of Session, privy council, parliament, Convention of Royal Burghs and the court itself — showed the new questioning of burgh authority, by discontented insiders as well as by outsiders, which accompanied the re-emergence of the burghs on the national stage. The questioning of burghs' legal status and authority was potentially more damaging, as well as harder to counteract, than the crude planting of royal nominees in burgh office.

The burghs provide clear evidence, akin to that which demonstrates the demise of the bond and feud as mechanisms for settling disputes in rural society,[63] that the unspoken balance between jurisdictions, local and national, which typified Scotland's feudal kingdom, was breaking up in the course of the sixteenth century. If the overlapping jurisdictions which existed in the localities had worked satisfactorily throughout the medieval period,[64] the same could not be said so readily for the increasing overlap — and competition — of burgh law and the king's law. It is not surprising that a number of burghs, caught up in this new challenge to their status and authority, took steps to draw together and preserve the physical symbols of their power — their records and charters. The depute town clerk of Aberdeen was ordered by the town council to draw up a register of all the property and privileges of the burgh in 1575 and a further inventory was compiled in 1591; in Edinburgh the town clerk spent much of the second half of the 1570s searching for and copying out the burgh's fragmentary early records; in Dundee a catalogue of ecclesiastical property gifted to it in 1567 and a register of burgesses going back to Flodden were compiled in 1582 – 3.[65] This was more than a sudden antiquarian fashion. It should perhaps be likened to the rash of histories of great noble families which were written at much the same time;[66] both the nobles and the burghs were intent, in their own way, to try to define and preserve the integrity of their community in the face of the challenge of a new monarchy. There were absurdities, of course, in some of this: Edinburgh in its panegyric of welcome on the occasion of the visit of James VI in 1617, claimed to trace its foundation back to 331 BC.[67] But if nobles could claim antiquity, why not burghs too? There was, however, a serious point amidst the mythology. The town council of Aberdeen made an elaborate and elegant plea before the young James VI at Dunottar castle in 1580, recalling the benificence of Robert I;[68] the message, even if coded, was an unmistakeable plea for a return to the old order.

The particular reasons for Aberdeen's anxiety in 1580 are clear enough. It had just beaten off a threat by the king's treasurer to levy a £20,000 fine on the burgh and it was desperate to regain the lucrative salmon fishings which had during Morton's regency been appropriated by one of his kinsmen, George Auchinleck of Balmanno.[69] Yet it had been the crown itself which had first jeopardised the fishings, the jewel in Aberdeen's fiscal crown, some twenty years before by questioning the burgh's charters and ordering them to be submitted for examination by the privy council. A chain of litigation, whose cost was creating concern as early as 1556, was set in motion.[70] It is small wonder that the burgh had decided by 1586 that it had to appoint a lawyer on a permanent retainer to look after its interests in processes before the central courts; in 1588 it appointed a resident political agent in Edinburgh as well.[71] The episode is a good example of the general point that even if there was an appreciable increase in law and order in sixteenth-century Scotland, the crown could, if it wished, be a law unto itself. The profits of justice, which had even in the fifteenth century constituted an important part of royal revenue, took on new dimensions as the sixteenth century progressed. By the 1590s the scrutiny of burgh charters was a routine ploy in the crown's treatment of the burghs.

Equally serious in its effects on the burghs was the fact that the crown and its courts frequently spoke with not one voice but many. In 1542 Perth had received two separate royal letters recommending different candidates as provost; inevitably, the decision had to be passed to the courts for resolution.[72] The troubles which convulsed Perth for much of the thirty years up to 1560 were exacerbated rather than eased by the tangled web of royal jurisdiction. The dispute between the Erskine family and the burgh of Stirling over the sheriffship of Stirling see-sawed for a century and more through the courts and royal administration until it was resolved in 1633.[73] Acts of parliament could be countermanded by decisions of the Court of Session, privy council or by royal fiat. It is little wonder that the first demand burghs made of new monarchs or regents was a confirmation of their charters: a general confirmation of burgh privileges was, for example, made in 1555, 1563, December 1567, August 1571, July 1578 and October 1579. In this context, it may become apparent that the very length of James VI's reign was not so reassuring to many contemporaries as it is habitually portrayed by historians; it was, in certain respects, positively alarming. A series of short, bland acts ratifying burgh privileges had been passed between 1593 and 1612 but they sat ill at ease with the crown's scrutiny of charters. This was the reason why in the parliament of 1621 the burghs wanted, above all else, a specific confirmation of their charters and privileges; they were prepared to meet the crown's exorbitant demands to secure them.[74]

Yet acts of parliament, legal precedent and even centuries-old burgh charters could be — and were — overridden by the crown. In 1546 the Court of Session affirmed its right to dismiss any burgh provost even if he had 'committed no fault in the execution of his office'; 'suspicion' of a lack of neutrality was enough to amount to due cause for the crown to dismiss him.[75] Part of the case against the crown's backing of Scrymgeour as provost of Dundee in 1604 was that an act of one of James III's parliaments stipulated that no constable of a royal castle should hold major office in that burgh.[76] Scrymgeours had, of course, been combining the two offices at various times for a century or more but the crown had never before been so intimately involved in defending the practice, except for the brief period of Arran's monopoly of the offices in Edinburgh in 1584–5.[77] Yet again, the emergency contingency of previous years threatened to become the norm in the long personal reign of James VI. In 1491 the king's council had decided that no burgh had the power to alienate its common good; a century later James VI gifted the burgh mails of Elgin and Forres, at a price, to the earl of Moray.[78] In effect, the crown had moved from the posture of defender of the burghs' liberties, condemning — if not preventing — interference by nobles, to the point where, by 1600, it was the chief offender in riding roughshod over legislation designed to protect the independence of burghs. James VI's granting of monopolies is the best-known example, but by no means the most serious. In 1550 the Court of Session had ruled that the crown had no power to enable unfreemen to buy and sell merchandise; yet in the last ten years of his reign James VI was prepared to grant to individuals, for a price, exclusive rights to buy and sell certain commodities.[79] In this, as in so many other aspects of policy, James VI was pressing hard against the boundaries of good lordship.

The clearest examples of the spiralling demands of the crown can be seen in two spheres: its ever-widening notion of the obedience owed to itself by its subjects, which by the 1620s included meticulous conformity to the unpopular, quasi-Anglican liturgical policy, and the more frequent and ever more novel fiscal demands it made, particularly from the 1580s onwards, which culminated in 1621 in what James VI himself claimed was 'the greatest taxation that ever was granted in that kingdom'.[80]

There was curiously little in the first generation after the Reformation of 1560 in the way of a concerted or determined effort by the crown — or by the Protestant elements at court — to impose a strict Protestant settlement on the localities, including the burghs. There was no religious test imposed on holders of burgh office until an act of parliament of 1573.[81] Queen Mary did, it is true, interfere with burgh elections after she returned from France in 1561 but largely confined her attentions to her capital; even there, she did not pursue a crude policy of promoting Catholics at the expense of Protestants.[82] In this respects, as in many others, Mary's personal reign was the most conservative of the sixteenth century in its attitude towards the burghs. This was hardly surprising in the light of the multi-faceted urban unrest which had marked her mother's regency, but the contrast between the two periods is striking. There were no general taxes imposed by the queen other than for her son's baptism in 1566; a proposal to tax the burghs to pay for the ministry ended up as a series of outright grants to them of the lands and revenues of the old church which lay within their precincts — a modest windfall but one which the burghs had campaigned for since 1562; and the queen's treatment of Dundee's involvement in the attempted *putsch* of 1565 was discriminating and moderate, in sharp contrast to her son's near-paranoid treatment of Perth after the Gowrie conspiracy in 1600.[83] The one clear exception to this fairly permissive policy was that of Aberdeen, the most obvious Catholic centre in the country, which was three times subjected to a royal visitation between 1562 and 1574; each visit, including that of Mary herself in 1562, marked an enforced, but remarkably small, step towards a Protestant setttlement.[84] If both Queen Mary and the regents who followed her had reservations about forcing a window into the souls of subjects, her son did not. Part of the novelty of the royal coup of 1583–4 was the extraordinary lengths taken to suppress Melvillian thought, not only amongst the ministers but throughout the capital. The whole of the Edinburgh kirk session was summoned in 1584 to the royal palace at Falkland to subscribe a letter condemning its ministers under pain of treason. It was not until the 1580s that a significant grass-roots enthusiasm for Protestantism emerged in the towns; it was countered, when it did, by a new royal authoritarianism.[85] These issues — and the tensions which they bred — receded somewhat until James VI's insistence on pushing the Five Articles through General Assembly and parliament between 1618 and 1621. By then the protagonists had both become more entrenched and extreme in their views; a new-style urban Calvinist, fuelled by an inner conviction verging on antinomianism as well as by political animus, collided with an increasingly intolerant royal Erastianism.[86] The focus of the struggle lay in Edinburgh, where the town council was subject to a barrage of demands from the court, not only insisting that its members — as well as those of future councils — subscribe the Five Articles but that the council enforce the new arrangements in all the town's churches. The Edinburgh council found itself cast in the role of reluctant agent of an anglicising monarchy. And when it demurred, it found itself interrogated before the privy council along with the dissenters it was supposed to police.[87] The revolt of 1637–8 was, in part, a response to still more anglicisation but, ironically, to rather less coercion by royal government than had obtained in the last years of the reign of James VI.

One of the main features of late medieval Scotland was how lightly it was taxed by the crown.[88] Occasional taxation did exist but the bulk of the crown's regular revenue derived from burghs came either in the form of burgh ferms, set for the most part in the fourteenth century, or the revenue from customs, which had been further extended in 1424 to cover export commodities such as herring, skins and woollen cloth.[89] Yet by the reign of James V customs brought in less to the exchequer than in that of David II. In 1597 a wholesale revision of duties, combined with an additional impost on the lucrative wine trade and a wholly novel, general levy on imports of 5 per cent, combined to double revenue to £8,000 per annum.[90] The vast bulk of this revenue, well over 80 per cent, accrued from the four largest burghs, which gave the crown a further motive to vet their affairs more closely, but there was well-founded suspicion of large-scale defrauding of the crown, either by deliberate under-declaration of goods or by smuggling.[91] The crown would find other ways of securing its share of the growing wealth of burgh merchants in the early seventeenth century.

It is fair to say that regular national taxation was established only in the 1580s.[92] Yet there had been a great deal of taxation raised, even if on an *ad hoc* basis, since the 1530s. In 1533, in the middle of a scare of likely war with England, the burghs had very large sums indeed levied on them — Edinburgh, Dundee and Aberdeen paid £225, £108 and £84 a month respectively.[93] Government records for the 1540s and 1550s are too fragmentary to make a satisfactory assessment of the total volume of demands made by the crown but indications of it can be found in the records of individual burghs. Twelve taxes were raised on Aberdeen between 1545 and 1550 and five on Edinburgh in the space of fifteen months in 1556–7.[94] Not surprisingly, the burghs found it increasingly difficult to meet these tax demands. More than twenty burghs were pursued for arrears or non-payment of tax in 1552–3.[95] Certain burghs were obliged to seek extraordinary means to comply, but their room for manoeuvre was limited as the crown had been careful to ensure, by vetting burgh tax rolls, as it did in 1533, that 'cardsters, spinners and such other miserable persons' should not be taxed.[96] The precaution was effective for Scotland experienced no tax riots, either in the towns or elsewhere, in this period. Edinburgh tried to extend the tax net to resident lawyers and sons of merchants before they had gained burgess-ship; not unexpectedly, the lawyers took the matter to court and won, but even the scheme to tax merchants' sons had to be abandoned as a 'novelty' in 1557.[97] Aberdeen in 1558 lowered the tax threshold to every inhabitant of 'value of £40 Scots in goods and land' — well beneath the level of £100 rent or 2,000 merks of moveable property which operated by the end of the century.[98] More seriously still, it was obliged to resort to feuing the town's common lands and fishings in 1551–2.[99] It was the weight of royal taxation which caused the church to set in motion the process of feuing of kirk lands; although Aberdeen may be an isolated case of a burgh feuing its lands, it provides some measure of the burden borne by all the burghs in the 1540s and 1550s.

That burden increased still further in the reign of James VI. The 'novelty' of merchants' sons paying tax became standard practice in Edinburgh after 1584 'in respect of the alteration of the time'. The numbers of those assessed for taxation in the capital rose by almost a third between the 1560s and the 1580s; wealthier craftsmen who had paid tax there but corporately until 1583 found their tax bills multiplying once they were individually assessed — the goldsmiths paid three times and the tailors two and a half times as much as before.[100] The phenomenon which most clearly distinguishes the characteristically medieval burgh of late fifteenth-century Scotland from the early modern town emerging by the late sixteenth century was the rise in its taxable population.

The crown was intent to raise revenue by extending both the number of taxpayers and the range of activities assessed for taxation. The package of new taxes accepted by parliament in 1621 introduced important new principles. Burgesses were no longer taxed only on the traditional forms of income they made within burghs; the new tax on annualrents, if it had not been commuted by burghs, would have forced them to pay tax on their activities on lending money secured by wadset of estates.[101] All burgh inhabitants, whatever their occupation — whether lawyers or not — paid tax on the profits they made from conventional money-lending. The growing wealth and widening activities of the urban economy were subtly mirrored in the legislation of 1621. The sums raised by the crown are difficult to calculate,[102] but the effects on the inhabitants of the burghs are clear enough: in Edinburgh, the numbers paying tax rose from 1,152 in 1605 to 1,653 in 1630.[103] That, coupled with the fact that Edinburgh was taxed twenty-three times between 1601 and 1624,[104] introduced a new and significant issue into urban politics; the burghs were, by the 1620s, arguably the most heavily taxed section of Scottish society. Taxation, it has been argued, jolted 'people in the localities . . . out of their relative isolation';[105] it also jolted the internal structure of urban society.

The effects of more and more regular taxation have to be linked to the other demands which central government made of the burghs in a period, between 1550 and 1625, of approximately a four-fold increase in general prices.[106] The crown was anxious to hold down prices, especially of basic foodstuffs, and it was the burgh craftsmen who bore the brunt of the sacrifice. Repeated exhortations were made to burgh magistrates, particularly between the 1530s and 1550s to control or reduce food prices.[107] Yet this pressure also had its effects on the structure of burgh government; in Perth the town council increasingly, from the 1540s onwards, encroached on the traditional powers over the town's economy of the dean of guild and his court.[108] And the rather different, political pressures of the mid-1580s persuaded the Edinburgh town council of the sense of its nominating the dean of guild's council, in order to reformulate the burgess oath and oversee its implementation.[109] The varied demands made of burgh government by the crown comprised one of the most important factors — if not *the* most important — in the reshaping of the medieval urban community, which was near complete by 1625.

It has been said that the later stages of the reign of James VI were a period when the internal frontiers — political and cultural as much as geographical and racial — which kept Scotland apart were beginning to come down, as part of the process of the growing maturity of the Scottish state.[110] There is a certain truth in the argument but much of it might be put a rather different way. This was a period when many of the familiar landmarks — respect, homage and authority — which had held a loose feudal kingdom together and staked out the relationship between the king and his tenants-in-chief, burghs as well as nobles, were becoming obscured. It was, as a result, an age marked by widespread uncertainty. The crown had adopted a variety of novel expedients, both fiscal and political. The institution of a Register of Sasines, recording all transactions in real estate, which had promised to lend a new security of tenure to owners of property, was followed by a new, swingeing tax on annual rents. The new respect within Scottish society for law and order, on which the crown built much of its policy, was accompanied by an evident disrespect on the part of the crown for many of the ancient traditions and privileges which had previously provided the basis for the relationship between the Scottish kings and the royal burghs. Far from there being a new harmony of understanding between the crown and the burghs, there was, it might well be argued, a fundamental and mutual misunderstanding of the new roles each had cast for the other. There was indeed a new 'violence of the state',[111] from which the burghs suffered as much as any other section of Scottish society: the Montrose town council imprisoned in Dumbarton castle in 1599 for rejecting the king's nominee as provost could testify to it, as could the 355 innocent inhabitants of Perth interrogated in 1600 after the Gowrie plot.[112] Yet the malaise ran deeper than this. It was symbolised by an episode in 1618, when the privy council complained of how it had been 'endlessly importuned' by the Edinburgh town council to withdraw a new tax on grain imports. This, the privy council claimed, was an 'intolerable . . . presumption' and it wondered how burgh magistrates would react if they found themselves confronted by any man who 'refuse to give obedience'.[113] The royal burghs, the tenants-in-chief of the king, had been reduced to the status of litigants. It was an attitude which lay at the core of the thinking of James VI but it also permeated his administration.

Notes

1. See J. Wormald, *Court, Kirk and Community: Scotland, 1470–1625* (London, 1981), 27–40, 160–75, and A. Grant, *Independence and Nationhood: Scotland, 1306–1469* (London, 1984), 168, 170, whose approaches underlie the very different periods they deal with.

2. Wormald, *Scotland*, 112, 119.

3. See *APS*, ii, 525, and *CSP Scot.*, i, no. 884 for lists of the burghs in attendance. Aberdeen's trio included David Mar, a protestant sympathiser (ACA, MS Town Treasury Accts., I (i), 1559–60, and see White, Chapter 4, this volume; their expenses amounted to 100 merks, more than the burgh raised to support the Congregation six months earlier. For Edinburgh see *Edin. Recs., 1557–71*, 71, and M. Lynch, *Edinburgh and the Reformation* (Edinburgh, 1981), 233. The Perth document is Craftsman's Book, nos. 23A, 34, see Verschuur, Chapter 2, this volume.

4. *CSP Scot.*, xii, no. 906. It is doubtful that Huntly had such undisputed sway over all towns in the north-east. Aberdeen itself held the earls at arm's length for the most part; this question is discussed more fully in the Introduction.

5. G. S. Pryde, 'Scottish Burgh Finances prior to 1707' (St Andrews Ph.D., 1928), 120; J. Wormald, *Lords and Men* (Edinburgh, 1985), 137–8; W. M. Mackenzie, *The Scottish Burghs* (Edinburgh, 1949), 133, who cites a shorter version of the report (*CSP Scot.*, v, no. 638), which was tentatively dated as 1580. It is also ascribed to 1602 in *CSP Scot.*, xii. Different copies no doubt existed, which explains the minor variations in text, but the political references make it clear that the document must have been composed in 1584.

6. See esp. J. Brown (ed.), *Scottish Society in the Fifteenth Century* (London, 1977), 33–65.

7. G. Donaldson, *All the Queen's Men: Power and Politics in Mary Stewart's Scotland* (London, 1983), 141–3.

8. *Autobiography and Diary of Mr James Melville* (Wodrow Society, 1842), 119.

9. Although it is true that in general nobles did not manipulate the burgh votes in parliament, the point takes on a different complexion if it is recognised that it was written in the circumstances of 1584; cf. Wormald, *Lords and Men*, 139.

10. *Estimate of the Scottish Nobility during the Minority of James the Sixth* (Grampian Club, 1873), 14, 24.

11. *Estimate*, 11–12, 14, 24, 32; *Glasgow Recs., 1573–1642*, 105–6; Perth, Sandeman Library, MS Burgh Court Bk., B59/12/2, fo. 34r.

12. *Roll of Eminent Burgesses of Dundee, 1513–1886*, ed. A. H. Millar (Dundee, 1887), 10, 12–13, 49–50, 57–8; *Estimate*, 32; *RSS*, viii, 965; *RPC*, iii, 573. See Donaldson, *Queen's Men*, 144–5, for a discussion of these nobles.

13. *CSP Scot.*, vi, nos. 654, 665; *Historie and Life of King James the Sext* (Bannatyne Club, 1825), 209; J. Spottiswoode, *History of the Church of Scotland* (Spot. Soc., 1847–51), ii, 325–6. Cupar's burgh records are wanting for most of the sixteenth century.

14. Lynch, *Edinburgh*, 161–3; Lynch, 'The origins of Edinburgh's "toun college": a revision article', *Innes Review*, 33 (1982), 3–14.

15. Although there are clear parallels with James II's treatment of English borough corporations from 1687, these have still to be investigated in Scotland; see T. Pagan, *The Convention of the Royal Burghs of Scotland* (Glasgow, 1926), 82–5.

16. This aspect is discussed more fully in M. Lynch 'Scottish Calvinism, 1559–1638' in M. Prestwich (ed.), *International Calvinism, 1541–1715* (Oxford, 1985), 236.

17. *Acts of Council*, 341–2, 367; *Abdn. Recs., 1398–1570*, 136–40; Wormald, *Lords and Men*, 40–1; A. White, 'Religion, Politics and Society in Aberdeen, 1543–1593' (Edinburgh Univ., Ph.D., 1985), 21.

18. *Acts of Council*, 281, 291; M. B. Verschuur, 'Perth and the Reformation: Society and Reform, 1540–1560' (Glasgow Univ. Ph.D., 1985), 317.

19. *Maitland Miscellany* (Maitland Club, 1847), 79. For the Hamiltons' own interests in towns, see E. Finnie, 'The house of Hamilton: patronage, politics and the church in the Reformation period', *Innes Review*, 36 (1985), 6, 26.

20. See White, Chapter 4, this volume, and his 'Thesis', 30–46.

21. *Acts of Council*, 542–3; Verschuur, 'Thesis', 360, 371–2; *Scottish Correspondence of Mary of Lorraine* (SHS, 1927), 118, 159–60.

22. See White, 'Thesis', esp. 16–17, 35, 44–6, 58–66, 187–96, 304–5, 310–16, for an important, extended discussion of the corollary — Aberdeen's ambivalent relationship with the earl of Huntly — which establishes that it, at least, was not as the 1584 report stated, 'at his command'.

23. White, 'Thesis', 216–7.

24. The 3rd earl of Huntly died in 1524; the 4th earl, born in 1515, was in England for a time after the fall of Angus in 1528; see *Scots Peerage*, iv, 532, 534.

25. *APS*, ii, 14, 497–8.

26. Craftsman's Book, no. 34; Verschuur, 'Thesis', 404–5; Lynch, *Edinburgh*, 71–3.

27. Verschuur, 'Thesis', 407–8, 426–8; see also *Edin. Recs., 1528–1557*, 236, 263.

28. In 1552 the Convention had admitted the 'great variance' in burgh government; see Chapter 1, this volume, n. 43.

29. Pagan, *Convention*, 20–1; *Burghs Conv. Recs.*, i, 6–10, 520–1. An otherwise unknown meeting at Perth in August 1555 is minuted in Scottish Catholic Archives, Fort Augustus MS A1, fos. 330v–333v.

30. Pagan, *Convention*, 22; *APS*, iii, 102.

31. R. Nicholson, *Scotland: The Later Middle Ages* (Edinburgh, 1974), 17.

32. In 1590 the Convention enforced, under threat of a fine, joint consultation amongst the burghs if any of them was approached by the crown for purposes of taxation or revenue (*Burghs Conv. Recs.*, i, 339).

33. *Mary of Lorraine Corresp.*, 427; *CSP Foreign, Eliz.*, ii, nos. 20, 111; Lynch, *Edinburgh*, 77; Verschuur, 'Thesis', 462.

34. *Scottish Historical Documents*, ed. G. Donaldson (Edinburgh, 1970), 254.

35. Lynch, 'Calvinism', 238–40.

36. *Abdn. Recs., 1398–1570*, 318, 322; *Peebles Recs., 1165–1710*, 258.

37. White, 'Thesis', 196; Lynch, *Edinburgh*, 113–14; *RPC*, i, 597; A. Mawell, *The History of Old Dundee* (Edinburgh and Dundee, 1884), 192; *Stirling Charters*, 106, 112–15. See also *RSS*, vol. viii, and Donaldson, *Queen's Men*, 145, for details of the conspiracy of 1584; the burgh of Stirling was given a blanket remission which exempted only thirteen from it. See Pitcairn, *Criminal Trials*, ii, 192–208, for the fruitless interrogation of Perth's inhabitants in 1600.

38. Spottiswoode, *History*, ii, 325–6.

39. *Eminent Burgesses of Dundee*, 25. See *CSP Scot.*, vii, nos. 62, 65, and I. Flett, 'The Conflict of Reformation and Democracy in the Geneva of Scotland, 1443–1610' (St Andrews Univ. M. Phil., 1981), 148.

40. Lynch, *Edinburgh*, 156–7, 162–4.

41. MS Perth Burgh Court Bk., B59/12/2, fos. 35–40, 43, 58, 60. Athol even took the burgh to the Court of Session in 1592 for dismissing him from office (ibid., fos. 54–5).

42. M. Lynch, 'Whatever happened to the medieval burgh?', *Scot. Econ. and Soc. Hist.*, 4 (1984), 9; Lynch, *Edinburgh*, 157–67, 218–19.

43. *RPC*, ii, 32–4; R. S. Rait, *The Parliaments of Scotland* (Glasgow, 1924), 302.

44. Cf. M. Lee, *Government by Pen: Scotland under James VI and I* (Chicago, 1980), 15.

45. *Burghs Conv. Recs.*, i, 340.

46. *APS*, iv, 435.

47. *Eminent Burgesses of Dundee*, 50; Maxwell, *Old Dundee*, 315, 350–1, 355–66; *RPC*, vii, pp. lxxxv–vi, 94–100, 735–7; Flett, 'Thesis', 148ff.

48. Pagan, *Convention*, 78–9; *Burghs Conv. Recs.*, ii, 411–12, 445; iii, 4, 19, 36, 79, 113.

49. J. W. Buchan, *A History of Peeblesshire* (Glasgow, 1925), 36–7.

50. See *Stirling Charters*, 213–15, 217, for details of the councils of 1563–5 and 1595-6, also *Stirling Recs., 1519–1666*, 106, 138–40. A

list of 'friends' of Lord Erskine is given in *RPC*, i, 11.

51. *Burghs Conv. Recs.*, i, 313–14; White, 'Thesis', 304–7.

52. *Edin. Recs.*, *1604–1626*, 142; *State Papers and Correspondence of Thomas, Earl of Melros* (Abbotsford Club, 1837), ii, 519.

53. Pagan, *Convention*, 48–9; *Burghs Conv. Recs.*, i, 318–19; *Melros Corresp.*, ii, 519; *HMC Mar and Kellie* (1904), i, 104–6, 165; *ACL*, i, 147–8, 150. See also Stevenson, Chapter 8, this volume.

54. T. C. Smout, *A History of the Scottish People, 1560–1830* (London, 1969), 107; Pryde, 'Thesis', 24.

55. See *Introduction to Scottish Legal History* (Stair Soc., 20 (1958), 430–32), for a discussion of the process of replegiation.

56. E.g. in *Acta Dom. Concilii, 1501–3* (Stair Soc., 1943), 113 (Inverness and Dingwall), 476–7 (two provosts of Aberdeen).

57. E.g. in *Acta Dom. Concilii et Sessionis, 1532–33* (Stair Soc., 1951), 46–8 (Ayr); Buchan, *Peeblesshire*, ii, 222–3, 258–9.

58. E.g. in *Acts of Council*, 515, 525 (Lanark), 487 (Elgin), 478 (Irvine), 620 (Ayr), p. lxvi (Dumfries).

59. In 1561, for example, the Dundee bakers appealed to the crown against their magistrates forcing them to sell bread at too low a price; A. J. Warden, *The Burgh Laws of Dundee* (London, 1872), 338.

60. Verschuur, 'Thesis', 326–7.

61. *Edin. Recs.*, *1573–1589*, 255–8, 264–75; Lynch, *Edinburgh*, 63; *Abdn. Recs.*, *1570–1625*, 612–13, 621; *RPC*, iii, 470–1, 481–4; White, 'Thesis', 325–7.

62. The burgh setts are conveniently printed in abbreviated form in *SBRS Miscellany* (1881), 161–295.

63. See Wormald, *Lords and Men*, 157–67, for a stimulating reappraisal of the notion of good government in early modern Scotland.

64. This is the persuasive argument put forward in Grant, *Scotland*, 157–9, although the evidence is slender.

65. ACA, MS Council Recs., xxviii, 355; *Abdn. Recs.*, *1570–1625*, 21, 70; White, 'Thesis', 2–3; the first volume of Edinburgh's printed records, *1403–1528*, is partly based on a collection brought together about 1580, see p. xxxii; *Eminent Burgesses of Dundee*, 51.

66. A. H. Williamson, *Scottish National Consciousness in the Age of James VI* (Edinburgh, 1979), 128, 133–4.

67. D. Calderwood, *History of the Kirk of Scotland* (Wodrow Soc., 1842–9), vii, 245–6; see also A. Skene, *A succient survey of the famous city of Aberdeen* (first ed., 1685, reprinted 1833), 27, for an impression of Aberdeen's flourishing mythology.

68. *RPC*, ii, 294–5. The plea was also, significantly, recorded in the council minutes, but not extracted in the printed record; MS Co. Recs., xxx, 340–2.

69. Ibid., xxix, 800–1.

70. *Abdn. Recs.*, *1398–1570*, 294–5.

71. MS Co. Recs., xxxii, 17, 300, 381; John Nisbet was paid 20 merks *pa*, but Alexander Hay, clerk of the rolls, was paid £105; see also *ACL*, i, 14ff, 46ff.

72. *Acts of Council*, 522; Verschuur, 'Thesis', 339.

73. *Stirling Chrtrs.*, 112–15.

74. These acts are conveniently collated in *Ancient Laws and Customs of the Burghs of Scotland*, ii, 1424–1707 (SBRS, 1910), 75, 85, 87, 93, 101. See ibid., 119, 121, 126, 127, 130, for the post-1593 legislation, which culminated in the promise, in the act of 1612, that a more complete confirmation would be drawn up.

75. *The Practicks of Sir James Balfour* (Stair Soc., 1922–3), 43.

76. Maxwell, *Old Dundee*, 358; *APS*, ii, 95.

77. *Eminent Burgesses of Dundee*, 10, 49–50; Lynch, *Edinburgh*, 159, 163.

78. Balfour, *Practicks*, 45; *Melros Corresp.*, i, 110, ii, 101.

79. Balfour, *Practicks*, 49; *Melros Corresp.*, i, 351; *Mar and Kellie*. i, 165; Lee, *Government by Pen*, 198–9. But some attempts to grant monopolies foundered; see *Mar and Kellie*, i, 351.

80. *Mar and Kellie*, i, 112.

81. *APS*, iii, 72.

82. Lynch, *Edinburgh*, 108–18.

83. The grants of 1567 are given in *RSS*, v, 3334ff. See *RPC*, i, 348, 501, 597–8, for Dundee in 1565, when Haliburton was dismissed as provost, but little else.

84. White, 'Thesis', 298.

85. Lynch, *Edinburgh*, 162; Lynch, 'Calvinism', 240–1.

86. Lynch, 'Calvinism', 241.

87. Calderwood, *History*, vii, 391, 596ff; *RPC*, xiii, 521–2. These troubles are discussed in W. H. Makey, *The Church of the Covenant, 1637–1651* (Edinburgh, 1979), 157–8.

88. Wormald, *Scotland*, 15–16.

89. Mackenzie, *Scottish Burghs*, 112–13; Nicholson, *Scotland*, 283–4.

90. *APS*, iv, 118; *Burghs Conv. Recs.*, i, 497–8; ii, 19–21; Lee, *Government by Pen*, 15.

91. I. Guy, 'The Scottish Export Trade, 1460–1599' (St Andrews M. Phil., 1982), 20, 24.

92. Wormald, *Scotland*, 161.

93. *Acts of Council*, 391, 394.

94. White, 'Thesis', 71–2; Lynch, *Edinburgh*, 72, 87n.

95. *Acts of Council*, 616–17, 619–20.

96. Ibid., 399.

97. Ibid., 635; *Edin. Recs., 1557–1571*, 14.

98. *Abdn. Recs., 1398–1570*, 309; the result in 1558 was that the stenters, who assessed individuals for taxation, refused to take office. *APS*, iv, 141–2.

99. White, 'Thesis', 73.

100. *Edin. Recs., 1573–1589*, 325–6; Lynch, 'Medieval burgh', 10–11.

101. The significance of the tax on wadsetters — and the reason for the stiff resistance put up against it by the burghs — is revealed in J. Brown, 'The Social, Political and Economic Influences of the Edinburgh Merchant Elite, 1600–38' (Edinburgh Univ. Ph.D., 1985), 313–54, which demonstrates extensive mortgaging of estates by nobles and greater lairds in this period.

102. See Stevenson, Chapter 8, this volume.

103. Brown, 'Thesis', 16, 18. In Aberdeen widows, sons and doctors

were all taxed in 1622; *ACL*, i, 198.

104. Brown, 'Thesis', 362, 364.

105. Wormald, *Scotland*, 159.

106. S. G. E. Lythe, *The Economy of Scotland in its European Setting, 1550–1625* (Edinburgh, 1960), 110.

107. See e.g. Balfour, *Practicks*, 63–5; *Edin. Recs.*, *1528–1557*, 230, 237–8; *RPC*, i, 3, 30, 36, 106–7, 139, 142, 488–9; Lythe, *Economy*, 106–8.

108. See Verschuur, Chapter 2, this volume.

109. Lynch, *Edinburgh*, 164.

110. G. Donaldson, 'James VI and vanishing frontiers', in *The Scottish Nation*, ed. G. Menzies (London, 1972), 112–14.

111. Wormald, *Lords and Men*, 165.

112. *RPC*, vi, 34; Pitcairn, *Criminal Trials*, ii, 192–208.

113. *Melros Corresp.*, i, 320.

4

The Impact of the Reformation on a Burgh Community: The Case of Aberdeen

Allan White

The sixteenth-century burgh of Aberdeen clustered around three hills which rose sharply from the northern banks of the river Dee. From the eastern edge of the burgh the ground fell away sharply to the harbour, the source of Aberdeen's wealth and its window on the world. The burgh's main commercial links were with the Low Countries, the Baltic and Scandinavia, although Aberdeen merchants were even to be found as far afield as Iceland.[1] The trading contacts between Aberdeen and Europe were paralleled by a busy traffic in the academic and ecclesiastical market. Links were forged not only between Danzig, Dieppe and Veere, but also between King's College and the university towns of Cologne, Louvain and Paris. Aberdeen was a definite part of the northern European cultural and intellectual commonwealth. The currents of opinion, academic and otherwise, emanating from across the seas were at least as strong as those stemming from the south and west of Scotland. However, although the burgh was a distinct community with a political and economic life of its own it was not totally divorced from outside influences. It was perennially vulnerable to forces outside its control: the interruption of trading contacts by war, the expansionist ambitions of the local gentry and nobility, and the vagaries of royal patronage. By keeping a balance between all of these potentially conflicting forces the burgesses of Aberdeen hoped to retain their distinctness and independence whilst recognising the interdependence of town and country, centre and locality.

The familiar hierarchical pyramid of wealth and status evident in many early modern towns was also seen in Aberdeen.[2] The social pyramid rested on a broad base and rose to a sharply tapering apex. However, the hereditary principle that reigned so inflexibly in the burgh ensured that upward mobility within the structure was closely controlled. The peak of the Aberdeen social pyramid was not regularly broken off, neither was the composition of the oligarchy that maintained control of the town regularly changing.[3] There was considerable immobility, even stagnation, within burgh society. As the sixteenth century progressed Aberdeen became a less open society and its privileged class less willing to admit newcomers qualified by wealth, if not by heredity, to share power commensurate with their status. In effect, by the end of the sixteenth century the oligarchy which had managed the town for over a century showed all the signs — inbreeding, intolerance and immutability — of an aristocracy in decline.

Throughout the sixteenth century the government of the burgh was vested exclusively in the hands of the merchant guild. Indeed the acts of parliament of 1469 and 1474, which related to the conduct of burgh elections, confirmed a dominance that the burgesses of guild had already achieved in the town.[4] Successive councils took full advantage of the acts of parliament to further establish themselves as a self-perpetuating oligarchy, excluding completely any representation of craftsmen on the council.[5] As a result the idea of the 'community of the burgh' had been applied in an increasingly narrow sense. By 1441 it was clear that the community of the burgh was understood simply in relation to the members of the merchant guild.[6] Real power was concentrated in the hands of an even smaller group of about a dozen merchant dynasties, all closely related by marriage and long-term family association, who often maintained seats on the council for decades. In some ways burgh society represented a series of concentric circles and it was possible to enjoy considerable mobility within one's own circle but difficult to move from one to another. It was almost impossible to penetrate to the town council, the charmed circle in which legislative and executive power was concentrated. At the heart of the council stood the Menzies family who formed the central link in an exceedingly complex chain of power, kinship and patronage.

The Menzies had arrived in the north-east from Perthshire towards the beginning of the fifteenth century, just before their more eminent local counterparts, the Gordons, who would secure the earldom of Huntly; a Gilbert Menzies was recorded as provost of the burgh in 1423.[7] During the course of the next century the Menzies, by administrative skill, astute political manoeuvering and a judicious scheme of alliance-building, were to emerge as the premier family in Aberdeen, rather as the Gordons were to do in the region as a whole. The Menzies did not come to exert a firm grip on the provostship until the end of the fifteenth century; before that they were simply one component part of the oligarchy. Their rise to power was built on the defence of customary privilege rooted in antiquity and having the force of law. One pillar of this policy was the exclusion of local nobles and lairds, including the Gordons, from interference in the internal affairs of the burgh. The Menzies oligarchs wished to redraw the boundary between town and country, a distinction which had become progressively blurred throughout the fifteenth century, and which was to be seriously challenged in the middle of the sixteenth by the greatest of the local nobles, the fourth earl of Huntly.

During the fifteenth century the Gordons had established themselves in the north-east where the Stewarts and the Douglases had held sway before them.[8] Their rise to power was due to an astute policy of marriage and local alliance building. The territorial possessions of the family increased in scope throughout the fifteenth century and contributed to their considerable fortune. The landed endowment of the earls of Huntly offered unrivalled opportunities for patronage and the creation of a gentry clientage. The earls made good use of these opportunities by settling cadet branches of the family on these lands in return for the traditional services due to kin and lord.[9] By the time the fourth earl succeeded to the title in 1524 the landed expansion of the Gordons had largely ceased and his interest was directed towards the expansion of his 'affinity' by entering into bonds of manrent with local noble and gentry families, and the acquisition of honours and titles which demonstrated the power and prestige of his lordship. The wisdom of the policy of territorial investment and the resulting increase in the Gordon fortunes can be clearly seen in a 1554 tax roll for the shire of Aberdeen.[10] The earl of Huntly paid just over 14 per cent of the total collected for the whole shire. His contribution of £200 exceeded that of his nearest rival, the earl of Erroll, by £100, with Lord Elphinstone next at £60. The Earl Marischal, who was to be the main Protestant in the locality after 1560, paid only £4 for his lands in Aberdeenshire, suggesting the meagre extent of his territorial patronage there in contrast to his holdings to the south in Angus and Mearns. Marischal's holdings were matched by those of Thomas Menzies of Pitfoddels, the provost of Aberdeen, who paid £4 for his lands in the shire at the same time. The earl of

Huntly's disposal of lands and money in favour of bonds of man-rent emphasised not only his fortune but also his determination that it should purchase him security and standing in the region. The foundation of Gordon policies in the north-east was the conviction that their power depended on royal favour, and royal favour in turn depended on their being able to execute the function of king's lieutenants in the north. Should they fail in that commission their whole position in the region would begin to crumble.

The north-eastern polity was thus composed of a number of distinct but related communities. Local rural society was led by the earl of Huntly, whose position rested on the loyalty and support of a network of kinship and clientage constructed over a century or more. The community of the burgesses of Aberdeen was related to this broader world by ties of family and business association, but it was never fully absorbed by it and often asserted its independence, albeit at some cost. On a number of occasions during the sixteenth century the town was the object of assaults by local lairds, by the Leslies and other Garioch gentry in 1525, the Forbes in 1530, the earl of Huntly during the civil war of 1567–73, and the Leslies once again in 1587.[11] During such attacks the gates were closed and chains stretched across the streets to prevent horsemen deploying. Even the architecture of the burgh's houses, with their high walls and low entrance gates enclosing a series of small courtyards, was incorporated into the defensive system of the burgh.[12] The burgh was not simply a community of individuals, it was a complex of households each with duties and responsibilities as well as rights and privileges; in Aberdeen privilege had to be earned and defended from the predatory interests of outsiders. In such a society the ties of kinship and family loyalty acquired a profundity and institutional expression of remarkable intensity. At the death of James V in 1542 Aberdeen presented a profile of a relatively small, increasingly close-knit and relatively static society, secure in its isolation and confident in its conservatism. It was just such a society that was most vulnerable to pressure for religious changes which questioned so many of the values for which it stood.

In many ways the events of 1543–5 were a rehearsal for those of 1559–60 in Aberdeen. The experience which the Menzies family and their associates gained from a brief alliance with the earl of Arran, the governor of the kingdom, in his attempts to pursue a Protestant and anglophile policy decisively influenced their reluctant adherence to the cause of reformation in 1559–60. One of the first of Arran's acts after he had been confirmed as governor in March 1543 was to name Thomas Menzies, the provost of Aberdeen, as his comptroller, and to appoint him to his council.[13] Such an appointment is all the more surprising since Menzies was totally new to central government. Moreover, Arran was in serious financial difficulty and needed all the help he could get simply to remain solvent.[14] The association between Menzies and Arran has two-fold significance. At the outset of Arran's governorship Scotland was militarily weak, politically dominated by a number of rival aristocratic interests, and faced with fending off an English invasion whilst avoiding absorption into the French interest. In order to defend his governorship Arran needed allies in the localities who would render his administration effective; to this end he turned to Thomas Menzies, Aberdeen's defender against the ambitions of the earl of Huntly, Arran's rival. The governor's need matched the provost's aspirations. Menzies was the representative of the gentrified townsmen who were pressing for a greater role in central government. It was this move out of the burgh, and out of the region, which was to place a severe strain on the traditional arrangement of local politics and lead to the temporary eclipse of the Menzies family by the earl of Huntly.

The earl of Arran was moved by the traditional considerations of a territorial magnate. When in 1543 Henry VIII offered to make him ruler of Scotland beyond the Forth Arran declined saying that 'all his land and living lay on this side of the Forth [the south], which he would not gladly change for any living beyond Forth'.[15] Alliance with Thomas Menzies gave him a valuable pocket of influence in what had hitherto been regarded as the territory of the earl of Huntly, his rival and opponent, as well as giving him control of a highly important burgh with a harbour and good roadstead. By establishing direct relations with the burgh of Aberdeen through the provost, and ignoring the earl of Huntly, Arran was by-passing the traditional royal agent in the region and finding new ways of executing policy.

One of the first fruits of the co-operation between Arran and Thomas Menzies was the implementation of a programme of religious preaching incipiently Protestant in character. Two renegade Dominican friars, both of them from the government's stable of reforming chaplains, were encouraged to begin the reformation of the religious life of Aberdeen with the support, both verbal and financial, of the town council.[16] Menzies also committed himself wholeheartedly to the governor's pursuit of an English alliance, thereby alienating the earl of Huntly whose sympathies lay with the French connection. Huntly had his own supporters in the burgh who were able to mount a serious challenge to the Menzies in August 1543.[17] Arran's volte-face and abandonment of the English marriage along with his former anglophile agents and clients in September 1543 further weakened the Menzies position in Aberdeen.[18] The key to their survival in power lay in the support they derived from central government, together with their domination of the council; should either be seriously threatened their fall was inevitable.

The ties between Arran and the Menzies were gravely threatened at the parliament of December 1544. Burgh politics were of secondary interest to the earl of Arran compared to the complexities of international relations and magnatial dynastic ambition. In order to consolidate a united front against the English Arran was forced to recognise the position of the great landed earls in government, and return to the traditional royal policy of rule through the magnates. In the end the earl of Huntly's support for the marriage of Arran's son to the young Queen Mary weighed more heavily with the governor than any loyalty to his former comptroller.[18] By conceding Huntly's pre-eminence in the north-east Arran effectively isolated Menzies. Accordingly, in January 1545, Huntly took office as provost of Aberdeen, with Menzies as his deputy.[19] Even this arrangement was ended at the next election in September 1545 when the Menzies influence was completely eradicated from the council which was then weighted with Gordon clients.[20] Thus, the Menzies fell victims to the earl of Huntly whose interests they have traditionally been held to have served. It was only Huntly's capture at the battle of Pinkie in September 1547 and the subsequent collapse of his influence in the burgh which allowed the Menzies to reinstate themselves on the council.[21] However, they were not to be secure in the burgh until 1556 when seats on the council became definitively hereditary. Henceforth the only movement within its ranks was confined to the office of bailie, an office which was to be dominated by the Menzies and their confederates.

The events of 1560 came as a severe shock to the various communities which composed the burgh of Aberdeen. Neither were the changes wrought then widely welcomed. A Protestant minister was appointed by the autumn of 1560 but no kirk session emerged until 1562, and only then as part of Lord James Stewart's programme of protestantising the north.[22] The failure of Lord James to take advantage of the temporary eclipse of Gordon

fortunes left the burgh's conservative establishment free to inter-
pret its own Reformation settlement. Consequently a valiant, if
discreet, rearguard action was fought for more than a generation
to preserve as much as possible of the old ways. The progress of the
Reformation was further impeded by the widespread survival of
popular Catholic belief and practice, enshrined both in the
Catholic household and the guild.

The appearance of Protestant opinion in Aberdeen before 1560
was, on the whole, infrequent and insignificant. In 1521 the
master of the grammar school, John Marshall, had expressed
doubts about papal supremacy, but even he had been allowed two
years to change his mind. A decade later Alexander Dick, a Franciscan, declared in favour of reformed theology. The reaction of
the people of Aberdeen may be judged by his having to flee to the
more bracing Protestant air of Dundee.[23] A more serious threat to
orthodoxy was presented by the importation of Protestant
literature by way of the east-coast ports. In 1525, and again a
decade later, such traffic was prohibited by the crown.[24] However,
such legislation only indicates a potential danger, it does not reveal
the character, composition or even location of possibly dissenting
communities. It was also the case that the ports were a means of
entry for Catholic reforming works. The prevailing Catholic
opinions of Cologne and the Low Countries were certainly well
represented on Aberdeen book shelves. Indeed the diocese of
Aberdeen was the first in Scotland to implement the decrees of the
Council of Trent and to draw up a scheme of Catholic reform.[25]
Aberdeen did not seem ripe for reformation in 1560, and such
reformation as there was came about largely through the pressure
of external circumstances.

The events of 1559–60 revealed something of the strengths and
weaknesses of the forces ranged on either side of the religious
divide, as well as the dilemma faced by the burgesses of Aberdeen
caught between an instinctive conservatism and a determination to
maintain their privileges and freedom of action. It was characteristic of the Reformation in Aberdeen to have been slow to take
initiatives. The burgesses, especially those who controlled the
council, seemed always to be responding to the negative influences
stemming from Edinburgh and Dundee. They had no desire to
repeat the history of 1543–5, when a brief flirtation with
Protestantism had led to the fall of the Menzies. Having carefully
re-established their position the Menzies were unwilling to risk all
in a cause whose outcome was uncertain. They were willing to ally

with the local magnates to delay the course of the Reformation, but they were not willing to become their satellites, or to be trapped in the middle of a power struggle between rival aristocratic camps.

During the critical latter half of 1559 the burgh of Aberdeen attempted to preserve a studied neutrality and remained away from the vigorous marching and counter-marching of the Lords of Congregation and the queen regent. Their distance from the drama gave the council the opportunity to reflect on events and produce a measured response to them. The burgesses were determined to ensure that the disorder which accompanied religious change in the southern burghs should not erupt in Aberdeen. They were also determined not to be dominated by a volatile, factious and radical ministry intent on pushing them further in the direction of reformation than they wished to go.

The focus of ecclesiastical life in the burgh in 1560 was the parish church of St Nicholas, of which Parson Gordon of Rothiemay said a century later: 'there is no church so neat and bewtifull to be seen in Scotland'.[26] The burgesses of Aberdeen, as well as those noble and gentry families who lived outside the burgh, had invested considerable pride as well as financial resources in it. Apart from sheltering thirty altars and supporting sixteen chaplains it also served as a burial place for the families of lairds such as the Leslies and the Irvines of Drum.[27] St Nicholas had also, half a century before, formed part of Bishop Elphinstone's plan to make his diocese a model of church government and religious practice, a scheme in which the burgesses had been willing collaborators. The university of Aberdeen, another of Elphinstone's foundations, also had its representatives amongst the chaplains of St Nicholas. The chaplaincy of St Mary Magdalen was customarily held by the bursar in civil law at King's College. Master Hector Myreton held it until 1563, having been presented in July 1518.[28] The successor to the bursary and the chaplaincy was Master John Kennedy, the depute town clerk of Aberdeen.[29] Thus, Kennedy, who was at the heart of the burgh's administrative life, brought together in his person the three principal influences on Aberdeen life: the town council, the university and the diocese.

The burgh's craftsmen also had an interest in the parish kirk where they maintained their own altars and chaplains. Their rights of patronage were limited however, since the council had to approve any chaplain appointed by the crafts. Nevertheless, the altar still acted as a focus for the piety and devotion of the craft guild, as well as contributing to its corporate sense of identity and distinction. The craftsmen regarded their altars with a pro-prietorial air; even after 1560 they considered themselves to retain certain rights which did not revert to the town on the abandon-ment of the structures of the old church. In 1564 a dispute broke out between the council and the hammermen over the endowment of St Eloy's altar in the parish kirk. The councillors were faced with co-ordinated opposition to their claims as patrons of the altar from the hammermen who were reluctant to see their rights over-ridden. In some ways this conflict was a test case, and in the end the council was forced to admit that it did not have undisputed sway over the disposal of the revenues of the old church which lay within its jurisdiction.[30]

The town council's control of the patronage of many of the altars in the parish kirk offered them opportunities for rewarding burgh servants; the master of the grammar school, the master of the song school, and the town clerk depute all held chaplaincies in St Nicholas.[31] The chaplains therefore formed a sizeable pro-portion of the burgh establishment. They were involved with their flocks at several levels, living amongst them on close terms in houses and chambers scattered throughout the town rather than in conventual buildings next to the church. Not unnaturally, relations were sometimes strained, since the chaplains depended for part of their incomes on revenues derived from small annual rents and allowances, and they sometimes found themselves involved in litigation with their flocks.[32] Such incidentals of social life should not always be taken as examples of pressure for religious reformation amongst the people, but might reflect the strains of everyday living in a small, densely packed burgh. The various members of the clerical establishment were thus not simply to be found serving the spiritual needs of the people, they appeared in all walks of life. Moreover, a strong sense of local identity and pride of place was planted in the clergy, and they were left in no doubt that they were burgh servants.

The ecclesiastical institutions of Aberdeen, its parish kirk, friaries, hospitals and chapels all formed part of the rich pattern of foundation, endowment and patronage which linked each con-stituent part of local society, magnate and bishop, canon and laird, burgess, craftsman and chaplain. These foundations were the out-ward and visible expressions of the interior, unarticulated relation-ships on which that society was based. The general impression of

Aberdeen in the mid-sixteenth century is one of fairly unadventurous orthodoxy, content with the practice of medieval religion. However, political experience elsewhere in Scotland had shown that where authority rested on force of character, and where loyalty was personal, religious conflict could tear great rents in the fabric of what was hitherto accepted. With the past history of the events of 1543–5 to reflect on, the conservative burgesses feared most the coalition of the small body of local Protestant sympathisers and the volatile strength of the Congregation. In order for the oligarchy to retain control of burgh life a unification of internal and external threats had to be avoided.

Thomas Menzies, the provost of Aberdeen, viewed the northward advance of Protestantism with considerable anxiety. He rightly sensed in it a threat to the established order of the burgh. His concern lay not simply in defending the interests of the Catholic church, but also in preserving the political stability of Aberdeen which was closely bound up with the destinies of about eighteen prominent families. Some impression of the relative strengths of the various parties within the burgh may be gained from an examination of the lists of those who served as bailies during these years. In the period 1556–9 twenty-seven men served on the council. Of these, three died in office and were immediately succeeded by their sons. These twenty-seven were drawn from the ranks of thirteen Aberdeen families. Fourteen of the twenty-seven served without interruption throughout the period, one served only one term, and two were added to the council in 1562, both of them sons-in-law of the provost; a further two were added in 1567. It becomes immediately apparent from such a scrutiny that the burgh was ruled by substantially the same people after the Reformation as before. Indeed, after the Reformation power became increasingly concentrated in the hands of a small inner grouping within the oligarchy. From 1563 to 1569 only five men held the office of bailie; two of them were sons of the provost, two were his sons-in-law, and the other, Master George Middleton, was married to a Catholic and had, in 1559, objected to the association of Aberdeen with the forces of the Congregation.[33] The Reformation prompted the Menzies to tighten their grip on the government of the burgh; paradoxically it increased their power rather than reduced it.

The first serious attempt to involve Aberdeen in the maelstrom of national politics came with an assault on the religious houses of the burgh by a reforming mob from Angus and the Mearns.[34] The nature of this enterprise was not entirely clear. At the time the tide appeared to be turning against the Lords of Congregation and this attack may have been prompted by resentment at the burgh's lack of involvement in the struggle against France, together with a determination to implicate it in the reforming efforts of the Congregation. However, as well as provoking a spirited intervention by the earl of Huntly in defence of the parish kirk and the university, the raid by the men of Angus was the catalyst that revealed a division of opinion on the council, and brought forward that dissension that the provost and his associates most feared. The arrival of the southern mob on 4 January forced an emergency meeting of the council. The raid appears to have continued during the meeting and some of the townsmen, for whatever reason, joined the raiders. In order to retain control of the situation David Mar, the dean of guild, proposed that the friars' revenues and buildings should be taken over and applied to the town's use.[35] The meeting had an additional and more threatening dimension. The provost was absent from the burgh during this episode and his failure to appear gave David Mar the opportunity to attempt a coup with the aim of replacing the Catholic establishment of the burgh with a Protestant one almost overnight.

David Mar, a Protestant sympathiser, had chosen the moment to associate Aberdeen with the Reformation with great care. The provost and six other members of the council, all of whom had expressed strong public opposition to the Congregation on 29 December 1559, were out of the town. Their absence gave Mar the chance of seizing control of the council and attempting to push through a comprehensive programme of legislation, including the diversion of the revenues of the friars to the support of Protestant preachers and the military endeavours of the Congregation. The language which expressed this purpose was taken, more or less directly, from the various bonds of the Congregation. The only member of the council to dissent at this meeting was Gilbert Collison, master of the kirk work and a consistent conservative in later years.[36] It was not until the head court of the burgh met on 8 January 1559 that general opposition to Mar's drive towards reformation began to grow. Gilbert Menzies, the provost's eldest son, acted as spokesman for the opposition during his father's continued absence from the town; over half the council associated themselves with him. It thus became clear that the coup was not going to succeed and that the initiative had been lost by the reformers.

The matter was taken up again at the guild court, customarily held a few days after each head court. The provost finally made an appearance at this court on 12 January and gave some indication of why he had not featured at the previous meetings. The truce which had been agreed between the queen regent and the Lords of Congregation expired on 10 January. Thomas Menzies simply kept out of the way until that date had passed, allowing his son to act for him in the burgh.[37] The acts carried out by Mar and, as Menzies said on 12 January, in collaboration with 'extranears' were clearly illegal after the expiry of the truce. Thomas Menzies was thus able to return to the burgh with his reputation untarnished as a defender of law and order. His hostility to the changes encouraged other burgesses to express their opposition also; he was thus able to countermand Mar's legislation and inhibit the payment of Protestant preachers from the town's revenues. The Protestant cause and its supporters on the council suffered from having declared too early and, as a result, had been left isolated and deprived of general support.

Hostility to pressure for the reformation of the burgh church very quickly spread outside the ranks of the Menzies family and their supporters, together with half the council who had gathered behind them. This group was soon joined by six other prominent burgesses who were prepared to take instruments on their dissatisfaction at the course of events; three were notaries, two were burgesses with kinsmen amongst the chaplains of St Nicholas' kirk, and a leading craftsman.[38] Although this mobilisation of opinion within the town was sufficient to prevent any further steps towards the establishment of a Protestant polity, it was not secure enough to reverse the prevailing trend of events. The Protestant party may have been in a minority, but it was too powerful to be ignored or overcome. The chief problem facing Thomas Menzies was how to draw the town back from the brink of rebellion without splitting the council irrevocably and precipitating the intervention of the most powerful local conservative, the earl of Huntly. The tactic he employed was to remain the keystone of Menzies policy for the next twenty years. All religious debate was to be strictly confined to the council chamber. He relied on his own network of patronage and influence, as well as his skills at political management, to aid him in defusing any potentially damaging sectarian strife.

It was not until the beginning of March 1560 that the first tentative steps were taken to associate Aberdeen with the Congregation.

Clearly Aberdeen had to take account of the drift of magnatial opinion; the earl of Huntly and the bishop of Moray had already begun to waver in their allegiance to the queen regent.[39] The other leading magnate in the area, the Earl Marischal, and his associates, the Forbes, had been linked with Protestantism since the 1540s. A Catholic Aberdeen was a definite threat to aristocratic and Protestant vested interest in the region, as well as presenting a useful port of entry for re-supplying foreign forces in the country in the event of a French-inspired Catholic revival.[40] In fact the vigour of anti-French feeling in the country was too strong to be resisted utterly by the burgesses of Aberdeen. Therefore on 11 March the council agreed to support the Congregation by offering to send a force southwards and to raise a tax to aid the enterprise.[41]

The co-operation offered to the Protestant lords was definitely limited, encompassing a mere forty men, a meagre figure compared with Huntly's boast of being able to muster a force of 20,000 men to support Queen Mary should she have chosen to land at Aberdeen instead of Leith in 1561.[42] The decision to support the Congregation was a reversal of Menzies' previous policy which had been expressed in the strongest terms. The treaty of Berwick in February 1560, taken together with Huntly's decision to associate with the Congregation, may have conditioned the adherence of the burgh to the same cause. The terms of the treaty were couched in a way that would have been acceptable to the burgesses of Aberdeen with their scruples about rebellion against legally constituted authority. The treaty allowed that it was possible to be anti-French without being disloyal to the queen.[43] Under these terms the town felt able to commit itself to the Congregation, and on this occasion the only objector was Gilbert Collison.[44] When the disposition of the properties of the religious houses was once more discussed at the same meeting of 11 March, the people who had formerly objected to the town's trafficking in the endowments of the old church renewed their protests. However, they did not object to alliance with the Congregation.[45] A compromise had obviously emerged which allowed hope for the preservation of some form of conservative opinion alongside a modified support for the forces of change.

The attitude of the earl of Huntly was clearly of great significance in influencing the burgesses in their decision. His hesitations were finally resolved in April 1560 when he half-heartedly signed the bond of the Congregation along with Leslie of Balquhain and Seton of Meldrum and other conservative lords.[46] Whereas

Gordon power had previously presented a threat to the burgh, the town soon found itself an ally of magnatial interests. The difficult task then facing the burgh was how to derive maximum strength and support from the alliance without being swallowed up by it. Their success in achieving an association with the right degree of distance may be partially measured in that in 1562, when Huntly's rebellion against the crown was put down at the battle of Corrichie, the town was not implicated in his fall.[47]

The death of Mary of Guise and the triumph of the Congregation left the burgh of Aberdeen at a loss as to how to respond. It was impossible to rely on a Catholic restoration during the queen's absence in France, and the earl of Huntly's alliance with the Protestants precluded any interference from that quarter. The burgh could not afford to abstain from the process of settlement of the realm. Accordingly three delegates were sent to the Reformation parliament of August 1560 to pursue a limited policy of co-operation with the new regime.[48] Their presence there gave them the invaluable opportunity of selecting the first minister of the reformed kirk in Aberdeen.[49] Clearly this was a key appointment; an enthusiast, a political opportunist or a radical evangelist would have provided a centre of agitation or a focus of discontent which might have polarised opinion within the burgh. The Reformation actually offered the council the opportunity of extending their control over the burgh; they had no intention of relinquishing any more of such control than was strictly necessary; it was also clear that they intended to control the pace and direction of reformation. In Adam Heriot, the town's first minister, they chose wisely and well. He was scholarly, retiring, and not even a pale shadow of his volatile counterpart in Edinburgh, John Knox. The choice of Heriot was not simply an expedient, it was a definite option for a particular kind of church, as well as being a gesture of friendship to the powerful Lord James Stewart, whose protégé Heriot was.[50] From the very outset it was clear that the Reformation settlement in Aberdeen was to be different to that in other major burghs.

The establishment of Protestantism as the official church of the burgh did not involve the disappearance or proscription of Catholicism. Catholicism survived not simply in the persons of its clergy, who were not forced to leave the burgh, but even in its theological and liturgical expression. After the Reformation the Catholic Church went underground; the public kirk became the privy kirk. Even after 1560 it was still possible to attend mass and receive the sacraments.[51] It was also possible to attend a Catholic university until 1569 at King's College in Old Aberdeen. The paradox of this situation was that some of the inhabitants of the burgh, from the highest to the lowest, managed to combine membership of both churches with little apparent sense of contradiction. There was thus a dual establishment whose membership overlapped. This was true of its laity, and even of some of its clergy, as with John Collison, the former sub-chanter of the cathedral and chaplain of St Nicholas who, having refused to support the ministers of the new kirk, for many years agreed to lead the psalm singing in the parish kirk on Sundays.[52]

A sign of the equivocal attitude of the burgesses of Aberdeen to the Reformation may be seen in their policy towards the former clergy of the Catholic Church. Considerable ties of blood and patronage existed between the various churches and religious houses of the burgh and its inhabitants. Nonconformity amongst the chaplains of St Nicholas was not likely to be severely punished since many of them were relations of the members of the town council. In resolving this problem the town adopted a gentle approach; its attitude was publicly correct whilst being privately considerate. A religious test was imposed on the chaplains, in accordance with the decision of the convention of nobility in January 1561.[53] Although some of the chaplains accepted the condition of attendance at the prayers and preaching in the parish kirk, others did not. The most significant of these latter was John Black, the former master of the song school.[54] For some years he remained aloof from conforming, and consequently was deprived of his chaplain's pension, but it was not until 1574 that the matter was resolved with his submission to the new order.[55] Another of the chaplains, Master Andrew Gray, left the country rather than conform, although he made arrangements that his brother should collect his revenues and forward them to him in the Low Countries.[56]

The attitude of the council was, on the whole, lenient and even generous to the members of the former Catholic clergy, both religious and secular. A number of former religious continued to live in Aberdeen after 1560, dependent on the tolerance and support of the council. Two Franciscans were paid by the council to act as guardians of their former friary.[57] The prior of the Carmelites, John Failford, was given shelter in the house of the provost of Aberdeen until his death in 1576.[58] Failford was in touch with the continent during all of this time and was receiving books from there as late as 1572.[59] In January 1568 the council ordered that Richard Garden, a Carmelite, should receive his board and lodging from the chief men of the town council until further notice.[60] Thus Garden, a Catholic priest, was given access to the chief men of the town with the blessing of the council, which provided him with the opportunity for that kind of 'ressonyng' about the scriptures which was so suspected by the kirk session. Similarly in 1566 John Wright, one of the former chaplains of St Nicholas, was appointed keeper of the lighthouse which had recently been established in St Ninian's chapel on the top of the Castle hill.[61] He was therefore available to the inhabitants of the burgh yet sufficiently apart to be unobtrusive. Against this gamut of Catholic clergy in the burgh Protestantism could muster only Adam Heriot and John Leslie, the reader.[62]

The proponents of the Reformation were also forced to confront another reality of life in Aberdeen: the extraordinary network of kinship and family ties. Even those who supported the Protestant cause were connected by blood or marriage to Catholic sympathisers. In the manuscript of the 1562 kirk session register a significant emendation has been made to one of the statutes formulated in December of that year concerning the treatment of those who refused to accept the new doctrines. In its original form penalties were laid on those who associated with excommunicates. However, in the manuscript this passage has been deleted. Plainly it would have been difficult, if not impossible, to enforce these penalties because non-conformity was so pervasive.[63] Catholicism was present amongst many members of the kirk session as well as in their households. The wife of the clerk to the kirk session, Bessie Seinyeor, was a convinced Catholic and the daughter of one of Edinburgh's leading Marian merchants.[64] The provost kept his private chaplain, John Failford, to minister to his needs. Alexander Knowles, a prominent burgess and member of the session, was on friendly terms with the bishop; his daughter, Janet, was on closer terms still, having borne the bishop several children.[65] The wife of Master George Middleton, a sessioner and regularly a bailie of the burgh, remained a Catholic until 1574 when she conformed under pressure.[66] Of the four members of the Menzies family on the session, three were periodically accused of papistry, whilst the wife of Gilbert Menzies the elder, the provost's brother, refused to conform even during the crackdown on the old kirk in 1574.[67] A pattern of determined and fairly healthy Catholicism may be seen in Aberdeen, a pattern which may also be traced right to the heart of the structures of the new kirk in the burgh.

Since a considerable amount of Catholic sentiment survived it is perhaps not surprising that certain pious practices associated with the old Church should also have remained. The recurrence of public demonstrations of traditional celebrations were associated chiefly with the burgh's craftsmen. The seasons and ceremonies of the Catholic Church had been of special significance to them, since they allowed for the public expression of corporate identity together with a demonstration of the rank and importance of the craft. The religious aspirations of the craft were focused on its altar in St Nicholas', and its place in burgh society was seen in the precedence accorded to it in public liturgical processions. There had been considerable friction at successive Corpus Christi processions in the 1550s because certain crafts had usurped the place of others in the order of the processions.[68] The place of honour was that nearest the Blessed Sacrament, and it was a matter of competition to see which craft could secure that place. On such occasions the whole hierarchy of the ordered burgh commonwealth could be seen, religious and secular, clerical and lay, burgess and craftsman, all joined together in a dramatic presentation of the internal coherence of burgh life. Needless to say, the Reformation called all of these basic assumptions into question, and in changing the expression of these principles it came very close to altering the foundations on which they rested. The burgesses of Aberdeen were well aware of the subversive power of the new kirk, which is one of the reasons they determined to control it.

The Reformation proved to be a shock to the craft guilds, striking at the root of their distinctive identity and traditions. The frustration of their religious character drove them to find other ways of promoting a sense of corporate identity and expressing it in distinction to the council. This process inevitably brought them into conflict with the burgess oligarchy. The liturgical celebrations of Corpus Christi may no longer have been possible after 1560, but in 1562 there were attempts to continue the traditional marking of the seasons of the year. In May of that year the town's bellman was punished for drawing people out into the fields to celebrate the coming of May.[69] Three years later certain craftsmen were again brought before the council and charged with an attempt to restore the ancient custom of celebrating the pageant of Robin Hood and Little John, a practice which had been forbidden by parliament in 1555. The ringleaders of this episode were later to become prominent as leading agitators for increased participation of the craftsmen in the political life of the burgh in 1587.[70]

97

More was swept away in 1560 than liturgical celebrations and the public nature of society. The large number of religious holidays in earlier times had ensured freedom from work for craftsmen and servants, but such opportunities were drastically reduced after 1560. It was not even clear that servants would be permitted to attend Sunday services in the kirk on a regular basis since it might take them away from their work. The kirk session merely stipulated that it was desirable for servants to attend the preaching every other Sunday.[71] Observance of traditional Catholic holidays seems to have been one of the most difficult traces of the pre-Reformation Church to eradicate. It survived very strongly amongst the craftsmen and was one of the principal targets of the Regent Morton during his visit to the burgh in 1574 in a further effort to plant Protestantism in the conservative soil of Aberdeen.

On numerous occasions the craftsmen were rebuked for taking Catholic holidays. In January 1576 the craft deacons were admonished for not preventing their crafts from sitting idle on Christmas day.[72] The custom appears to have been so deeply ingrained that it was necessary to warn the masters of the grammar and song schools to enforce attendance by their pupils on feast days. Despite this injunction parents still kept their children at home. The council therefore ordered that the names of non-attenders should be reported to them.[73] A few years earlier the council had actually encouraged the keeping of such holidays by permitting the pupils at the grammar school to remain absent from 21 December to 6 January.[74] Despite the council's apparent change of heart, public celebrations, especially at Christmas time, proved difficult to stamp out. In December 1574 a sizeable group of people, mostly women, were charged with dancing and singing 'off fylthe carrolles' on Christmas day.[75] While Catholic doctrine may not have been widely preached, traditional Catholic practices, so firmly entwined with local custom and social life, proved difficult to uproot. Catholic sympathies were found throughout every stratum of burgh society and were protected by a powerful group of conservative burgesses at the heart of the patriciate that ruled the burgh. Any attempt to root out Catholicism involved an inevitable conflict with vested interest, and the odds were against immediate success.

The ecclesiastical settlement in Aberdeen after 1560 came about through a combination of external pressure and the conjunction of national politics with local minority opinion; it was not the result of a steady growth of Protestant opinion within the burgh. The small Protestant party within the burgh was not strong enough to bring about a Reformation on its own; it was constantly dependent on outside encouragement. Protestantism was largely an alien movement facing a burgh elite which was experienced in government and the manipulation of burgh institutions. Even the minister, who should have been one of the leading exponents of reformed doctrine, was an outsider who faced a daunting web of kinship, wealth, patronage and compromise. A more dynamic character might have found the going easier and made a greater impact. Adam Heriot faced the additional difficulty of the survival of much of the structure and personnel of the old Church inside the town. The staff of the pre-Reformation parish kirk still played a notable role in burgh society, and even the parish kirk itself was not fully adapted to the Protestant form of service until 1574.[76] Both the town council and the kirk session maintained Catholics in their ranks, and many of the other members of both bodies had Catholics in their families. The situation was untidy and unsatisfactory to say the least, and was to remain so well into the 1580s.

Notes

1. *CSP Foreign, Eliz., 1561–62*, no. 302.
2. P. Clark and P. Slack (eds.), *English Towns in Transition, 1500–1700* (Oxford, 1979), 111.
3. See W. G. Hoskins, 'English provincial towns in the early sixteenth century' in P. Clark (ed.), *The Early Modern Town* (London, 1977), 102 (for an English comparison).
4. *APS*, ii, 95, 107.
5. *Burghs Conv. Recs.*, i, 313.
6. *Early Records of the Burgh of Aberdeen, 1317, 1398–1407*, ed. W. C. Dickinson (SHS, 1957), pp. ciii–civ, 21.
7. *Registrum Episcopatus Aberdonensis* (Spalding and Maitland Clubs, 1845), i, 219.
8. J. M. Brown, 'The exercise of power' in J. M. Brown (ed.), *Scottish Society in the Fifteenth Century* (London, 1977), 52.
9. *Spalding Miscellany*, iv, 203–4.
10. *Scottish Notes and Queries*, 7, 178–80.
11. *Abdn. Recs., 1398–1570*, iii, 131; *CSP Scot.*, ii, nos. 799, 836; *ACL*, i, 7–46.
12. G. Cadenhead, 'The Aberdeen Burgh Territories', *Transactions of the Aberdeen Philosophical Society*, 1 (1884), 78–9.
13. *APS*, ii, 414; *ER*, xviii, pp. lxi, 33.
14. Marcus Merriman, 'The Struggle for the Marriage of Mary, Queen of Scots: English and French Intervention in Scotland, 1543–1550' (London Univ. Ph.D., 1975), 34–5.

15. *Miscellany of the Maitland Club* (Maitland Club, 1847), 78.

16. *Abdn. Recs., 1398–1570*, 189.

17. Ibid., 190.

18. *Hamilton Papers*, ii, no. 425.

19. *Abdn. Recs., 1398–1570*, 214.

20. ACA, MS Council Register of Aberdeen, xviii, fo. 535.

21. MS Council Register of Aberdeen, xix, fo. 339.

22. *Abdn. Recs., 1398–1570*, 98, 107.

23. *Acts of Lords of Council in Public Affairs, 1501–1554*, i, 371–2.

24. *Abdn. Recs., 1398–1570*, 110–11; *Acts of Council*, i, 423.

25. W. J. Anderson, 'Some documents of the Scottish Reformation', in *Essays on the Scotish Reformation*, ed. D. McRoberts (Glasgow, 1962), 369–70.

26. J. Gordon, *Abredoniae utriusque decriptio: A description of both touns of Aberdeen* (Spalding Club, 1842), 14.

27. *Aberdeen St Nicholas Cartularium*, ii, 406.

28. *Aberdeen Fasti*, 127–8.

29. Ibid., 127–8.

30. A. J. White, 'Religion, Politics and Society in Aberdeen, 1543–1593' (Edinburgh Univ. Ph.D., 1985), 144–6.

31. MS Council Register of Aberdeen, xxi, fo. 296; xxiii, fo. 55.

32. Ibid., xix, fos. 67, 176; xxiii, fo. 266; xxix, fo. 226.

33. White, 'Thesis', 154–6.

34. *Abdn. Recs., 1398–1570*, 315.

35. Ibid., 315; White, 'Thesis', 160–2.

36. *Abdn. Recs., 1398–1570*, 319.

37. G. Donaldson, *Scotland: James V–James VII* (Edinburgh, 1965), 94; *Abdn. Recs., 1398–1570*, 318.

38. Ibid., 319.

39. Donaldson, *James V–James VII*, 93.

40. Knox, *History*, i, 126; *RSS*, iii, no. 820.

41. *Abdn. Recs., 1398–1570*, 322.

42. J. Lesley, *The History of Scotland from the death of King James I, in the year MCCCCXXXVI to the year MDLXI* (Edinburgh, 1880), 294.

43. Donaldson, *James V–James VII*, 101.

44. *Abdn. Recs., 1398–1570*, 322.

45. Ibid., 323.

46. Knox, *History*, i, 314–15.

47. Ibid., ii, 61.

48. *APS*, ii, 525.

49. Knox, *History*, i, 334.

50. White, 'Thesis', 166–9.

51. *BUK*, i, 254.

52. MS Council Register of Aberdeen, xxviii, fo. 544.

53. Ibid., xxiv, fo. 195.

54. Ibid., xxiv, fo. 159.

55. Ibid., xxv, fo. 662.

56. Ibid., xxiv, fo. 613.

57. W. M. Bryce, *The Scottish Grey Friars* (Edinburgh, 1909), i, 324.

58. *Spalding Misc.*, ii, 43.

59. *CSP Scot.*, iv, no. 168.
60. *Abdn. Recs., 1398–1570*, 364.
61. *Abdn. Recs., 1398–1570*, 158.
62. MS Council Register of Aberdeen, xxvi, fo. 646.
63. *Selections from the Records of the Kirk Session, Presbytery and Synod of Aberdeen* (Spalding Club, 1846), 17.
64. M. Lynch, *Edinburgh and the Reformation* (Edinburgh, 1981), 146, 195.
65. *RMS*, iv, nos. 829, 2028.
66. SRO, CH2/448/1, fo. 40.
67. *Kirk Session Register of Aberdeen*, 17.
68. MS Council Register of Aberdeen, xxi, fos. 423, 425.
69. *Abdn. Recs., 1398–1570*, 343.
70. E. Bain, *Merchant and Craft Guilds, a history of the Aberdeen Incorporated Trades* (Aberdeen, 1887), 63–4.
71. *Kirk Session Register of Aberdeen*, 6.
72. Ibid., 21.
73. Ibid., 16.
74. *Abdn. Recs., 1398–1570*, 366.
75. *Kirk Session Register of Aberdeen*, 18.
76. *Aberdeen St Nicholas Cartularium*, ii, 384–5. When the Regent Morton arrived in Aberdeen in 1574 he found the organ in the parish church intact together with the finely carved choir stalls and the timber choir screen. The reredos of at least one of the side altars was also in place; the burgesses protested that it helped to keep the draughts off the congregation during services.

5

Burghs, Lords and Feuds in Jacobean Scotland

Keith M. Brown

The bloodfeud is not usually associated with an urban environment, except perhaps in Italy where an urbanised nobility appears
to have introduced it during the course of the fourteenth and
fifteenth centuries.[1] Yet during the reign of James VI feuding was
found in the Scottish burghs, involving their inhabitants both as
active participants and as reluctant bystanders. The numbers were
not great — around forty cases have been identified to date — and
their violence was unspectacular when contrasted with the types of
violence found in continental cities and towns. The bread riots and
tax strikes which engulfed urban communities in days and even
weeks of vandalism and terror were alien to Scotland, and even
religion failed to inspire the same kind of manic butchery experienced throughout many of the urban centres of Reformation
Europe.[2] The disturbances created in Perth and Edinburgh at the
Reformation, or in the civil war a decade later, pale into insignificance when compared to the events in Antwerp in 1566, or Paris in
1572, and it was not until 1736, in the Porteous Riots, that a
genuinely urban revolt took place in Scotland.

The relative peacefulness of the Scottish burgh has been widely
recognised for some time,[3] but does this mean that 'The townsmen
could be counted on, in the interests of law and order . . .',[4] as
though they inhabited a quite different physical and ideological
world from their rural neighbours? Urban communities in the
sixteenth century were simply not large enough to be able to evolve
such a distinctiveness, especially in a kingdom like Scotland where
only Edinburgh was of any appreciable size.[5] Certain distinctions
did emerge, like the tensions which created 'the feud betwixt the
merchants and craftsmen' of Edinburgh,[6] which has no parallel in

the relationships of comparable rural status groups. These differences, however, were superficial and, as was the case in most of the rest of Europe, rural and urban economies and politics were closely identified with one another. Where urbanisation was less advanced, that identification was all the greater, and thus in Scotland town and country were very much a part of the same landscape. In a century where the independence of towns may have been declining throughout Europe, there has been no evidence to suggest that Scotland was following a contrary course.[7] In Edinburgh, 'burgh politics had been swallowed up, in the factionalism that enmeshed Scottish politics as a whole',[8] a development which occurred throughout France during this same period.[9] It has also been pointed out that 'in burgh society, as in Scottish society as a whole, the pull of family and kin was usually more potent than that of ideas',[10] and even in England it has been suggested that kinship survived the splitting of families into urban and rural environments.[11] Clearly the town was not the same as the countryside, and one can push the idea that common bonds and interests united them too far,[12] but so can distinctiveness be overemphasised, and thus false polarisations are created in describing communities and their values.

The encroachment of noble power into burghs was, therefore, part of a wider European experience, exaggerated in Scotland by the crown's failure to seize as great a share of urban patronage as was the case in, for example, Castile or England.[13] This can be exaggerated,[14] but there was a great deal of truth in the English report that 'the burroughs and burgess towns are wholly at the devotion of some nobleman or other, few excepted'.[15] The mistake would be to see in this a slavish obedience to over-mighty magnates whose relationship with the burgh was essentially an exploitative one from which the burgh desperately wanted to escape. In fact many burghs were content with the security a powerful local lord could guarantee them.[16]

In south-west Scotland the Maxwell kindred controlled a large dependancy of lesser lairds and families and held all the major offices in the region, including that of warden of the west march. Lord Maxwell was clearly the man to have on one's side, and both the burghs of Dumfries and Annan sought his friendship. As a small, fairly insignificant burgh, Annan simply entered into a bond of maintenance and manrent with Maxwell,[17] but Dumfries occupied a less obvious client status. Maxwell had a town house there, and the provostship of the burgh was effectively in his gift,

103

being 'in the disposicion and choise of the Lorde Maxwell, with thassent of the burgesses'.[18] It was an arrangement which suited the burgh as much as it did the Maxwells, and when in 1584 the earl of Arran tried to interfere by imposing a crown nominee, the laird of Johnstone, to the provostship, both Lord Maxwell and the burgh united to drive him from the town.[19] Such outside intervention was deeply resented, and it drove Maxwell into a rebellion which resulted in the defeat and death of Johnstone, the complete overthrow of royal power in the region and Arran's own downfall.[20] Consequently, Maxwell's already vast regional power was enhanced, and Dumfries found itself at its centre. Like its patron, the burgh remained sympathetic to Catholicism, and religious dissent may have cemented the relationship. Shortly after his triumph against Arran, Maxwell held mass 'in publique manner' close to the burgh, and followed this with another in his town house. The burgh's Protestant minister was silenced, and Dumfries threatened to become the heart of a Catholic regional revival.[21] Swift royal action in 1587 and 1588 resulted in a temporary lapse in Maxwell power, but Dumfries remained secure in the hands of Lord Herries who took over the provostship, and continued to ensure the Maxwell influence there.[22] By 1592 Lord Maxwell had been fully restored, and again threatened to dominate the region, but was killed by the Johnstones in 1593 at the battle of Dryfe Sands.[23] Real decline followed this military disaster, especially as the ninth Lord Maxwell was a wildly uncontrollable young man whose excessive behaviour finally led to his forfeiture in 1607. Along with his estates and titles Maxwell lost the Dumfries provostship, but the family remained popular in the burgh, and when in 1608 Lord Maxwell treacherously murdered the laird of Johnstone in revenge for his father's death, the burgh protected him and mobbed the royal guards sent to arrest him.[24] The town was fined by the king and four years later Maxwell was executed after foolishly returning from exile;[25] but in spite of this collapse of the family's fortune the old loyalties remained. In 1621 the earl of Melrose wrote to John Murray about some disturbances in the locality, commenting that 'It kythes that the town of Dumfreis cairies their olde respect to the name Maxuell, and that they affect the towne, and will be ready to protect them.'[26]

The relationship between Dumfries and the Maxwells was clearly one that had been worked out over a long period of time to mutual satisfaction. The earl of Mar had an equally harmonious arrangement with Stirling where he controlled the imposing royal castle. In 1595 the earl's enemies murdered one of his dependants who also happened to be a bailie of the burgh, thus uniting lord and town in a bitter feud with the Livingstone and Bruce families, and with their court patrons. Here royal messengers were mobbed by the townsmen while Mar looked on, irritated by the king's refusal to take his side openly.[27] Yet not all burghs were happy with the attention they received from the landed elite, and from the fourteenth century parliament had been persuaded to pass legislation discouraging uninvited interest in burgh affairs by noblemen or other neighbours.[28] A small burgh like Elgin could do little to avoid being sucked into the dependency of the earls of Huntly, but Aberdeen's growing disenchantment with their lordship shows the dangers in treating such a powerful client without sufficient regard.[29] The problem for a burgh like Aberdeen was similar to the 'fear–security' cycle used to describe the relationship between French provincial governors and the towns of their provinces. The town elites were reluctant to become clients but, especially in unsettled times, they needed the security which the protection of regional magnates offered them.[30] Too little protection and a town could fall prey to the violence of predators, too much and it could, like the once mighty Florence, lose its independence.

While magnates like Huntly required the most careful of handling, burghs were less inclined to be deferential to men of lesser status. When in August 1592 Robert Bruce of Clackmannan prepared to leave Perth, he was halted by the burgh authorities and asked to pay custom on some of his goods. He refused, the burgh confiscated them and Clackmannan went home mouthing threats. Shortly afterwards he attacked a party of Perth townsmen as they passed his house. Instead of frightening the burgh this simply angered it all the more, and a number of townsmen went out to Clackmannan's lands where they trampled his corn. Not surprisingly, fighting broke out and Clackmannan captured two of the Perth men, both of them friends of a burgh magistrate. Again the burgh responded decisively, and that night the town council led an assault on Gaskenhall, Clackmannan's house. The house was surrounded, shot at, and finally set alight, forcing the laird to surrender. Furious and humiliated by this defeat Clackmannan took his case to the king, but the privy council was unsympathetic, and imprisoned both sides for their behaviour. More positively, pressure was put on them to come to an agreement and Clackmannan appears to have received some compensation, while mutual assurances were exchanged. However, honour remained unsatisfied, and a few months later Clackmannan attacked another party of Perth men. Two of them were singled out for particularly rough treatment, 'being baith hurt and wounded in divers parts of their bodies, to the effusion of their blood in great quantity, the said laird and his accomplices maist shamefullye tirrit them baith naked, and in maist barbarous and shameful manner scourgit them with horse bridles through the town of Abernethy, as gif they had been thieves or heinous malefactors.' This time Clackmannan appears to have got away with his attack, and nothing more is heard of the feud, though one presumes that it was some time before he or his men traded in Perth again.[31]

Perth was a big enough burgh to act tough like this, and Clackmannan was a small enough laird for the burgh to take him on, but there was nothing exceptional about such behaviour. Here the burgh was acting like any rural dependency, protecting its interests, becoming involved in a feud to pursue them and using violence.[32] In 1586 the burgh's provost, bailies, council and the deacons of the crafts had all had to give assurance before the privy council that they would not harm the earl of Gowrie whose family was used to wielding the sort of influence in the burgh that Maxwell enjoyed in Dumfries.[33] The earl was a minor at the time, and his father had been executed two years before, so the Ruthven power was at a low ebb, but it is still significant that a rich and powerful noble family felt the need to extract such guarantees. Similar assurances were made by a long list of Kinghorn inhabitants for the safety of John Boswell of Malmuto,[34] and by the entire burgh of Lanark for the safety of William Livingston of Jerviswood.[35] These communities were clearly capable of handling their affairs with the sort of muscle which was understood by their rural neighbours; force was a normal weapon in the political arsenals of burghs.

To explore this in more detail it is worth returning to Aberdeen. The burgh's protracted wriggling free from Gordon domination was greatly helped by the difficulties the Gordons found themselves in from the 1560s onwards, but in 1587 the sixth earl still succeeded in having his dependant, Menzies of Pitfodells, re-elected as provost. It was in this context in February 1588 that trouble broke out in Aberdeen over the possession of salmon fishing rights and teinds in Banff. Ownership was disputed by a number of burgesses who either were on, or had friends on, the town council and Thomas Leslie, a burgess who had the backing of John Leslie of Balquhain, an important local laird. On 4 February the Leslies attempted to force their rivals' tenants to abandon their fishing, but had to withdraw when the burgh magistrates intervened. Balquhain was then denied entrance to Aberdeen, prompting him to send a message to Alexander Rutherford and Alexander Cullen, two councillors with stakes in the questionable fishing, announcing that he had 'dischargen kyndnes and denuncen his evill inimitie to thame'.[36] The burgh immediately complained to the king, and Balquhain was ordered to dissolve his forces and to find caution not to harm his enemies.[37] Furthermore, the town council then took steps to crush dissent within Aberdeen by charging the Lesie brothers, Thomas and John, of having 'purchest lordship' from Balquhain against the burgh gates. Both were found guilty by assize, fined and deprived of their freedom of the burgh. On the same day Cullen and his friends wrote to agents in Edinburgh asking them to block the Leslie efforts to persuade the king to ask Huntly to intervene, while on the next day the humiliation of the Aberdeen Leslies was completed when the bailies searched John Leslie's house in connection with his alleged adultery with a Janet Hunter.[38]

Within the course of two weeks the burgh appeared to have driven off an external threat and suppressed internal dissent. Huntly did leave court and journeyed north to pacify both parties, and he may have been responsible for having caution given to the Aberdeen Leslies by their enemies before he quickly hurried south again.[39] Then on 16 March Balquhain's son attacked, wounded and robbed a party of Aberdeen men.[40] The burgh began intensive lobbying of Huntly, of the privy council, and even of Edinburgh town council, both to impress on them that Balquhain had 'declairit his feid' and to frustrate efforts by Thomas Leslie and his brother to have the town council's judgement against them overturned.[41] In order to make their point more effectively it was decided to send the bloody shirts of the wounded burgesses to the kind, a recognised means by which justice was demanded, but they had to tell their Edinburgh agents that as yet they had been unable to get their hands on the shirts. Not wishing to miss the opportunity for some colourful propaganda they wrote:

. . . we mich not haiff the bludie sarks to send to you thairfor ye man do the best ye can thairin and furnes sarks and putt bluid thairon for the mater is trew quhowbeit we can not haiff the sarks to send presentlie. We are laith to delay in this. At the leist tak ane sark and schaw to his Maiestie and his council. . .[42]

They also succeeded in lobbying both the justice clerk and Chancellor Maitland, but when the issue was raised in council the king intervened 'and fand fault that sic billis war past abefoir in favour of the townschipe of Abirdene'. This time he agreed with the Leslies that both parties should be summoned south to answer for their actions.[43] On the following day the two burgesses gave caution for Balquhain's safety through one of their Edinburgh friends.[44]

While the Leslies were having this success in Edinburgh, Balquhain's son was again active in the locality. At the end of March he and his men attacked Cullen's country house in Buchan, breaking into it, looting it and killing two servants. This incident was followed by a number of other provocative shootings, and Thomas Leslie warned his fellow townsmen that 'thair wald be folks schortlie in this town quha wald rip up our houssis and buthis in despyte of us and all that wald assist us . . .'[45] The burgh responded by preparing to raise a defence force,[46] and an escalation of the conflict appeared very likely. In fact there was no more violence, and following Balquhain's complaint to the privy council over his exclusion from the burgh, the entire affair was put into the hands of Huntly who was given just over a month to calm everybody down.[47] In this Huntly succeeded, everyone was put under caution, and the dispute was channelled into a legal struggle.[48] By the summer the affair had died down,[49] but more important than the details of any settlement was the giving of a bond of manrent by the provost to Huntly in June.[50] Although the bond was in Menzies' name, his family's long tenure of the provostship meant that, in effect, Aberdeen was again recognising Huntly's lordship.[51] As Balquhain was a close dependent of Huntly, the role of the Gordon earl begins to look more suspicious. If Aberdeen had been resisting his overtures for a formal recognition of his lordship, as appeared to be the case, then in unleashing Balquhain, or at least failing to restrain him, he had made the burgesses rethink their need for protection. This was not the end of the story, but in this short episode one sees something of the tension which existed between a burgh, a local laird capable of being a considerable nuisance and a great magnate who was demanding recognition of his regional stature from the burgh.[52]

Smaller burghs had much less success in retaining their independence when faced with similar circumstances. During the civil war which followed the deposing of Queen Mary in 1567 the border burgh of Jedburgh had sided with the king and the laird of

Cessford, chief of the Kerrs, against the Marian leader, and Cessford's rival within the kindred, Kerr of Fernihurst.[53] In 1573 Cessford and his allies, Rutherford of Hunthill and Turnbull of Bedroule, complained to the privy council that in spite of the ending of hostilities Fernihurst was continuing to oppress the burgh.[54] However, the burgh had also been exploiting the fact that it had ended the war on the winning side and had the protective presence of a friendly English garrison, by making raids against Fernihurst's lands.[55] With the removal of that protection the Kerrs were able to gain the upper hand, killing a John Rutherford and a number of other Jedburgh men, and forcing Jedburgh to turn again to Cessford, who was also warden of the middle march, for help. In 1578 an agreement was drawn up before the privy council committing the burgh, the Kerrs, and the Rutherfords to keep the peace under pain of 'perjury, infamy and tinsell of perpetual credit, honour and estimation in tyme cuming.'[56]

Tension, however, continued, especially after the fall of the Regent Morton and the gradual restoration of favour to the Fernihurst Kerrs. In 1586 the burgh complained of the 'deidlie feid and grite inimitie standing betuix the maist part of the baillies and inhabitants of the burgh on the ane part . . .' and William Kerr of Ancrum, a kinsman of Fernihurst, who had slaughtered three townsmen a few months before.[57] This time a solution was sought in a bond of manrent by Rutherford of Hunthill, whose family was the most prominent in the burgh, to Fernihurst, and by the temporary banishment of Ancrum.[58] When Fernihurst died Ancrum took over the leadership of his kindred and in 1590 he was elected provost of the burgh in what looks like a further effort to cement the alliance between Jedburgh, the Rutherfords and the Fernihurst Kerrs. However, the election was carried through against a royal order to elect Cessford so that the burgh could function as the administrative centre of his wardenry. Cessford then sought the assistance of Chancellor Maitland, and he and the king agreed to overturn the election. Yet Ancrum still represented a threat both to Cessford's leadership of the Kerrs and his pre-eminence in the locality, and a month after this success at court, Cessford's son, Sir Robert Kerr, murdered Ancrum in an Edinburgh close, for which he suffered no more than a few months exile.[59] Jedburgh, however, continued to be the source of further sniping among local kindreds, and in September 1601 a bloody skirmish took place on market day between the Turnbulls and the Kerrs which left one man dead and half a dozen wounded.[60]

Being overawed by local lords and kindreds was a fact of life most burghs had to live with at some point in their history. In 1600 Peebles was feuding with James Gledstanes of Coklaw over some lands lying close to the town, and was unable to prevent the Gledstanes riding into the burgh and shooting dead a minor burgh official, James Dickson.[61] Two years before this William Lawther, bailie of Lauder, injured one of the Hume family in a fight, and shortly afterwards Lord Hume and his men went to the burgh, set fire to the tolbooth where the bailie was hiding and cut him to pieces when he emerged from it.[62] In 1588 the burgh of Leith complained of oppressions it was suffering from the earl of Bothwell who was extorting money from their merchant shipping through his office of lord high admiral, and there was some slaughter between his men and those of the town.[63] Chancellor Maitland manipulated the rivalry of the master of Glamis and the earl of Crawford over Forfar and tried to 'awake this sleping dogg to byte Glames'. Crawford was himself no respecter of authority, and in 1581 had one of his men forcefully freed from prison in Dundee,[65] while in 1578 Ayr complained that power in the burgh was being usurped by Campbell of Loudon.[66] In 1593 Inverness was occupied by Huntly's dependant, MacRanald of Keppoch, who drove out the Mackintoshes, only to be in turn driven out by the vengeful Mackintosh chief who forced the burgh to sign a bond promising to resist Huntly or 'accept the deadly feud of the said Lachlan'.[67] St Andrews narrowly avoided violence in a feud over the provostship in the early 1590s,[68] but in Glasgow in 1606 a feud erupted between Sir George Elphinstone, the newly elected provost, and Sir Matthew Stewart of Minto, the outgoing provost. The rivalry finally took a violent form when a riot broke out between their supporters in which one man was killed and 'sundry hurt with staves'.[69]

Edinburgh was never subjected to such overt interference by noblemen in the later sixteenth century, but a number still made the effort to court support there. Anger in the burgh over the murder of the earl of Moray by Huntly in 1592 caused the king to leave for the west. When he returned a few weeks later 'many spiteful libels' were still being 'cast in the streets . . . where sundry banished men are now held to lodge, and most men arm themselves ready for troubles'.[70] A year later Huntly's friends were trying to stir up support among the Edinburgh crafts as part of their campaign to effect his restoration.[71] Also in 1593 the appointment of Alexander Hume as provost was a severe blow to Bothwell who had a feud with the Humes. In 1594 it was Lord Hume and his dependants who led the defence of Leith against Bothwell's last and most daring raid, but marching behind him were the townsmen of Edinburgh.[72]

Even more common than conflicts of this type, in which the burgh had some stake in the outcome, were those in which they acted as little more than arenas for the feuds of landed kindreds and dependencies. The burghs were commercial and, in the cases of the larger ones, cultural and political meeting places for localities and regions. They were, therefore, hosts to lords with their large armed retinues, and in the narrow streets or crowded market places there was every likelihood that rival feuding families would clash. Individual combats, brutal assassinations and running street battles which had nothing to do with the inhabitants of the burgh itself were features of urban life which were largely imported from the countryside. Aberdeen was the setting for fighting between the Gordons and the Forbes in 1573, the Gordons and the Keiths in 1587,[73] 'a great fray' took place there between the Keiths and the Hays in 1598,[74] and in 1616 Aberdeen was the setting for a judicial murder of Francis Hay by the Gordons.[75] In 1580 Jardine of Applegarth and Kirkpatrick of Closeburn battled out their differences in Dumfries, wounding in the process the provost and a number of bystanders who tried to intervene.[76] In 1578 Chancellor Glamis was among those killed when he and the earl of Crawford met one another in the confined road up to Stirling castle, and 'thair servands in pryde strave for the best part therof'.[77] Incidents like this arose from what Sir Robert Gordon described as 'a custome among the Scots (more than any other nation) to contend for the hight of the street; and among the English for the wall'.[78] Sir John Maxwell of Nether Pollok complained to the privy council that in Glasgow in September 1581 John Pollock of that Ilk had attacked him and his friends, and had 'chassit and followit thame on horsbak to have slayne thame with swordis and dischargit pistolettis at thame'.[79] In 1590 one man was killed and many others were injured at Dumbarton fair when the feuding Buchanans and MacAulays clashed,[80] and there was bloodshed at Cupar market in 1610 between Sir Andrew Small and Robert Patillo.[81]

Edinburgh's position as the major centre of the royal court, of government and the law meant that it was more exposed to such violence than other burghs. More than anywhere else Edinburgh drew powerful magnates and their dependants into its claustrophobic and populous environment, and there both local and court rivalries overlapped. Robert Birrel, the burgh's gossiping diarist, conveys an environment of casual and common violence such as 'Robert Cathcart slaine pisching at the wall in Peiblis wynd heid be William Stewart',[82] but his reporting is sensationalised. Nevertheless, the potential for explosive violence in the Edinburgh streets was much more acute than anywhere else. In February 1593 the duke of Lennox and Sir James Sandilands with their usual retinues were on their way to Leith to play golf when they were seen by Sandiland's enemy, Mr John Graham, a senator and lord of session. Graham mistakenly thought the duke's party were brandishing weapons at him when in fact they were only carrying their golf clubs aloft, and so he and his friends began shooting. A minor battle developed which resulted in many injuries and the deaths of both Graham and another gentleman.[83] Two years later Sandilands attacked the earl of Montrose, the chief of the Graham kindred, outside the Edinburgh tolbooth, making 'a furious onset on the erle, with gunnis and swordis in great number'. An estimated forty shots were fired, and there were a number of casualties, including the laird of Kerse who was killed, and Sandilands who narrowly escaped dying from head wounds.[84] In 1589 the Scotts and Kerrs fought a similar gun battle in the streets in which a number of the latter were killed,[85] as did the lairds of Johnstone, Cessford and Drumlanrig in 1597.[86] Another outbreak of violence was narrowly frustrated by royal intervention in 1588 when a personal quarrel between the earl of Bothwell and the master of Glamis over some 'braggings' between them spilled over into the streets.[87] Even after 1603 violence of this nature could still appear, and in 1605 'ane combat or tuilzie' was fought in the centre of the burgh between the younger laird of Edzell and the laird of Pittarrow and their friends. 'The faucht lastit frae 9 hours at night till 11 at night, twa houris!' wrote the shocked Birrel.[88]

Less troublesome than these tuilzies, but just as bloody, were the murders committed by feuding parties taking advantage of an enemy's vulnerability away from his own locality. Sir William Stewart, a royal favourite, was trapped and killed in a close by Bothwell in 1589 after he had insulted the earl.[89] James Geddes of Glencoquo and his kinsmen, 'all bodin in feir of weir', cut down a Mr David Baillie on the High Street,[90] while another Geddes laird was murdered in Edinburgh by the Tweedie family.[91] Lord Spynie was slain one evening in July 1607, when, in a feud within the Lindsay kindred the young laird of Edzell made an attack on the master of Crawford, wounding him, but killing his uncle by mistake.[92] In July of the following year William Stewart, the nephew of the former Chancellor Arran, stabbed to death Lord Torthorwald in revenge for his uncle's murder twelve years before.[93]

Edinburgh was not a sort of early modern Chicago in which rival gangs headed by tough bosses waged war on one another. That, of course, would be a caricature of both the feud and the social and political relationships which sustained it. It was, however, a town troubled by the violence of the feud. How violent the burgh was in terms of ordinary crime is not yet known, but one suspects that it was less so than a city like Madrid where it has been estimated that a murder took place every day in the year.[94] In London too 'the city and even the main arterial roads were continual scenes of upper-class violence',[95] and a more detailed study of Elizabethan Colchester has concluded that 'feuding amongst the gentry was certainly an almost regular part of life'.[96] One doubts if quite the same thing is meant by feuding in this late Tudor context as is found in Scotland, but clearly Scottish towns were not unique in having this problem amongst them. The important issue is one of degree, but to be at all authoritative on that, greater analysis of violence in the Scottish burghs is necessary.

There was little that burghs, even Edinburgh, could do to restrain the violence of lords and their retinues as distinct from controlling the criminal violence of their own populations. Legislation existed and was being constantly improved upon which was intended to limit the carrying and use of guns, particularly small hand-guns which could be easily concealed. Both the wearers of such weapons and the craftsmen who made them were liable to be brutally punished, but even the threat of amputation of the hand could not persuade men in a feuding society to go about without their guns, while the burghs themselves were the major suppliers of the weapons.[97] Convocations were also limited by statute but little attention was paid to this; when the earl of Huntly was summoned to Edinburgh to a day of law and was reminded to limit his followers, it was assumed that 'he will bring such a company as will bring him safe away however the matter will go'.[98] Tuilzies, duelling and feuding itself was attacked by the privy council and parliament, but with little effect before the late 1590s.

The major criticism of the feud came from the church, for reasons which were both theological and ethical. To this the crown added its own political objections, and the nobility acquiesced, sensitive both to the church's arguments and to more secular

113

changes in how honour, nobility and gentlemanly conduct were understood.[99] Among townsmen many of these ideas would also be found, as no doubt was a general feeling that such behaviour was not good for business. However, too much can and has been made of the notion of Scotland's peace-loving burgesses at the expense of understanding the relationships which bound town and country together. In 1578 James Melville was attacked in Glasgow by two university students whom he had recently disciplined. Both were charged by the university authorities, but the two were related to the locally powerful Boyd and Cunningham kindreds, and threatened that 'the Boids and Cunninghams wald slay the maisters and burn the College'. Undeterred, Andrew Melville, the principal, refused to give way to 'bangsters and clanned gentlemen', and confronted the earl of Glencairn and Lord Boyd when they rode into the burgh with a few hundred men apiece. In the end the two lords agreed with Melville and approved the university's discipline of Alexander Cunningham, the more intransigent of the students. Then their followers who 'for the maist part, knew nocht for what cause they cam, luche him to scorn, spendit thrie or four hounder mark in the town, and returned as they confessit, graittir fulles nor they cam a field'.[100] In writing this Melville revealed some of the clergyman's distaste for the obligations of the kindred, but he had also lived long enough in towns to see the profit to be made from the influx of lords and their men into a burgh, even for a short visit. The burgesses could not have wanted the rural elite to stay away from their towns, nor would they have been very happy if men like Glencairn and Boyd had come unaccompanied. On the other hand the problem they created was perceived. Richard Abercrombie, an Edinburgh bailie, complained to the privy council of raids he had suffered on his lands from a neighbour, telling them that such behaviour was especially unacceptable 'in a cuntrie [county] quhilk sould be peciabill, sa neir the seat of justice, and sould rather gif exampill to the far Hielandis and Bordouris, quhair sic forme of unqueist is usit'. In Abercrombie's mind the feud, and any behaviour associated with it, was clearly barbaric, being 'in comtempt of God and of his Majestie'.[101] Yet one has to avoid identifying this as the authentic voice of the burgess class who 'had always been interested in peace'.[102] It was one strand of thought within the burgess community, but it was one inspired by weakness as much as by deep-felt convictions, and when, as in Perth in 1592, burgesses believed they could get away with it, they seized on the opportunity to employ violence themselves.

The part played by the burgh community in changing public attitudes to violence at the end of the century was not simply one defined by bourgeois attitudes to law and order. The commissioners of five burghs, including two from Edinburgh, were present at the convention in June 1598 which passed the important 'Act anent Feuds', but they were a very small minority in a body which was predominantly landed and noble.[103] Similar points can be made about other legislation on this whole issue, and in fact most of the work was handled not by parliament but by the privy council in which the burghs had no direct voice at all. Where the burgh magistrates did have greatest say was within their own jurisdictions, and even here the extent to which they were able to, or even showed much interest in, imposing law and order on the lords who came within their bounds was limited. Earlier in the century Edinburgh had come to an agreement with the constable of the castle, the earl of Erroll, in which the burgh magistracy would supply the deputes to his court of verge, that area of four-miles radius around the king. Obviously this only applied when the king was in the Edinburgh area, but this and the additional legislation passed to try and pacify this highly charged area was useful, and, for example, it was the burgh magistrates and watch who were used by the king in 1588 to restrain Bothwell and Glamis.[104] Efforts were made by the burgh, working in conjunction with the privy council, to anticipate potential violence, as in 1607 when Lord Maxwell and his father-in-law, the marquis of Hamilton, with whom he had quarrelled bitterly, both turned up in Edinburgh at the same time. The privy council meticulously defined the limits of their movements, ensuring that they would not both be out of their lodgings at the same time, even telling them which church to attend and how to get there.[105] Control of this kind was, however, a delicate business since noblemen of this status were not easily restrained.[106] Nor was it always possible to maintain an effective surveillance of men's movements in a town with the population density of Edinburgh. In 1607 the privy council tartly reminded the king of this, telling him that 'your maiestie knowis that malefactors may be in Edinburgh, without the Counsellis knowlege . . .'[107]

Faced with larger scale difficulties, like the holding of parliament in Edinburgh in 1584, the burgh magistrates added their own security arrangements to those of the privy council. On this occasion thirty citizens were armed to augment the standing town guard and fines were imposed for a range of offences, from twenty shillings or a two-hour stand in the market place for slander to ten pounds for drawing blood.[108] Enforcing those fines was another matter, especially where noblemen and their dependents were involved, and one imagines that on the whole burghs sweated their way through such events, and hoped that the profits made during them outweighed any disturbances which might accompany them. Where an incident did take place, as at the Perth parliament in 1606, the privy council was the more effective means of enforcing any punishment.[109]

Evidence that burghs were not simply natural constituencies for royal absolutism in contrast to feudal violence comes from behaviour within the urban population itself. In 1578 the government had to intervene and establish procedures for settling a feud between the burgh and the university of St Andrews, and fighting broke out again between the two in 1592.[110] Of course, the university had a high proportion of the sons of landed families in it, and this example is in a sense a very special one. Acts of caution between two Ayr burgesses in 1585,[111] or among a number of Crail inhabitants in 1588,[112] do, however, show similar tensions to those existing in the countryside. More dramatically, in 1600 a private combat was fought in Edinburgh between two burgesses, one of whom was killed, the other of whom was executed to discourage others from duelling.[113]

In 1609 Andrew Henderson, the son of an Edinburgh merchant burgess, mutilated the hand of Adam Montgomery, another merchant burgess, while resisting the attempts by Montgomery and a burgh bailie to arrest him for assault. Henderson was brought to trial, found guilty of demembration and banished for life. Six months later Henderson was still in prison, but had succeeded in getting his case brought to the attention of the king. James wrote to the council, criticising Montgomery for having refused compensation through 'malicious and revengefull heate', and agreeing that Henderson should be banished rather than remain in prison, as he had suffered enough. Then in the summer of 1617 Henderson returned with a year's remission from his banishment, but was seized on his arrival and thrown into ward by Montgomery. On hearing Henderson's complaint the privy council freed him on condition that he stayed away from the Montgomeries and left the country by October never to return. In fact he was still in Scotland in February 1618 when both he and Montgomery appeared before the privy council to submit their feud. Henderson's banishment was confirmed, but he had no money for assythment and instead made Montgomery assignee to all his goods, giving him power to intromit with them. This was renounced by Mongomery who stated that he had no wish to make any material gain from the agreement. What was more important was what did satisfy him. Henderson also agreed to do homage to Montgomery on his knees and to beg his forgiveness. Here was the full symbolic ritual of the feud enacted in a peace settlement between two Edinburgh burgesses.[114]

That agreement was purely a private one, helped along by a privy council which always preferred private justice to enforcing the rigour of the law through the courts. In another case in Stirling in 1613, however, the burgh authorities sanctioned and participated in a similar settlement. A feud had broken out in the burgh between Duncan Paterson, dean of the guild, and the Donaldson family who were of burgess status. In March 1610 the affair was brought before the burgh council who

> Ordines Johnne, William, and James Donaldsonnes, to be inhibit and discharget at ony tyme heirefter during the inimitie and feid betuix thame and Duncane Patersoune, deane of gild, ather to croce, pas, or repair throw the said Duncanes clos, or within ony uther the said Duncannes boundis, or yit to contend with him for the gait quhen they salhappin to meitt togidder, bot that they giff him the gaitt as becumes thame to do to ane magistrate, under the pane of ten pundis, toties quoties.[115]

This decision in Paterson's favour appears to have kept the peace for some time, but the Donaldsons' sense of grievance remained, heightened no doubt by Paterson's elevation to the provostship. Three years later another of the family, Adam Donaldson, was charged by the burgh council of having attacked Paterson, 'dispersoning of him and minting to ane quhinger to have struik him thairwith, also with ane gold club' which he grabbed from the unsuspecting hand of John Skerar, the astonished dean of guild. The burgh council found Donaldson guilty, fined him thirty pounds and ordered that he be held in ward until the day he could be taken to the market cross where he 'sall thair oppinlie crave God, the Kingis Maiestie, the said provest and haill magistratis of this burgh, forgiveness of his offence foirsaid'. In effect Donaldson was both paying assythment and doing penance and, while the important act of homage was missing, the similarity with other feud settlements is clear. Here both the dignity of the burgh and the personal honour of Paterson were satisfied. Furthermore, as in the Edinburgh case, Donaldson was banished from Stirling, having been stripped of his freedom of the burgh and being warned that if he ever returned he would be heavily fined.[116]

This keen awareness of the obligations of the feud in its settlement as well as in its more violent aspects demonstrates the common values shared by those who lived in the town and those living in the countryside. In 1597 Andrew Stalker, an Edinburgh goldsmith, accidentally killed the master stabler of the earl of Angus. Stalker was imprisoned, pending trial for his life, but some young men of the town, who were then acting as the town guard during the sitting of parliament, went to the king to plead for him. James gave them a sympathetic hearing, but he had no intention of offending the Douglases, besides which a remission would not have saved Stalker's life if Angus still wanted revenge. He therefore sent them to Angus to 'satisfy and pacify his wrath' which they did by offering him the manrent of the entire company in exchange for Stalker's life.[117] A man's life was thus saved, and Angus fulfilled his obligations to his servant, an obligation the townsmen quite clearly recognised as legitimate. In contrast to this is an agreement in 1576 between Lord Livingston and Robert and John Moffat, both Edinburgh burgesses. The Moffats' elder brother, Thomas Moffat of Glenkirk, had been killed by two of Livingston's men. Lord Livingston took responsibility for these men and agreed to pay the Moffats seven hundred merks to be distributed between Glenkirk's wife and children, and to infeft Robert Moffat in some of his own lands. Having assythed the Moffat family, Livingston also agreed to bring the killers to Glasgow to offer the point of a sword to the Moffat brothers in an act of homage and penitence.[118] In a sense this is more remarkable as here one has a lord negotiating the settlement of a feud with two burgesses and agreeing to enforce its terms, while the burgesses were fully prepared to insist on everything which the feud entitled them to, including homage.

Such agreements were not confined to cases involving noblemen. In 1585 Christine and Violet Kellie, with the consent of their brothers and their 'haill kinsmen and freindis of the surname of Kellie', made separate settlements with David and Andrew Home, indwellers in Dunbar, for the slaughter of their father, Cuthbert Kellie, burgess of Dunbar. As compensation each of them was to receive an infeftment in land worth twenty merks annually.[119] The Arthur kindred, including two lairds and a commissioner of

Edinburgh, made a similar peace with a number of St Andrews men for the slaughter of James Arthur. The St Andrews men were to go into exile, and in return the Arthurs forgave them.[120] In 1591 John Cock, baxter burgess of Edinburgh, accepted two hundred merks on behalf of his daughter, whose husband had been killed, and on behalf of the rest of his son-in-law's kin, from John Crombie, maltman burgess of the same burgh.[121] Forgiveness was also granted in the form of a letter of slains from John Rollock, burgess of Dundee, to George Ross of Balnagowan for the killing of Patrick Rollock by one of Ross's kinsmen.[121]

Scottish burghs were not bloody, violent places where feud incessantly raged. Even in the countryside the feud was not that disruptive. How criminally violent the burghs were is unknown, but whatever the level of violent crime was, it was not greatly added to by feuding. Yet feuding was there. It was there in the burghs' relations with surrounding lords and lairds, though those relations were more often mutually beneficial than destructive. That point was also borne in mind when the rural elites brought their own feuds into burghs. Resentment there may have been, but the violence was too episodic to be unbearable, and there was no chorus of protests from the urban community about the presence of these men in their midst. Sound business sense as well as political realism may explain that, but so did lower expectations of what was tolerable, and an appreciation of why feuding took place. Men living in towns shared in the ideology of the feud and participated in and approved of its violence, when necessary, its justice and its ritual. Their view of how politics should be conducted, and what should be expected by way of justice, was one they shared with their rural kinsmen and neighbours. There was no antithesis between a bourgeois world in the towns and a feudal countryside. The burgesses were not patiently awaiting the advent of royal absolutism to save them from the excesses of aristocratic violence. It would be equally wrong to argue that an Edinburgh merchant burgess perceived the world he lived in in exactly the same way as a rural laird, but neither were they worlds apart. There was a very good chance that both understood revenge and assythment, that for them both the feud was a legitimate right and obligation. It was the church which altered that, and then the crown in co-operation with the nobility, firstly making the violence of the feud unacceptable, and half a century later, during the civil war, rejecting its concept of justice. There is, however, no evidence to suggest that the feud disappeared any faster in the burghs than it did in the lowland countryside. Until that point in time when it did become disreputable, in the seventeenth century, the feud remained a powerful and useful tool for those who governed and lived in the burghs, its language universal, its violence tolerated and its justice seen as an effective means of restoring the peace.

Notes

1. H. G. Koenigsberger and G. L. Mosse, *Europe in the Sixteenth Century* (London, 1979), 55.

2. For urban rebellion see P. Zagorin, *Rebels and Rulers, 1500–1600, volume 1, Society, States and Early Modern Revolution* (Cambridge, 1982), 228–74. For a more detailed analysis of one riot see E. Le Roy Ladurie, *Carnival in Romans* (Harmondsworth, 1981).

3. This has been most recently emphasised by J. Wormald, *Court, Kirk and Community* (London, 1981), 46, 'urban life in Scotland, and certainly relations between towns and government were peaceful to a degree rare in Europe'.

4. M. Lee, *Government by Pen* (Illinois, 1980), 5. This is also the belief of C. Smout, *A History of the Scottish People* (London, 1969), 110.

5. For Edinburgh's size see M. Lynch, *Edinburgh and the Reformation* (Edinburgh, 1981), 9–14. During this period and certainly by the 1630s Edinburgh was probably the second most populous town in Britain; see Makey, Chapter 9, this volume.

6. D. Calderwood, *The History of the Church of Scotland* (Wodrow Society, 1842–9), iv, 411.

7. Zagorin argues that the identity of interests between rural and urban elites bound them together politically, a contrast to a division between noble or feudal, and bourgeoisie (*Rebels and Rulers*, 71–7). The economic relationship was also a close one: see F. Braudel, *Capitalism and Material Life* (London, 1979), 376–9, and Le Roy Ladurie, *Carnival in Romans*, ch. 1, 'The Urban and Rural Setting'. The decline of the towns in the face of growing aristocratic power is stressed by G. R. Elton, *Reformation Europe, 1517–1559* (London, 1974), 306–7, and by J. H. Elliot, *Europe Divided, 1559–1598* (London, 1977), 46. F. Braudel, *The Mediterranean and the Mediterranean World in the Age of Philip II* (London, 1973), ii, 725–34, goes further and writes of 'the defection of the bourgeoisie' to the values and aspirations of the nobility.

8. Lynch, *Edinburgh*, 156.

9. This is discussed in R. H. Harding, *Anatomy of a Power Elite, The Provincial Governors of Early Modern France* (Yale U.P., 1978), 53–4, 88–9, 97–8, 201–2.

10. Lynch, *Edinburgh*, 208.

11. P. Clark and P. Slack, *English Towns in Transition, 1500–1700* (Oxford, 1976), 14.

12. Thus M. H. B. Sanderson, *Scottish Rural Society in the Sixteenth*

Century (Edinburgh, 1982), 146–7, rightly pointed out that not all burgesses simply aimed at becoming landed gentry.

13. J. Lynch, *Spain Under the Hapsburgs, volume 1, Empire and Absolutism, 1516–1598* (Oxford, 1981), 206–8; Clark and Slack, *English Towns in Transition*, 126ff.

14. G. Donalson, *Scotland: James V – James VII* (Edinburgh, 1971), 12.

15. *CSP Scot.*, xiii, pt. 2, p. 1118. But see Lynch, Chapter 3, this volume, for the date and provevance of this report.

16. J. M. Wormald, *Lords and Men in Early Modern Scotland* (Edinburgh, 1985), ch. 8, 'Uncertain allies: burghs and politicians'.

17. Ibid., 340, no. 34.

18. *The Calendar of Letters and Papers Relating to the Affairs of the Borders of England and Scotland [CBP]*, ed. J. Bain (Edinburgh, 1894–96), i, 151.

19. *The Historie and Life of King James the Sext* (Bannatyne Club, 1825), 209; *RPC*, iii, 767–8; J. Spottiswoode, *History of the Church of Scotland* (Spottiswoode Society, 1847–51), ii, 325–6.

20. For the details of this see K. M. Brown, 'The Extent and Nature of Feuding in Scotland, 1573–1625' (University of Glasgow Ph.D., 1983), ii, 474–82.

21. *CBP*, i, 216–17.

22. Brown, 'Thesis', ii, 494–500. For evidence that the Maxwells were still running the burgh, see *RPC*, iv, 349.

23. Brown, 'Thesis', ii, 510–21.

24. Ibid., ii, 531–9. For the loss of the provostship see *RPC*, viii, 36–7, and for the mobbing incidents ibid., viii, 86–7, 97–8, 119, 125, 169.

25. Brown, 'Thesis', ii, 539–41. Strictly speaking Dumfries was not fined, but it did forfeit the £1,000 caution it had advanced for Lord Maxwell (*RPC*, viii, 169).

26. *State Papers and Miscellaneous Correspondence of Thomas, Earl of Melros* (Abbotsford Club, 1837), ii, 433. Maxwell's brother had been restored and created earl of Nithsdale by this time.

27. *Historie King James*, 346–7; *CSP Scot.*, xi, 575, 584, 624, 625, 637; xii, 123.

28. Wormald, *Lords and Men*, 138–9.

29. Ibid., 141–3. See also A. White, 'Religion, Politics and Society in Aberdeen, 1543–1593' (Edinburgh Univ. Ph.D., 1985), 304–5, 310–16.

30. Harding, *Anatomy of a Power Elite*, 88, 98, 202.

31. *RPC*, v, 6–8, 80–1.

32. For the Scottish bloodfeud see J. M. Wormald, 'Bloodfeud, kindred and government in early modern Scotland', *Past and Present*, 87 (1980), 54–97; K. M. Brown, *Bloodfeud in Scotland, 1573–1625: Violence, Justice and Politics in an Early Modern Society* (Edinburgh, 1986).

33. *RPC*, iv, 115.

34. Ibid., iv, 178, 182, 193–4.

35. Ibid., iv, 239.

36. *ACL*, i, 7.

37. Ibid., i, 7, 10.

38. Ibid., i, 11–18; *RPC*, iv, 203, 209.

39. *ACL*, i, 13 – 14; *RPC.*, iv, 260, 261; D. Moysie, *Memoirs of the Affairs of Scotland, 1577 – 1603* (Maitland Club, 1830), 66.

40. *ACL*, i, 18 – 19, 20 –.4.

41. Ibid., i, 18 – 28, 31 – 7.

42. Ibid., i, 31 – 4.

43. Ibid., i, 37 – 8.

44. *RPC*, iv, 265.

45. Ibid., iv, 38 – 41; 'The Chronicle of Aberdeen', *The Miscellany of the Spalding Club* (Aberdeen, 1842), ii, 58.

46. *ACL*, i, 40 – 1.

47. *RPC*, iv, 267 – 8.

48. *ACL*, i, 41 – 7; *RPC*, iv, 272 – 3, 275 – 6, 276 – 7, 278 – 9, 280, 281.

49. *RPC*, iv, 304.

50. Wormald, *Lords and Men*, 293, no. 72.

51. Ibid., 143.

52. *RPC*, iv, 533, and see the decreet arbitral in SRO, Register of Deeds, 1/44/19. For the events of 1593 see Moysie, *Memoirs*, 118; *Historie King James*, 331.

53. *Domestic Annals of Scotland from the Reformation to the Revolution*, ed. R. Chambers (Edinburgh, 1859), i, 75 – 6; *RPC*, ii, 110 – 11, 115 – 18, 266 – 71; *CSP Scot.*, 112, 134, 383, 531. At this time the provost was a Rutherford.

54. *RPC*, ii, 266 – 71.

55. *CSP Scot.*, iv, 624.

56. *RPC*, ii, 684 – 5. This led to further peace discussions in 1579 (*RPC*, iii, 160).

57. *RPC*, iv, 57 – 8, 63 – 4; *Historie King James*, 338.

58. Wormald, *Lords and Men*, 323 – 4, no. 4; *Historie King James*, 338.

59. *RPC*, iv, 529 – 30; *CSP Scot.*, x, 416, 430, 439, 562; Spottiswoode, *History*, ii, 411; *Historie King James*, 245. The Rutherfords did, however, have the provostship back by September 1592 (*RPC*, v, 13). Within a few years it was lost to Kerr of Fernihurst (ibid., v, 490).

60. Pitcairn, *Criminal Trials*, ii, 370 – 82. There had been serious fighting in the burgh six months earlier (*RPC*, vi, 261 – 2).

61. *RPC*, vi, 152; R. Renwick, *The Burgh of Peebles, 1604 – 52* (Peebles, 1911), 9; In 1605 a Gledstanes appeared in court on a charge of having killed a Peebles burgess in 1561, and two years later the feud was still unresolved (Pitcairn, *Criminal Trials*, ii, 472).

62. *CSP Scot.*, xiii, pt. 1, 207; Chambers, *Domestic Annals*, i, 300 – 1. The king tried to have this affair settled quickly, but Haddington presbytery excommunicated Lord Hume, and while negotiations began in 1598, within a month of the murder, it was 1606 before Hume received his remission (*CSP Scot.*, xiii, 214; Pitcairn, *Criminal Trials*, iii, 116).

63. *CSP Scot.*, ix, 641; *Edin. Recs., 1573 – 89*, 150.

64. *CBP*, i, 375 – 6; *CSP Scot.*, x, p. 468.

65. *RPC*, iii, 572 – 4.

66. Ibid., iii, 44 – 5.

67. SRO, Mackintosh Muniments, GD 176/162.

68. J. Melville, *Autobiography and Diary of Mr James Melville* (Wodrow Society, 1842), 210.

69. *RPC*, vii, 233, 234–5, 240–7, 249–50.

70. *CSP Scot.*, x, 645, 637; Moysie, *Memoirs*, 91; Calderwood, *History*, v, 146.

71. *CSP Scot.*, xi, 91.

72. For Hume's appointment and its effect, *CSP Scot.*, xi, 170, 188; *CBP*, i, 492, 498. Most of the details of the Leith raid are found in *CSP Scot.*, xi, 227, 304; *CBP*, i, 524–5, 525–7; Spottiswoode, *History*, ii, 448.

73. *Historie King James*, 139; 'Chronicle of Aberdeen', 59; Moysie, *Memoirs*, 154; National Register of Archives, Moray Muniments, 217/2/3/245; *CSP Scot.*, ix, 531.

74. *CSP Scot.*, xiii, pt. 1, 338.

75. Sir R. Gordon, *Genealogical History of the Earldom of Sutherland from its origin to the year 1630* (Edinburgh, 1813), 340–2; *RPC*, x, 496–502.

76. *RPC*, iii, 263, 268.

77. Calderwood, *History*, iii, 397; *Historie King James*, 148–9; Spottiswoode, *History*, ii, 206; Moysie, *Memoirs*, 4; 'Chronicle of Aberdeen', 44; J. Melville of Halhill, *Memoirs of His Own Life* (Bannatyne Club, 1827), 264; D. Hume of Godscroft, *A General History of Scotland from the Year 767 to the Death of King James* or *History of the House of Douglas* (London, 1657), 341–2; Sir J. Balfour, 'Annals of Scotland', in *The Historical Works of Sir James Balfour*, ed. J. Haig (Edinburgh, 1824–5), i, 364.

78. Gordon, *Sutherland*, 144–5.

79. *RPC*, iii, 436.

80. *RPC*, iv, 535.

81. *RPC*, viii, 435–6.

82. 'Diary of Robert Birrel, 1532–1605', in *Fragments of Scottish History*, ed. J. G. Dalyell (Edinburgh, 1798), 46.

83. *Historie King James*, 267; *CSP Scot.*, xi, p. 49; Calderwood, *History*, v, 223.

84. *Historie King James*, 345; *CSP Scot.*, xi, pp. 527–30; *CBP*, ii, p. 12.

85. *CSP Scot.*, x, 122.

86. Ibid., xiii, pt. 1, 57.

87. Ibid., ix, 640; Moysie, *Memoirs*, 71.

88. Pitcairn, *Criminal Trials*, iii, 61.

89. Birrel, 'Diary', 24.

90. *RPC*, iv, 656.

91. Ibid., v, 36–7.

92. Ibid., viii, 383; Pitcairn, *Criminal Trials*, iii, 61–5.

93. Pitcairn, *Criminal Trials*, iii, 65–72.

94. Braudel, *The Mediterranean*, ii, 713.

95. L. Stone, *The Crisis of the Aristocracy, 1558–1641* (Oxford, 1977), 111.

96. J. B. Samaha, 'Hanging for felony: the rule of law in Elizabethan Colchester', *Historical Journal*, 21 (1978), 766.

97. Gun control was an issue for Jacobean governments from 1567 onwards, see Brown, *Bloodfeud in Scotland*, 246–9. For gun production in the Scottish burghs see D. Caldwell, 'Royal Patronage of Arms and Armour Making in D. Caldwell (ed.), *Scottish Weapons and Fortifications, 1100–1800* (Edinburgh, 1981), 82. Some burghs attempted to introduce

their own by-laws on the carrying of weapons (Renwick, *Peebles*, 10).

98. For legislation on convocations see Brown, *Bloodfeud in Scotland*, 251–2. *CSP Scot.*, ix, p. 532.

99. Brown, *Bloodfeud in Scotland*, pt. 3.

100. Melville, *Diary*, 53–5.

101. *RPC*, iii, 109–12.

102. Smout, *History of the Scottish People*, 100.

103. *RPC*, v, 462.

104. W. C. Dickinson, 'Courts of Special Jurisdiction', in *Introduction to Scottish Legal History* (Stair Society, 1958), 396–7. Additional legislation was passed in 1593, 1597 and 1600 (*APS*, iv, 28–9; *RPC*, v, 403; vi, 77–8). For the Bothwell-Glamis incident, see Moysie, *Memoirs*, 71.

105. *RPC*, vii, 295.

106. See comments on this by G. S. Pryde, 'The Burgh Courts and Allied Jurisdictions' in *Introduction to Scottish Legal History*, 384–5.

107. *Melros Corresp.*, i, 32.

108. *Edin. Recs., 1573–89*, 295.

109. *RPC*, vii, 221–3, 247, 288, 498, 646; Spottiswoode, *History*, iii, 175–6; *Melros Corresp.*, i, 17; Balfour, *Works*, i, 17.

110. *RPC*, iv, 370; Melville, *Diary*, 206–7.

111. *RPC*, iv, 18.

112. Ibid., iv, 355.

113. Birrel, 'Diary', 48; *RPC*, vi, 860; Pitcairn, *Criminal Trials*, ii, 112–24.

114. *RPC*, viii, 621; xi, 202, 318; Pitcairn, *Criminal Trials*, iii, 58.

115. *Stirling Recs., 1513–1666*, 124.

116. Ibid., 133.

117. Chambers, *Domestic Annals*, i, 394–5.

118. SRO, RD 1/15/241.

119. SRO, RD 1/38/231, 1/34/322.

120. SRO, RD 1/34/38b, 1/34/40; Melville, *Diary*, 182–5.

121. SRO, RD 1/39/172.

122. 'Ross MSS', *Report of the Royal Commission on Historical Manuscripts*, (London, 1870–), vi, p. 717, no. 15.

6

Merchant Princes and Mercantile Investment in Early Seventeenth-Century Scotland

James J. Brown

Most economic studies of seventeenth-century Scotland have either virtually ignored the pre-Restoration economy or, if dealing with the endeavours of merchants between 1600 and 1660, have approached it in a somewhat pessimistic fashion. They tend to stress the economic shortcomings, to dismiss Scottish merchants as either essentially conservative or lacking the basic initiative necessary to attempt to align the Scottish economy with the more mainstream European nations which, from the end of the sixteenth century, were experiencing commercial revolutions.[1] Indeed, it has been recently written that it was only in the final years of the seventeenth century that Scottish merchants began to demonstrate any sort of business acumen or even to utilise the most basic of commercial skills — developing 'proto-banking' systems, using both long-term credit arrangements and partnerships, as well as investing for the first time in any significant way in small-scale industries. The combined effect of these novel practices, it is argued, was fundamentally to change what had been up to that time an essentially medieval and antiquated system of merchandising and allow the Scottish business community to enter the eighteenth century, and union with England, as profitable and efficient traders.[2]

However, as a group whose prime aim was to merchandise their products successfully in the increasingly competitive and sophisticated European market places, Scottish merchants of the early seventeenth century were dependent to a larger degree than ever before upon their ability to develop, utilise and manipulate these very trade mechanisms. In many respects the seemingly profound alterations in the character of Scottish business life alleged to have

125

taken place after 1660 may be little more than a re-establishment of practices which had germinated and been common enough in the early years of the seventeenth century. Most, if not all, of the apparently new developments in Scottish commerce in the Restoration period were also part of the backdrop against which certain Scottish traders, who could be termed the nation's merchant princes, worked during the first forty years of the century. An examination of a few of the important aspects of their commercial practices — their involvement in partnerships; the ownership and commercial chartering of ships; their growing dependency upon the employment of factors in foreign cities; the development and use of a credit system which involved transferable and heritable bonds, bills of exchange and an awareness of the international money-markets; as well as the channelling of surplus capital into manufacturing enterprises — when taken in combination indicates the relative sophistication of at least the wealthiest Scottish merchants' entrepreneurial activities between 1600 and 1640.

In purely economic terms Scotland was a nation whose trade had been dominated by the merchants of a handful of burghs from the fifteenth century, if not before. Between 1460 and 1600 approximately 80 per cent of the customs revenue collected by the Exchequer was generated by the three largest burghs of the realm — Edinburgh, Aberdeen and Dundee.[3] However, from the mid-sixteenth century, a period in which Scotland's economy experienced a boom which was similar to the general upswing in most other European nations,[4] it was, above all, Edinburgh's merchants who increasingly dominated the Scottish export trade. The capital's contribution to the total customs revenue grew from just over a half collected in 1480 to 59 per cent in 1530 and 65 per cent in 1578. Indeed, most of the goods exported from Scotland left through Leith, Edinburgh's port. Between 1460 and 1600 76 per cent of all wool leaving Scottish ports was exported from Edinburgh, as was 70 per cent of all wool cloth, 70 per cent of all sheepskins and 63 per cent of all hides — these being the staple Scottish exports. By the last years of the sixteenth century Edinburgh held a virtual monopoly over Scotland's export trade. It was from Leith that over 80 per cent of all Scottish sheepskins, 83 per cent of all hides and 73 per cent of all cloth left the country.[5]

Edinburgh's merchant community further consolidated its pre-eminent position in Scottish trade during the early years of the seventeenth century. Within a burgh of approximately 25,000 inhabitants[6] it has been estimated that there were, in any one year during the first forty years of that century, between 450 and 500 men described as merchants.[7] In Edinburgh, as in Scotland as a whole, both a wealthy overseas trader as well as an insignificant street pedlar who rarely ventured beyond the burgh's walls would have been termed as merchants,[8] but those involved in foreign trade must have been a select body and those of Edinburgh the most exclusive. In Edinburgh it is doubtful that more than a third of the 400–500 men described as merchants in the burgh tax rolls were in fact involved in trade beyond the Scottish borders.[9] The merchant community of Aberdeen, the third largest burgh in Scotland, could boast in the 1620s of perhaps 300 active traders, of whom a mere seventy-five were in any year involved in overseas trade.[10] The merchant community of Glasgow even as late as the 1680s numbered only between 400 and 500 men, of whom no more than a quarter were overseas traders and this out of a total population of less than 12,000 inhabitants.[11] Edinburgh, although a larger burgh, did not in fact have a proportionately larger merchant community than these two places. Its merchants were able to consolidate their hold on its expanding trade due to their smaller numbers and intimate connections. This may have made possible the branching into new areas of business.

In purely fiscal terms the wealth of Edinburgh's merchant community during the century's first forty years was a recognised fact. The burgh never paid less than 28 per cent of any of the taxes for which they were assessed by the Convention of Royal Burghs. Indeed, the Convention's revision of the rate in 1649 resulted in Edinburgh's inhabitants paying 36 per cent of any Convention taxation, although some felt that it should pay as much as half.[12] Between 1600 and 1637 Edinburgh's tax payers were assessed for a variety of crown, Convention and burghal purposes no less than thirty-five times.[13] The total levied was well over £425,000.[14] On average 1,400 people were assessed in each tax roll but 45 per cent of the money raised was paid by less than 8 per cent of the taxable population. These over the period numbered some 300, virtually almost all of them merchants. Almost half of the tax within the burgh during the first forty years of the century was paid by its merchant princes; they represented only one in every 200 of the burgh's inhabitants.[15]

This was the core of the Edinburgh merchant community — held together by links of various kinds, political and financial as well as those of family — which dominated both the burgh's affairs and its overseas trade.[16] The early seventeenth century saw this elite make attempts at a certain diversification away from the traditional overseas markets and staple commodities. An integral part of this partial shift in patterns of trade to and from Scotland was the adoption of novel business practices. The recourse to new markets and business methods, combined with a secure grip on most of the familiar trade routes, was to make Edinburgh's merchant princes by 1640 the most advanced as well as by far the most important merchandising group in Scotland.

The elite — numbering some 310 — which emerges from the evidence of the tax rolls was not wholly comprised of overseas traders. No more than 195 of them were directly involved in overseas trade and only 120 engaged in both importing and exporting.[17] Yet this group exported on 60 per cent of the ships leaving Leith in 1611–12, 1624–5 and 1626–8, imported goods on almost half of the ships arriving in Leith between 1621 and 1623, and imported almost 30 per cent of the goods arriving at that port from 1636 to 1639, these being the only years for which customs lists of the burgh survive.[18] During the 1620s the elite were the chief exporters of skins, plaiding and fish from the burgh, as well as the most important importers of cloth, grain and luxury goods. The Edinburgh elite never specialised totally in one particular commodity — as did the merchants of Aberdeen at the same period — but they were for the most part involved either in the grain trade with the Netherlands and the Baltic or with the lucrative cloth trade from England or the Continent.[19] It was through their particular interests in these forms of merchandising that the elite's trading patterns differed from the traditional areas which were of interest to the less wealthy Edinburgh merchants. The elite showed little desire to compete with either the smaller merchants in Edinburgh or with ports like Dundee or Aberdeen in trade with Scandinavia, Denmark and Germany, the areas which supplied such industrial raw materials as timber, although they were involved in the Baltic grain trade. Although the Scottish staple at Veere in the Netherlands remained an important European clearing centre for the elite's exports, they were diversifying their interests in the Low Countries by trading directly with Rotterdam and Amsterdam, the wealthiest city in early seventeenth-century Europe. The lucrative markets of northern France — Dieppe, Rouen and La Rochelle — from which many of the luxury goods imported to Scotland were purchased, as well as the blossoming cloth markets in England — in London in particular

— were the near-exclusive preserve of the burgh's wealthiest merchants.[20] The alterations made to the pattern and dominance of trade by the elite during these years were inextricably linked to, and were in turn affected by, the growing sophistication in the business practices implemented by Scotland's leading merchant community.

One of the basic urges felt by early-modern merchants must have been the desire to enter into commercial partnership with other traders. Not only would this provide merchants with a greater pool of capital and contacts from which to draw business but it also provided a limited form of risk insurance. It was with the most sophisticated form of partnership — that in which both partners involved contributed labour and services as well as capital and shared equally the risks and profits, a form of 'joint sale and purchase' arrangement similar to the *collegantia* or *compagna* of Italian merchants — that the elite were most likely to deal.[21] Certainly members of the elite made use of each other to form recurrent associations which may have been nothing more than occasional partnerships without the relationship being formalised into permanent companies. However 'joint-business' partnerships did exist, involving joint ownership of stock, goods and sharing of profits. And, more importantly, they were often of a long-standing nature. This form of partnership was in itself a significant departure from the forms of business relations practised by Edinburgh's wealthiest merchants who even only half a century before had rarely entered into 'joint stock' partnerships.[22] It was also different from Aberdeen where even the wealthiest merchants did not enter partnerships in the early seventeenth century.[23]

The most obvious reason for merchants to enter into partnership was for the purpose of trade. The surviving customs lists of Leith regularly mention men described as both 'partners' and joint owners of merchandise aboard the vessels, which gives some indication of the new links which were being formed within the tight-knit Edinburgh business community. The customs lists of 1622 reveal that Gilbert Williamson and Alexander Spier were involved in partnerships in order to import from the Netherlands.[24] In June 1612 John Sinclair, John Trotter and a group described as their 'partners' exported 400 bolls of bear and oats from Leith to Dort;[25] ten years later the same John Sinclair imported peas from Danzig with many of the same men who were still described as 'his partners'.[26]

The customs lists also make clear that the elite were involved in joint-stock ownership. The import lists of 1621–3 reveal that on almost eighty occasions merchandise brought into Leith harbour was registered as being jointly owned by at least two members of the burgh's merchant aristocracy, in addition to whatever else these men may have imported under their own names. The export lists of 1611–12 and 1626–8 indicate that it was less important, or perhaps less necessary, for members of the elite to enter into joint-stock ownership for the purposes of exporting goods. On fewer than twenty occasions did the elite export directly in partnership. This reflects the dual character of Scottish trade which had newly emerged by the 1620s. The export market, limited as it still was to fairly traditional items and marketing areas, was more readily open to a single merchant's endeavours; the import trade was more complex, involving new markets and commodities, and was more suited to the merchant combine.

Perhaps one of the most permanent of these joint-stock operations between members of the elite was that of Alexander Brown and Alexander Monteath. These two merchants, combined at times with other members of the elite, traded in jointly owned stock on no fewer than ten different occasions in the 1620s indicating a regularly conducted partnership, if not a legally formalised one. In May 1622 Monteath and Brown imported fifty lasts of bear from Middelburg.[27] A month later a group described as consisting of 'Alexander Brown, William Wilkie, Alexander Monteath and partners' imported rye from Danzig; in August 1622 the two partners imported grain, wax and ash on four different occasions from the Baltic, Middelburg and Amsterdam, although ownership of the goods was shared with certain other merchants including Robert Fleming, George Suttie and David McCall, all members of the merchant elite.[28] Brown and Monteath together imported beans from Rotterdam in March 1623, beans and bear from Amsterdam in May, rye and wainscotting from Königsberg in June; they also exported forty-five lasts of herring to the Baltic in joint ownership with three other elite merchants in September 1628.[29]

Significant as these joint-stock ventures were to them both, Brown and Monteath were also regularly trading goods under their own names. Monteath imported fifteen lasts of bear in July 1622 on the *Lamb of Leith* under his own auspices. However, Brown imported fifteen lasts of rye on the same vessel.[30] Monteath imported grain into Leith from Veere, Rotterdam and Amsterdam, as well as wax and flax from Danzig, either on his own or with merchants other than Brown a total of ten times from August 1622 to September 1623.[31] These investments, however, never matched in value those advanced with Brown. Similarly Brown, either on his own or with men other than Monteath, imported cereals, flax, iron and pitch from Danzig, Veere, Stralsund, Königsberg, Rotterdam and Middelburg between May 1622 and September 1623 on a total of eighteen different vessels.[32] That Brown was more willing than Monteath to expand beyond the limits of their partnership and to import a wider range of goods from a more varied number of European ports indicates a subtle difference in the two merchants' skills and trading practices. In terms of the export trade Monteath exported goods twice under his own name in September 1627, including six lasts of herring on the *Pelican of Lübeck*; Brown exported thirty lasts of herring on the same vessel as part of a separate combine.[33] Brown exported goods, such as herring, deals and wheat, from Leith to a wide variety of places including Danzig, Bordeaux, Stockholm, Veere, Amsterdam, Königsberg and Elsinore a total of twelve times between November 1626 and October 1628 either as his own stock or with men other than Monteath.[34] While the partnership between the two men was not the dominant factor in Brown's commercial life it was important to him and probably the most permanent of any of the elite's combines. Even when not trading directly in joint stock the two men tended to import or export on the same vessels. Although they were not connected by kin or marriage, the two men were members of the same social circles, an important prerequisite in determining relationships in burgh society. They were prosecuted together as partners before the privy council in 1618 for illegally exporting grain, swore an oath together with a group of men described as Easterly traders in 1622 about the importance of exporting coinage, and Brown replaced Monteath as Edinburgh's kirk treasurer in December 1628.[35] Their relationship is typical of the awakening realisation among Edinburgh's wealthiest merchants of the important role which joint-stock partnerships could play.[36] The new opportunities in overseas trade also had the effect of further consolidating the burgh oligarchy: in over 80 per cent of the joint-stock partnerships in which members of the elite were involved their partners were also drawn from the same privileged circle.[37]

The willingness on the part of the elite to enter into partnerships of both a long-standing and potentially profitable nature is also revealed in the growth in ownership and commercial chartering of trading vessels.[38] It has been generally assumed that the mechanisms operating behind the ownership and chartering of cargo space on sea-going vessels were conducted very much on an *ad hoc* basis of the master of the ship — he being the actual owner — renting out available cargo space for a particular voyage to whatever merchants required that their goods be transported. The division of the vessels into fractions — halves, quarters, eighths, sixteenths or even thirty-seconds — was a practice prevalent throughout Europe and has been taken to have been merely a temporary sharing-out of the vessel's cargo space amongst the merchants chartering it for that particular voyage. Subsquent importing or exporting would require renegotiation of terms between the merchants and master, over both cargo space and handling charges. Indeed, as far as seventeenth-century Scotland is concerned, it has been plainly stated that there existed no such thing as a separate ship owning group and that the skipper/owner hired out his vessel for particular voyages.[39] Yet evidence from the testaments of the wealthiest of Edinburgh's merchants during the first forty years of the century reveals a substantial capital investment by them in shipowning, something their fathers had not invested in.[40] At least 13 per cent of the 310 wealthiest individuals in Edinburgh viewed shipowning as a commercially profitable sideline to their role as merchandisers. Their investment in this area represents both the growth of a corps of men who could be termed as merchant-shipowners and the first significant development of this form of investment in Scotland.

Between 1600 and 1652 a total of forty-three testaments of members of the elite or their spouses show ownership of shares in vessels at the time of their death; on average almost 26 per cent of the total value of the inventory was made up of this form of investment. If each of the first four decades of the century are viewed separately, it can be seen that there was a definite growth in interest in the commercial ownership of vessels. By the 1640s a group had emerged with more than a third of the value of their inventories tied up in shipowning.[41] The importance of this investment could run from as little as the £200 which William Rae had invested in John Lookup's ship in 1619, worth less than 2 per cent of Rae's total inventory of goods, to the £5,833 6s 8d, almost 90 per cent of the value of his inventory, which George Stirling had invested in seven different vessels at the time of his death in 1648.[42] It was unusual for such a large part of any merchant's assets to be so tied up in shipowning, although three other members of the elite had invested at least 60 per cent of their inventories value in ships between 1611 and 1645.[43] Men such as Charles Hamilton, John Kniblo, Gabriel Ranken and Thomas Inglis, with about a quarter of their inventory of goods invested in ship shares, are more representative of the growth of this form of investment.[44]

The actual investment in shipowning could make up a substantial sum even if it formed a fraction of the merchant's inventory. David Jenkin had over £4,000 invested in five ships at the time of his death in 1641, although this amounted to only 10 per cent of the value of his inventory.[45] John Fleming's shares in four vessels, amounting to 17 per cent of his inventory, were worth £3,300.[46] One of the most substantial investors in commercial shipowning during the first half of the seventeenth century was Patrick Wood. At the time of his death in 1638 he held shares in thirty-six different vessels — an investment of £21,264 — although this amounted to less than 16 per cent of the total value of his inventory. His shares in vessels included the outright ownership of the bark *Isabelle* worth £1,583 6s 8d, a quarter of the *Dolphin of Preston* worth £1,333 6s 8d, half of the *Blessing of Kinghorn* valued at the same, a quarter of the *James of Leith* worth £2,266 13s 4d and the ownership of a one-eighth share of the *James of Kirkcaldy* worth £1,600.[47] His only rival in this field in Edinburgh was William Dick of Braid, the wealthiest merchant in Scotland at that time. By 1642 Dick had invested over £46,000 in shipping.[48]

The evidence also indicates that this form of investment was regarded as being of a long-term nature rather than merely the result of the renting of cargo space in a vessel for a particular voyage. Shipowning was seen as a potentially lucrative venture as well as a means of transporting one's own goods at as cheap a rate as possible. James Forsyth owned shares valued at 5,000 merks in the *Gift of God* at the time of his death in 1625 but had actually used that vessel to ship his goods in April 1622 to Leith from Dieppe.[49] Charles Hamilton exported his produce to Veere on the *John of Leith* in 1628 and owned shares worth £700 in that vessel at the time of his death in 1640.[50] Thomas Inglis, David Jenkin, Alan Livingston, David Murray, George Stirling, John Ritchie and Andrew Purves all showed a long-term interest in particular vessels which they used to transport their goods.[51] Indeed, Jenkin was part of an Edinburgh-based consortium which had commissioned the construction of the *St John of Leith* in Rotterdam in 1624.[52]

It is equally clear that the owners of a particular ship were not necessarily involved in using that vessel to transport their own goods but chartered the ship to other merchants for considerable profits. The owners would not only levy freight charges but also claim a portion of the profits of the voyage. In 1626 James Loch, as owner of a one-sixteenth part of the *Gift of God*, sued Andrew Mitchell, the master of the ship, for payment of his just sixteenth part of the freight charges and 'fee monies' made from that ship's voyages since October 1624.[53] Four years later, when Loch purchased a portion of the *Archangel of Leith*, it was stipulated in the contract that his sixteenth part should include 'the haill ornaments and pertinents belonging to the ship as she was entered to the sea in her last voyage from Leith with all profit, benefit or commodity to one sixteenth part . . .'[54]

Substantial profits could be made from investment in commercial shipping. In 1632 Alan Livingstone was owed £422, which represented the profit of the voyages of three of his vessels, in addition to the value of his shares in those ships.[55] Clear instructions were drawn up to maximise profits. In 1636 George Wauchope and George Stirling, who each received £75 as their share of the profits made by a voyage of the *Andrew of Burntisland*, endorsed a letter to the master of the ship giving him precise directions to sail to Dunkirk to purchase salt at a profitable rate which was to be taken to Danzig and resold at a profit, indicating not only their ability to respond promptly to market pressures but also that there was some direction and order behind the sailing of Scottish vessels rather than merely a haphazard sailing from port to port in search of profits, as has usually been assumed.[56] The owners of a vessel made sure that it was those chartering the vessel who were made responsible for paying for the crew's provisions while the vessel was lying idle in foreign ports awaiting the loading of cargoes.[57] While the elite were aware of the existence of a primitive form of ship insurance against the dangers of shipwreck or piracy, its purchase was based in London rather than in Edinburgh itself and they rarely resorted to it.[58] It was more usual that in cases of shipwreck it was the owners of the vessels themselves who were made responsible for the loss of the ship and its recovery and the owners of the goods aboard who were responsible for recovering their property, if possible.[59]

Not only did Edinburgh's wealthiest merchants involve themselves in long-term partnerships based on trade, joint-stock or shipownership but they also entered into partnerships through the regular employment of factors — most notably in employing resident factors in such places as Danzig, Dieppe, Bordeaux, Rouen, Paris, London, Bilbao and Veere. As well as allowing them the best opportunities possible to sell their goods to those with a practical knowledge of various European trading centres, such long-distance relations with financial partners, whom a merchant might never have met in person, aided the development and regular use within the elite's circles of various rudimentary forms of banking practices. These included transferable letters of credit, the use of what was in effect overdraft facilities in major trading centres, as well as granting the elite the opportunity of lending money in foreign cities. This points to a knowledge of the financial exchanges, brokerage systems and money markets of Europe on the part of the wealthiest merchants in Edinburgh. The use of factors in foreign cities, particularly in the Low Countries, dated, of course, from at least the fifteenth century and by the late sixteenth century certain wealthy Edinburgh merchants employed resident factors in Veere, Rouen, Bordeaux and Danzig. But it was more general practice that business was conducted on a personal basis with the merchants involved travelling with their goods and bartering them at dockside for whatever merchandise was available.[60] By the late 1630s it would have proved almost impossible for members of the Edinburgh merchant elite to have conducted the range of business they did had they not made substantial use of and placed considerable trust in their factors.

It was not unusual for less well-off Scottish merchants, let alone members of Edinburgh's merchant aristocracy, to commission temporarily other merchants to escort and sell goods on their behalf, particularly if they had no apprentice to act for them in this function.[61] However, it was chiefly members of Edinburgh's wealthiest trading circles who made long-term use of factors resident in foreign cities, usually employing expatriate Scots to work for them. In Dieppe their main factors were James and Michael Maill; in Bordeaux John Shegray, Jean Raoul and Manuel Beaupré, the only non-Scots factors employed by the elite; in Danzig Arthur Hutcheson; in Bilbao James Brown; in London Archibald Boyle, John Johnston, Robert Inglis and Francis Dick; in Paris Andrew Robertson, John Clerk and Andrew Beaton, and in Veere members of the Weir and Wallace families. At least a third of all the regular overseas traders amongst the elite employed at least one of these men at some point between 1600 and 1650. For the most part the relationship between Edinburgh's wealthiest men and their factors were amicable.[62]

Important as the use of factors in Veere, Dieppe and Bordeaux was for members of the élite, it was the employment of resident factors in London and Paris which indicates the growing sophistication on the part of the burgh's wealthiest merchants and their desire to establish trading links with the mainstream European commercial centres. Those members of the elite with factors in these cities employed them to lend money, to issue notes of credit and oversee international money transfers, something which they rarely demanded from their factors in other cities, not even those based at the staple port of Veere. Only a handful of Edinburgh's merchant princes employed resident factors in London, indicating that in general the majority of their business deals in that city, traditionally an environment hostile to Scottish merchants, were conducted through private business connections. However, by 1616 William Dick's affairs in London were sufficiently complex for him to pay his debts there through his factor, John Jossie.[63] Dick used Jossie to lend money at 10 per cent annual interest to a Scottish traveller in London in the early 1620s, but by 1626 he had been replaced by David Muirhead.[64] Muirhead continued Jossie's rôle as Dick's banker, lending money on his behalf to Scots in the English capital in 1629 but was himself replaced by Francis Dick by 1631.[65] By 1634 Patrick Wood too had secured the services of John Johnston to act as his resident factor in London. Wood operated a sophisticated service involving both money lending and issuing of bonds payable upon fourteen, twenty or forty-two days sight through his London factor.[66] Indeed, Wood not only spent several months in London between 1636 and 1638 but also complained in 1637 that he was in fact hard pressed to find money there.[67] Robert Inglis, himself a member of Edinburgh's wealthy merchant circles, acted as a resident factor in London for various members of the elite, granting them six and eight months credit for their purchases in that city.[68] Inglis's main rôle, however, appears to have been to establish a link for Edinburgh merchants between himself in London and John Clerk in Paris. Certainly the two men were in regular contact from 1633, transferring considerable amounts of Edinburgh capital between them. By the late 1630s they too were bemoaning the lack of 'good bills' available for their use on the exchanges.[69]

By 1638 Edinburgh's wealthiest merchants had invested a considerable amount of capital in Paris. A lack of personal connections, combined with greater distance and the linguistic

barrier meant that merchants trading in Paris made more use of a
resident factor than did those trading in London. As early as 1622
Scottish factors were employed in Paris. Andrew Beaton loaned
money in Paris to Scottish travellers in the names of William Dick,
Peter Blackburn and Henry Morison in the early 1620s, usually
charging interest payments.[70] It was part of Beaton's duties to
arrange for transfers of the elite's goods and money from Paris to
Dieppe, Bordeaux and Veere as well as to introduce them to
businessmen in French cities in which they had no previous
connections.[71] However, by the mid-1630s his relations with
Edinburgh merchants had become somewhat strained through his
failure to remain in regular contact with them and he was replaced
by John Clerk, an Edinburgh merchant who had taken up
residence in Paris in 1633.[72] After 1635 Clerk acted as the sole
factor in Paris for Edinburgh merchants, allowing them considerable overdraft facilities. In 1635 John Smith drew bonds worth
£12,389 on Clerk, transferring money from Dieppe to meet the
overdraft. In 1636 Smith drew almost £20,000 on Clerk and transferred £21,564 from his factor in Dieppe to cover the debt. At least
eleven other Edinburgh merchants also utilised Clerk in this
fashion, transferring funds from Dieppe at the end of a financial
year to cover the overdrafts which they had run up with him.[73]
Clerk was also used by various members of the elite to lend money
to Scottish travellers, usually Scottish gentry, in Paris during the
1630s.[74] Indeed, Patrick Wood wrote to Clerk in March 1637
chiding him for being so indiscreet as to force his customers to
endorse their bonds in front of his factor before handing over the
loan, which ultimately reflected badly on Wood himself.[75] Wood
was, nevertheless, impressed by Clerk's business acumen and
honesty, paying him a commission of 2½ per cent to work as his
factor, a full 1 per cent above the standard rate.[76] There was
indeed some competition amongst Edinburgh merchants in
lending money, in particular between Wood and John Dougal,
although both used Clerk as their factor. In January 1635 Dougal
wrote to Clerk that Sir Alexander Seton, son of the 3rd earl of
Winton, had complained of the rate of exchange offered him by
Clerk in Dougal's name of forty in the hundred between Paris and
Rome. Wood apparently had offered Seton ten in the hundred
between London and Rome. Dougal begged Clerk to give Seton
his money as cheaply as possible 'without any gain or commodity
thereon for it will make my Lord Winton to take some other by the
hand to furnish his son'.[77] This use of factors in London and

Paris by Edinburgh's merchant princes to lend money upon the international market, in addition to the more normal purchasing duties, indicates that by the late 1630s the wealthiest merchants in Scotland at least were aware of the complexities of the wider European financial scene. It also shows a definite change in the ways in which Edinburgh's merchants invested their money, for at no time in the sixteenth century had such dealings existed nor would they again until the early years of the eighteenth century.[78]

The first forty years of the seventeenth century also witnessed a certain amount of diversification of capital by the elite into another form of speculation which, although modest in outlay, was a marked departure from their traditional merchandising rôles. The involvement in industrial pursuits shows a willingness on the part of the elite to gamble with their capital, something, it has been stated, that their forefathers would not have ventured.[79] The wealthiest merchants of Edinburgh invested considerable sums in the mining of lead ore and coal, in establishing salt-pans, herring-curing, cloth-making, beer and vinegar brewing and rope-making. An examination of the manufactory movement in early modern Scotland has concluded that few manufacturing enterprises of any note were established in early seventeenth-century Scotland; the establishment of even small-scale manufactories belonged, it was argued, rather to the post-Restoration economy.[80] Yet, at least twenty of Edinburgh's wealthiest merchants were involved in investing their capital in industrial efforts — of whatever form or ultimate success — between 1600 and 1638.

The most substantial investment in manufacturing by these men, and probably the most profitable, was in the mining or processing of natural resources, such as coal, lead and salt, rather than in manufactories as such. A small group of wealthy Edinburgh entrepreneurs almost completely dominated these types of activity in early seventeenth-century Scotland. The most important lead ore mine in Scotland before the Civil Wars, Leadhills in Lanarkshire which produced 300–400 tons of lead ore a year and had been opened in 1590, was by 1613 under the control of John Fairlie.[81] At the time of his death in 1620 Fairlie had invested £8,100 in the mine and was owed 500 merks by David Foulis, son of the man who had opened the mine.[82] Fairlie worked in close cooperation with two other Edinburgh merchants, Ninian and John MacMorran, in the export of lead ore to the Netherlands from 1613 onwards. Various contracts entered into by these men in 1613 and 1614 gave the MacMorran brothers the right to two-

thirds of the profits made on the sale of 115,000 stones of lead ore
in Middelburg, amounting to over £42,000 by 1621.[83] In addition
to supplying at least 178,000 stones of lead ore on the foreign
market between 1613 and 1620, Fairlie also furnished lead for the
refurbishment in Linlithgow Palace in July 1620 and had dis-
bursed some £3,600 towards this before his death in September of
that year.[84]

The Edinburgh merchant elite were also involved in investing in
the production of salt and the mining of coal, in particular along
the Forth coast and in Fife. This was in direct competition to the
capital invested by the local Fife lairds which itself developed
markedly at this time.[85] By 1606 John Porterfield, who although
an Edinburgh merchant was from a wealthy Culross family,
owned two salt pans in Culross and two in Kincardine and by 1610
had purchased a further salt pan in Kincardine.[86] Edward Edgar
in 1610, Patrick Wood in 1629 and Peter Blackburn in 1632 were
all in possession of the right to coal and salt in Fife — Edgar and
Wood from Torryburn and Blackburn from Tulliallan.[87] It would
appear that the most important salt pans in Fife in the early seventeenth-century — those in Culross, Kirkcaldy, Torryburn and
Tulliallan — were all invested in and developed by members of
Edinburgh's merchandising circles rather than by local lairds.[88]
Indeed, the boom in the production of salt in these very areas in
the first three decades of the century may have arisen directly as a
result of Edinburgh capital. Certainly when the Fife salt industry
entered into a period of recession due to the lack of capital investment in the late 1630s it was at a time when Edinburgh's
wealthiest merchants, the most likely source of capital, were also
beginning to feel hard pressed financially.[89]

Beyond investment in salt panning and mining members of
Edinburgh's wealthiest merchant circle combined to invest in
producing cured herring. A consortium involving Joseph Marjori-
banks, James Arnot and George Todrig in 1615 purchased the
right of monopoly to make red herring from Tweedmouth to the
Pentland Firth. The combine invested a considerable amount of
capital in establishing a herring curing and packing factory in
Dunbar and had also spent some 2,200 merks in order to bring
skilled foreign workers to the area.[90] Despite initial difficulties the
Dunbar enterprise flourished well into the 1620s, attracting the
money of other wealthy Edinburgh merchants.[91] It is likely that
William Dick purchased the factory from the consortium for in
1642 he owned a herring works in Dunbar worth 60,000 merks.[92]

It was also members of the Edinburgh elite who were involved in the origins of what was to become by the late 1630s the only substantial industry within the burgh itself, beer brewing. In 1596 Edinburgh town council decreed that a society for beer brewing should be established due to the lack of any such industry in the town.[93] In February 1598 a Society of eighteen merchants was established and constructed its premises at Greyfriars Port.[94] From that time Patrick Cochrane, John Jackson, James Nisbet, George Todrig and Alexander Miller were all involved in the industry.[95] When the town council purchased the Society's property in 1618 for 40,000 merks the Society was owned by a consortium of eight of the town's wealthiest merchants.[96] The Society was re-established in Leith and in 1627 was set in tack for 4,400 merks to William Dick,[97] who made £16,000 in profits in 1636–7; and by 1642 he had 100,000 merks invested in the business.[98]

While there were various other attempts to promote industry in Scotland by members of the elite during the first forty years of the century it is doubtful that these were either of an enduring or profitable nature. Although it was Edinburgh town council's policy to establish cloth-making within the burgh from at least 1601 all attempts at this failed.[99] Although by 1632 Alan Livingston had invested at least £1,800 in a clothwork at Canonmills, to the north of the burgh, there is no evidence that cloth in any quantity was produced there. Livingston also owned a vinegar works in Leith worth £1,100.[100] The last significant investment made in establishing industry by any of the burgh's merchant princes before the Wars of the Covenant was made by Patrick Wood, just months before his death in 1638. He established a rope works in Newhaven, to the north-west of the burgh, and built workmen's houses. This investment was worth some £54,000, and outstanding sum even for one of the burgh's wealthiest entrepreneurs.[101]

Between 1600 and 1640 the wealthiest merchants of Edinburgh developed a number of important mechanisms of economic life for the first time in Scotland. They established long-term partnerships, developed commercial shipowning and chartering businesses, invested in small-scale manufactories and were well aware of the niceties of, and profits to be made from, involving themselves in the mainstream European money and banking markets. This took place as part of the process of consolidation of the grip which Edinburgh's merchants had over the bulk of overseas trade and it was the wealthiest men of the burgh who set the pace in establishing these new practices. These men were different from

Aberdeen's wealthiest merchants who remained throughout the period traditionally based traders.[102] Even the merchant elite of Glasgow, who were to figure so largely in Scottish trade in the later years of the seventeenth and early years of the eighteenth century, were before then chiefly small-scale traders using Leith or Bo'ness as their ports. The Glasgow manufactories and joint-stock enterprises belong, almost without exception, to the period after 1655.[103]

The vital years for Edinburgh's merchant princes lay in the early seventeenth century rather than after the Restoration. The strength of the Edinburgh merchant community was recognised in 1637 when it was proposed to establish in the capital a merchant company similar to the Merchant Adventurers of London.[104] However, it is probable that at no point prior to 1600 had such a small group of merchants controlled and dominated the economic future of Scotland's most important trading centre. While there did not exist in Edinburgh society merchant princes on the scale of the Medici or Fuggers, there was a group of men living on credit, expecting future benefits from their investments and maintaining large overdrafts in foreign cities. Patrick Wood and William Dick were pre-eminent amongst Edinburgh's merchant princes. Their careers — and their bankruptcies — underline both the breadth of investment of the Edinburgh merchant community and its precarious nature. Dick was ruined by the Wars of the Covenant[105] but Wood was bankrupt by the time he died in 1638 with debts amounting to over £61,000.[106] The progress of Edinburgh's merchants was already faltering before it was dramatically checked by the Scottish Revolution of the 1640s. There was a certain recovery in the Scottish urban economy after 1660, although in few towns was it on the scale reached by Glasgow.[107] Edinburgh's merchant community shared in this general economic revival but at no time did there emerge a group who achieved quite the dynamic or the near-monopoly of trade and credit enjoyed by the Edinburgh merchant princes of the early seventeenth century.

Notes

1. R. Mitchison, *Lordship to Patronage* (London, 1983), virtually ignores the economy prior to 1660. See also T. S. Colahan, 'The Cautious Revolutionaries: The Scottish Middle Classes in the Making of the Scottish Revolt' (Columbia University Ph.D., 1962), 112; S. G. E. Lythe, *The Economy of Scotland in its European Setting, 1550–1625*

(Edinburgh, 1960), 35–6; T. C. Smout, *Scottish Trade on the Eve of the Union* (Edinburgh, 1963), 27–8. H. R. Trevor-Roper, 'Scotland and the Puritan revolution', in *Religion, the Reformation and Social Change* (London, 1967), 395–6, even states that Edinburgh was destitute of mercantile spirit.

2. T. M. Devine, 'The merchant class of the larger Scottish towns in the seventeenth and early eighteenth centuries' in G. Gordon and B. Dicks (eds.), *Scottish Urban History* (Aberdeen, 1983); T. M. Devine, 'The Scottish merchant community 1680–1740' in R. H. Campbell and A. S. Skinner (eds.), *The Origins and Nature of the Scottish Enlightenment* (Edinburgh, 1982); T. C. Smout, 'The Glasgow merchant community in the seventeenth century', *SHR*, 48 (1968); T. C. Smout, 'The development and enterprise of Glasgow 1556–1707', *Scottish Journal of Political Economy*, 7 (1960).

3. I. Guy, 'The Scottish Export Trade 1460–1599, from the Exchequer Rolls' (University of St Andrews M.Phil., 1982), 166–7, 174.

4. S. G. E. Lythe, 'The economy of Scotland under James VI and I' in A. G. R. Smith (ed.), *The Reign of James VI and I* (London, 1973), 73; S. G. E. Lythe, 'Economic Life' in J. M. Brown (ed.), *Scottish Society in the Fifteenth Century* (London, 1977), points out the limitations of the Scottish economy in the fifteenth century; J. Brown, 'The Social, Political and Economic Influences of the Edinburgh Merchant Elite, 1600–38' (University of Edinburgh Ph.D., 1985), 108–10.

5. Guy, 'Thesis', 10, 20, 72, 77, 93, 97, 170, figs. 1A, 1D, 3.1A, 3.5A, 4.1A, 4.5A, 4.9A for all information.

6. Brown, 'Thesis', 12–15.

7. Ibid., 27. It has been argued that there were 600 merchants in Edinburgh in 1600 but this figure is far too high. See J. McMillan 'A Study of the Edinburgh Business Community and Its Economic Activities, 1600–1680' (University of Edinburgh Ph.D., 1984), 34, 38. It has been suggested that there were no more than 120 overseas traders in Edinburgh in 1583; see M. Lynch, *Edinburgh and the Reformation* (Edinburgh, 1981), 10, 51–2.

8. Ibid., 50; Brown, 'Thesis', 24–5, 112.

9. McMillan, 'Thesis', 114, guesses there were 170 overseas traders in the 1620s.

10. D. Macniven, 'Merchant and Trader in Early Seventeenth-Century Aberdeen' (Univeristy of Aberdeen M.Litt., 1977), 134.

11. Smout, 'Glasgow merchant community', 61–2; Smout, 'Development and enterprise of Glasgow', 195.

12. See Stevenson, Chapter 8, this volume; see also R. Baillie, *The Letters and Journals*, ed. D. Laing (Bannatyne Club, 1841–2), iii, 98.

13. Brown, 'Thesis', 362–4.

14. Ibid., 364.

15. Ibid., 21–2.

16. Ibid., 442–544, for a description of the merchants involved and their connections.

17. Ibid. See also SRO, E71/29/5, 6, 7, 8, 9, 11; E71/30/30 for Leith Customs Records.

18. Brown, 'Thesis', 424–37.

19. Ibid., 114–16, 118–27; Macniven, 'Thesis', 279.
20. Brown, 'Thesis', 138–68.
21. Ibid., 176; M. M. Postan, *Medieval Trade and Society* (Cambridge, 1973), 65–71; J. N. Ball, *Merchants and Merchandise: The Expansion of Trade in Europe 1500–1630* (London, 1977), 24; D. C. Coleman, *The Economy of England, 1450–1750* (Oxford, 1978), 53, 58–9, for a discussion of forms of partnerships.
22. M. H. B. Sanderson, 'The Edinburgh merchants in society, 1570–1603: the evidence of their testaments' in I. B. Cowan and D. Shaw (eds.), *The Renaissance and Reformation in Scotland* (Edinburgh, 1983), 190–5.
23. Macniven, 'Thesis', 241. W. Coutts, 'Social and Economic History of the Commissariot of Dumfries from 1600–1665 as Disclosed by the Register of Testaments' (University of Edinburgh M.Litt., 1982), 94, also states that partnerships were of a temporary nature.
24. SRO, E71/29/7, 14 Aug., 12 Sept. 1622.
25. SRO, E71/29/6, 9 June 1612.
26. SRO, E71/29/7, 16 July 1622. Trotter is not stated as having been involved.
27. SRO, E71/29/7, 6 May 1622.
28. SRO, E71/29/7, 26 June, 5, 10, 17, 29 Aug. 1622. That same month Monteath also imported stock with John Sinclair, as did Brown (SRO, E71/29/7, 12, 14 Aug. 1622).
29. SRO, E71/29/8, 22 Mar., 24 May, 13 June 1623; E71/29/11, 29 Sept. 1628.
30. SRO, E71/29/7, 2 July 1622.
31. SRO, E71/29/7, 12 Aug. 1622; E71/29/8, 7 Mar., 4, 24 Apr., 26 June, 8, 29 Aug., 17, 18 Sept. 1623.
32. SRO, E71/29/7, 13, 21 May, 16, 31 July, 14, 27 Aug. 1622; E71/29/8, 10 Nov., 26 Dec. 1622, 22 Mar., 25 Apr., 4 June, 4, 7, 13, 23 July, 13 Aug., 8 Sept. 1623.
33. SRO, E71/29/9, 19 Sept. 1627.
34. SRO, E71/29/9, 11 Nov., 6 Dec. 1626, 24 Apr., 19, 28 Sept. 1627; E71/29/11, 8 Apr., 12 May, 9 June, 24 July, 22, 29 Sept., 30 Oct. 1628.
35. *RPC*, xi, 431–2; xiii, 120–1; ECA, MS Council Recs., xiv, 28 Dec. 1627, 26 Dec. 1628.
36. Brown, 'Thesis', 183–5. Andrew Purves, William Wilkie and Andrew Ainslie also established partnerships.
37. Ibid.
38. Ibid., 189–99.
39. Coleman, *Economy of England*, 60; Postan, *Medieval Trade and Society*, 86–8; Macniven, 'Thesis', 242; McMillan, 'Thesis', 195; Lythe, *Economy of Scotland*, 125–7; W. G. Hoskins, 'The Elizabethan merchants of Exeter' in P. Clark (ed.), *The Early Modern Town* (London, 1976), 152; M. Reed, 'Economic structure and change in seventeenth-century Ipswich' in P. Clark (ed.), *Country Towns in Pre-industrial England* (Leicester, 1981), 117, 119.
40. Sanderson, 'Edinburgh merchants', mentions that only nine testaments out of over 200 examined reveal investment in ships.
41. Brown, 'Thesis', 190.

42. Edin. Tests., 28 Oct. 1619; 2 June 1649.
43. Edin. Tests., Agnes Graham, 21 Apr. 1612; Christian Voirie, 24 Dec. 1628; 6 July 1631.
44. Edin. Tests., 27 Mar. 1640; Margaret Philp, 29 May 1634; 27 Oct. 1621; Janet Morison, 14 Feb. 1609; 27 Oct. 1637.
45. Edin. Tests., 15 June 1642. Sixteen years earlier his wife had over £2,200 invested in ships, almost half of her inventory's value (Edin. Tests., 10 June 1626).
46. Edin. Tests., 15 June 1642.
47. Edin. Tests., 22 Mar. 1639; 30 Dec. 1640; 19 Mar. 1641; 27 May 1642.
48. SRO, GD 331/28/31.
49. Edin. Tests., 5 Apr. 1626; SRO, E71/29/7, 10 Apr. 1622.
50. SRO, E71/29/11, 4 Oct. 1628; Edin. Tests., 27 Mar 1640.
51. Brown, 'Thesis', 194.
52. *RPC*, xiii, 586–7; i (1625–7), 570.
53. ECA, MS Dean of Guild Court Recs. [DGCR], iv, 22 Feb. 1626. This sum amounted to over £1,000. In 1613 John Porterfield also sued the master of his ship for his profits (SRO, CS7/279, 12 Mar. 1613).
54. ECA, DGCR, iv, 10, 20 Feb. 1630. The profits amounted to 100 merks.
55. Edin. Tests., 30 Jan. 1633.
56. SRO, GD172/1755; Lythe, *Economy of Scotland*, 125, 127.
57. For example see ECA, DGCR, ii, 15 July 1618; ibid., iv, 23 June 1624. When Mr James Strachan chartered a vessel he was made responsible for the ship's company's payments while in port. These charges could be substantial as a vessel could carry at least twenty persons. See ECA, MS Council Recs., xv, 27 Sept., 6 Oct. 1637.
58. ECA, DGCR, iii, 7 Mar. 1621. William Cochrane insured his vessel in London in 1619.
59. Brown, 'Thesis', 198.
60. Sanderson, 'Edinburgh merchants', 192; Lythe, *Economy of Scotland*, 128; Brown, 'Thesis', 199–201.
61. Ibid., 201–3.
62. Ibid., 204–6; SRO, GD 18/2380/1/28; M. D. Rooseboom, *The Scottish Staple in the Netherlands* (The Hague, 1910), 165–6.
63. ECA, DGCR, iii, 22 May 1616.
64. SRO, GD 109/1411/1, 2; *Edin. Recs., 1604–26*, 295.
65. SRO, GD 30/1211/1, 2; NLS, Charters 5677; NLS, MS 83, no. 33; SRO, GD 18/2379/1/7.
66. ECA, DGCR, iv, 19 Mar. 1634; SRO, GD 18/2379/2/8, 38.
67. SRO, GD 18/2379/2/14; GD 18/2368/84, 110, 114, 141. Wood was in London in March 1636.
68. Brown, 'Thesis', 211.
69. SRO, GD 18/2358/7; GD 18/2361/fos. 29, 31, 33, 64; GD 18/2379/2/2, 3, 24, 25.
70. Brown, 'Thesis', 213.
71. SRO, GD 7/1/33/8, 9; GD 7/2/39.
72. SRO, GD 18/2358/3; GD 18/2361, described as the Account Book of John Clerk.

73. SRO, GD 18/2361/fos. 1, 3, 4, 12, 15, 22, 24, 27, 29, 30, 31, 33, 38, 40, 40a, 41, 42, 50, 51, 52, 55, 56, 57, 60, 64, 70, 72; GD 18/2368/40, 41.

74. Brown, 'Thesis', 215.

75. SRO, GD 18/2368/103.

76. SRO, GD 18/2368/110–11, 114.

77. SRO, GD 18/2380/2/2.

78. Brown, 'Thesis', 269.

79. Lythe, *Economy of Scotland*, 87; Sanderson, 'Edinburgh merchants' makes no mention of any investment in industry or manufacturing.

80. G. Marshall, *Presbyteries and Profits* (Oxford, 1982), 129, 131.

81. T. C. Smout, 'Leadmining in Scotland, 1650–1850' in P. L. Payne (ed.), *Studies in Scottish Business History* (London, 1967), 104; SRO, GD 237/216/4/12.

82. Edin. Tests., 15 Mar. 1621.

83. SRO, GD 237/216/4/12, 30.

84. *RPC*, xii, 335; Edin. Tests., 15 Mar. 1621.

85. For a discussion of the role played by lairds in this type of activity see T. M. Devine (ed.), *Lairds and Improvement in the Scotland of the Enlightenment* (Glasgow, 1978).

86. SRO, B22/8/9, 1 July 1606; SRO, CS7/283, 31 July 1613.

87. Brown, 'Thesis', 224–5.

88. C. A. Whatley, *That Important and Necessary Article; The Salt Industry and Its Trade in Fife and Tayside, c1570–1850* (Abertay Historical Society Publications, no. 22, 1984), 24–6.

89. Ibid., 26–7; Brown, 'Thesis', 117.

90. SRO, E71/29/6, 12 Dec. 1611; *Burghs. Conv. Recs.*, ii, 408; iii, 26–7, 34, 67, 72, 88–9; *RPC*, x, 436–9.

91. Brown, 'Thesis', 227; ECA, Compt of the General Gadger of Herring, 1620.

92. SRO, GD 331/28/3.

93. *Edin. Recs., 1593–1604*, 158.

94. Ibid., 213, 216.

95. Brown, 'Thesis, 228–9.

96. *Edin. Recs., 1604–26*, 172, 173, 174, 188, 189, 190, 191, 192, 193, 203, 209; ECA, DGCR, iii, 29 July 1618. James McMath, one of the original investors in 1598, was still involved.

97. ECA, MS Council Recs., xiv, 28 Nov. 1627, 28 Sept. 1632.

98. SRO, B22/8/26, 16 July, 11 Sept., 6 Nov. 1630; B22/8/29, 19 Feb. 1636, 6, 8, 12, 15, 18, 22 Dec. 1637; B22/8/30, 21, 28 July 1638; SRO, GD 331/28/3.

99. Brown, 'Thesis', 230.

100. Edin. Tests., 30 Jan. 1633.

101. Edin. Tests., 22 Mar. 1639, 29 June 1647; ECA, MS Council Recs., xv, 9 Feb. 1638.

102. Macniven, 'Thesis', 206–11.

103. Smout, 'Development and enterprise of Glasgow', 198–202; W. S. Shepherd, 'The Politics and Society of Glasgow, 1648–74' (University of Glasgow, Ph.D., 1978), 12, 323, 327, 335, 340, 344, 355; McMillan, 'Thesis', 114, 170.

104. *Edin. Recs., 1626–41*, xv.
105. See Chapter 8, this volume.
106. Brown, 'Thesis', 543–4.
107. Devine, 'The merchant class of the larger Scottish towns', 106–8.

7

Provincial Merchants and Society: A Study of Dumfries Based on the Registers of Testaments 1600–1665

Winifred Coutts

Dumfries, a royal burgh situated on the River Nith about nine miles upstream from the Solway Firth, was the seat of the commissariot court. The boundaries of the commissariot were based on the old diocese which had fifty-six parishes. It was bounded in the north by the main watershed of the Southern Uplands and in the south by the Solway. Hill-cattle and sheep could be raised in the mountains in the north whereas arable farming and the pasturing of dairy cattle were the occupations in the low-lying valleys of the Rivers Nith, Annan and Esk and on the stretches of land along the Firth.

The registers of testaments proved to be a rich store of information about the merchant community. Inventories of goods and gear and debts to and by the deceased were listed, each with its current market price (not an accounting price, since nearly contemporary prices varied). The wills which were quoted in the 'testaments testamentar' amplified the information gleaned from the inventories, and the habit in the earlier part of the period, of designating the occupation of executors, intromitters, overseers, tutors and cautioners was helpful in assessing the role played by merchants in contemporary society.

However, there are many years for which no registers are extant; earlier entries were more meticulously recorded than later ones; some moveable goods like hens and dogs were never mentioned. Furthermore, since the inventories dealt with moveable goods (though the wills often referred to the disposition of land and buildings) it appeared as if some merchants left moveable estates which were comparable in value to those of some landowners. While some merchants owned land, landowners were far wealthier

147

than the added value of their animals, grain and the debts owed to them — mainly in the form of rent — would suggest. If the value of land had been included, a different pattern of wealth would have emerged. In addition, the nature of the evidence gave undue weight to the presence of merchants and craftsmen burgesses. Ordinary craftsmen and servants were mentioned mainly when something was owed to them. Educated men are under-represented: only four notaries public appeared in the registers as leaving goods, although many more are known because they wrote wills for others;[1] schoolmasters were referred to but only one appeared in his own right;[2] many clerks wrote the register but only two merited entries.[3] Lastly, though there were some who technically should not have been included because their moveable estates were worth less than £10[4] and there were several whose debts exceeded their goods in value,[5] there was a substratum of which only a glimpse was caught — those with whom a cow or a sheep was grazed, presumably in return for wool or milk since no money was owed to them,[6] and below them were the nameless poor to whom many bequests were made.[7] Thus the registers do not allow estimates of population to be made and the entries refer only to a family in which a death had occurred. There were difficulties inherent in the statistics due to forisfamiliation, and children who had already been portioned were not recorded (though this was not invariable).[8]

A study of merchants cannot ignore the activities of other burgesses from a variety of occupations. Some clearly indulged in merchandising[9] and eight of them sold malt.[10] Some may have been craftsmen who had asserted their right to sell direct to the customer instead of through the merchant guild. Thus one sold barked leather and hides;[11] another sold bark and lime;[12] another sold herring.[13]

The growing of unconventional crops is one facet of the enterprise shown by merchants and burgesses. It reflects minds broadened by contact with a world whose horizons were much wider than those which bound the peasant farmers. Merchants and burgesses had a measure of economic independence which allowed them to experiment. Their livelihoods depended on their mercantile activities or their crafts, though most of these depended ultimately on the produce of the farms. They could afford to risk a little capital. The peasant farmer could not.

Both the possession of animals (not horses which could have been a means of transport) and the existence of grain 'sown' or 'lying upon the ground' provide indisputable evidence of farming. On this basis, thirty-six of the sixty-six individual merchants' estates within the town of Dumfries showed evidence of farming. Thirty had no agricultural interests,[14] which implies that they were buying their food. Supplies of grain were available in the stock of several merchants. A widow's crop of corns such as 'corn, bear, pease and wheat sown upon seven and a half acres' was sold by her executors 'to John McLean and George Rome, merchant burgesses of Dumfries, for the sum of 500 merks'[15] and Thomas McBriar, late bailie and merchant burgess of Dumfries had 'in the barn the teind of the Kirkland of Dumfries' bought by him 'from Mr. James Hamilton, minister at Dumfries, for the sum of 300 merks'.[16] Food could have been bought from merchants who had 'victuals' in their booths[17] or who 'furnished meat and drink'[18] — though this may have implied caterers. It is likely that milk was brought from indwellers who kept cows.

Some merchants clearly farmed within what was considered as the town of Dumfries. Thus entries specify 'with himself in this town, three "ky" with followers and a nag';[19] 'in his possession in Dumfries, one cow';[20] and 'with the defunct's spouse one cow with calf, one stot'.[21] When the inventories list a few animals but do not specify where they were kept, it is reasonable to assume that these were either within the town or on the outskirts. Some merchants looked after animals only. Thus one had two cows, two stirks and two sheep;[22] another had seven nolt and a nag;[23] another had three cows with followers and two horses;[24] another twelve sheep and a mare.[25] A cow provided milk, butter and cheese for domestic consumption or for selling and, later, meat and a hide; a sheep provided wool for domestic spinning or for selling and, later, meat, tallow and a skin. More merchants kept cows than kept sheep. None kept a bull in town. A few merchants concentrated on cultivation to the exclusion of animal husbandry. One had 'two acres sown in bear and pease'[26] while another had sown eleven pecks of bear and seven pecks of pease.[27] Others preferred mixed farming.[28]

Farming on a small scale probably took place in the 'yards' which are mentioned in wills[29] or for which mail (rent) was owed.[30] Those who farmed on a greater scale, owning sixteen nolt and twenty sheep,[31] or owning a cow, a calf, twenty-four sheep, a nag and the crop of five acres,[32] must have been farming on the outskirts. John Maxwell of Middlebie was owed by a merchant burgess for 'the mail and duty of certain acres of land lying within the burgh of

Dumfries'.[33] Twenty-eight of the thirty-six merchants with farming interests in Dumfries pursued at least some of these interests within or just outside the town. Many had a few animals in town but also others further afield. Thus a merchant with cows in Dumfries had sheep in Dalstepton 'with Thomas Grindlay there';[34] another kept two cows and a horse in Dumfries but had fifty-seven cattle and five oxen in the care of twenty-three different farmers and forty sheep with two other farmers.[35] Others had farming interests entirely outside Dumfries on a far greater scale. For instance, one had twenty-four cattle and six oxen 'pasturing with' eighteen farmers and thirteen sheep with a further two.[28]

Some merchants who farmed at some distance from Dumfries specialised in grain. Thus one merchant who grew oats, barley and pease owed 110 merks in rent in 1652 to the laird of Crawfurdton.[36] Others were 'mixed' farmers. William Lawrie owed 110 merks in 1640 for the mail of 'The Haughe' where he kept· cattle, sheep and horses and grew oats, barley, wheat and pease.[37] It is noticeable that whereas the peasant farmers were conservative, generally growing oats and bear and keeping cows and sheep, the merchant-farmers were often enterprising. Ten merchants cultivated pease[38] and of these three grew wheat.[35] With the exception of the merchant's crop in 'The Haughe'[37] all these crops were grown either inside Dumfries or so near to it that the place was not designated. As a leguminous plant, pease, with the nitrogen-fixing 'bacillus radicicola' in its root nodules, would have grown well and been seen to be beneficial to the soil as well as lending itself to cultivation in a 'yard'.

Eighteen of the non-merchant burgesses did no farming;[39] these included the notaries, the customer, smith, slater, two fleshers, and deacon of the wrights. The pattern was similar to that of the merchants, with only some keeping animals in Dumfries, others concentrating on arable. Thus one burgess had 'standing shorn upon the defunct's part of land of Baxter's Close, 30 thraves of oats, estimated to one boll oats'.[10] Others preferred mixed farming.[40] Like the merchants, some kept animals in Dumfries 'in the defunct's own hands' and others elsewhere with different farmers.[41] They were equally enterprising in the crops they grew 'upon the ground': four grew pease,[42] two grew wheat[43] and one grew rye.[42] Wheat 'in the barn in Dumfries'[44] and milled pease[45] could, however, have been bought.

Trading activities of both merchants and other burgesses are more easily deduced from the early entries. Those in the

Edinburgh registers list and price the inventories of merchant stock whereas those in the Dumfries registers generally estimate the value of the merchant wares in the booth and only some of the goods being traded can be ascertained from analysing debts. Here again most are referred to as 'wares' or 'merchandise'. The lists were taken from the merchants' account books[46] and it is in the nature of such evidence that more significance was attached to the name, occupation and amount owed than to the goods which were sold. Thus unspecified debts were owed to Thomas McBurnie by farmers, merchants, a tailor, chapman, saddler, mason, potter, horner, flesher, the commissary and a smith.[47] Nevertheless, among the unexplained debts there are some which provide an indication of what was traded. Thus the contents of a booth were estimated as worth 200 merks but the debts were for soap, frieze and plaids.[7]

Thirty-two of the merchants operating in Dumfries ran booths[34] and one had two.[31] The estimated value of their stock ranged from 800 merks[73] to a mere £40.[77] In only ten cases is there no evidence of what was sold.[48] From the remaining twenty-two booths and one 'shop',[49] it is clear that most functioned as general merchants, selling a wide range of raw materials like iron, hemp, lint, wood, manufactures like belts, jewellery, haberdashery and spoons and commodities like salt;[21] or iron, salt, alum, haberdashery and bonnets;[47] or brimstone, dyes, linen, bonnets, haberdashery, leather sheaths for knives;[50] or iron, honey, sack, cloth, weaving cards, scythes, books, spoons,[51] hemp, lint, paper, parchment, files, twine, arrows, fabrics, bonnets, gloves, needles and thread;[52] or timber, wood, linen and skins.[34] Some sold cramery — small wares like cards, tobacco and needles.[53] Sixteen merchants sold cloth and seven sold iron in their booths. A few sold 'victual'[17] or, more specifically, butter and cheese.[19] Even a chapman, who would not have belonged to the merchant guild, had a range of stock, valued at £80, which included linen cloth, belts, girths, saddles, buckles, thread and thimbles.[78] There was, however, evidence of specialisation in the stock of skins to the value of £1,000 and hides to the value of £200 in one Dumfries merchant's stock[54] and in the enormous quantity of linen (amounting to some £720 in value) which Matthew Forsyth dealt in, although not to the exclusion of other wares.[52] These clearly formed the basis of trade beyond the locality but the merchant who dealt in grain[29] must have been providing for the indwellers of the town who did not grow their own.

A variety of commodities, grain or animals can be used to demonstrate how little inflation took place over the period as a whole as the analysis in Table 7.1 shows:

Table 7.1: Prices of animals, oats and barley, 1600–62

	Cow	Ox	Sheep	Horse	Oats per boll	Barley per boll
1600	£8	£10	£1.1/3	£20	£6	£10
1609	£10	20m	£2	20m	£10–£6	£12–£10
1624	£15–£8	20m	£2–£1.1/3	20m–10m	£6–10m	£13–10
1630	£12–£8	20m	£2–£1.2/3	30m–10m	£5	£13–£10
1638	25m–20m	16m–10m	£2	£30–20m	20m–£10	£16–20m
1643	£12	£16–20m	£2–£1.2/3	£40–£20	£16–12m	20m
1656	£13.1/3–£8	£10	£3.1/3–£1.1/2	£30–20m	£20–£7	£16–£12
1659	£12–£10	£18–£10	2m	40m–20m	£12–£8	£10–£8
1662	£16–£12	£14	£2–£1.1/2	£40–£20	£10–£8	£20–£10

Source: SRO, Dumfries and Edinburgh Commissary Court Records.

The fluctuations in prices found within a year, which doubtless reflected the quality of the harvest, were more significant than variations over a longer period. There was a slight upward movement in the price of cattle but no significant price inflation. It is difficult to find goods for which quality and prices are both given but linen cost 13s 4d an ell in 1601,[55] 1607,[56] and 1658;[25] blue bonnets cost 13s 4d in 1605[50] and 16s in 1657;[57] a scythe cost 28s in 1626,[58] 1630,[59] 1638[60] and 1640;[51] iron cost 30s a stone in 1607[21] and 36s in 1627,[61] with the price variation perhaps reflecting quality.

Inventories of the booths and debts owed show that the merchants provided for the needs of rural farming, stocking reaping hooks at 5s each;[59] scythes at 28s;[60] soap at £3 4s a stone[62] and tar at 16s the pint[62] for cleaning the 'laid' wool, the sheep's wool which had been smeared with tar and butter as a winter protection;[7] stirrup irons at 5s the pair,[52] stirrup leathers at 8s 8d the pair,[52] bridles at 6s,[52] bridle bits at 2s 6d[52] and girthing straps at 6s 8d the ell,[52] and twine at 10s the ounce.[52]

They sold cloth for everyday wear — linen,[34] tweed,[63] London cloth,[64] Holland cloth,[65] Yorkshire cloth[64] and kelt,[64] harden,[56] Dundee 'gray',[52] frieze,[56] plaiding,[57] walked cloth,[23] drugget,[21] fustian;[64] finer fabrics like dornick,[21] steming,[57] English shirting,[64] English cotton[52] and lawn;[21] stiffening like buckram;[21] luxury fabrics like Spanish taffeta,[64] bombasine,[21] Ypres grosgrain,[65] velvet[21] and raw silk.[65] These were only specified in the earlier entries. Later entries rarely mention specific fabrics other than linen.[25] Thus only the prices of linen can be compared. In 1611 an ell cost 13s 4d;[56] in 1657 the stock of 400 ells was worth £266 13s 4d[56] — still one merk per ell. Most dealers in cloth also dealt in haberdashery — selling buttons;[64] silk buttons at 16s the gross,[52] tartan silk buttons;[65] needles at 4s the dozen[52] and pins on paper at 6s 8d each;[52] thread, white stitching,[64] embroidery silks at 26s the ounce;[47] laces;[57] decorating passments of silk,[50] pearling,[58] lace,[50] satin,[65] velvet[65] and fringes of gold sold by weight.[21]

Salt for the preservation of meat and fish was sold at £6 for a hogshead[21] or in barrels at 30s;[47] oil cost 5 merks a gallon[50] and vinegar was available at £12 for a barrel;[52] mace cost 10s an ounce;[65] ginger was 12s for a pound.[65] Herring[34] was sold but all references are to partly paid debts so it cannot be priced. Sugar cost 32s a pound,[68] an unspecified amount of honey cost £5 5s[9] and an unknown amount of prunes, 20s.[9] Curiously there is only one reference to wine. A minister owed 14s for sack.[51] Grain was widely available at varying prices.[69] Writing materials could be bought — parchment skins at 5s each;[52] wax for seals at 20s the pound;[65] pens and ink-horns at 2s 6d each[52] and paper at 25s the pound.[52]

Goods were sold for domestic industries — lint at prices varying between £6 the stone[34] and £3 for 'worst lint';[21] Flanders hemp at 40s for a dozen[52] (implying that it was packed in bundles) or at £3 the stone;[21] weaving cards at 18s the pair.[52] Dyes like red-violet orchardlitt cost £3 the stone;[50] red madder, 40s the stone;[50] an unknown amount of medhop, 35s.[56] Leather laces and points were available, though it is not clear how much was sold for 20s.[57] Files cost 3s 4d each[52] and nails, 12s for a hundred.[52] Malt sold at £20 the boll.[34] Fir deals sold at 20s[21] or 10s each,[34] depending on size or quality. Alum could be bought at 4s 2d the pound;[70] brimstone at 30s the pound.[50] Tallow cost 40s the stone.[56] Lead prices are unknown but prices for iron varied. Swedish and Danish iron could cost 30s a stone[21] although some Swedish iron was cheaper at 24s the stone.[65] Pewter was 10s[55] or 12s for a pound;[52] copper, curiously, was £3 for a dozen,[52] implying that it was transported in bars or blocks, and lead sold at 24s the stone.[52] 'Broken' silver was valued at 52s the ounce.[52] Household goods like candlesticks were also sold by weight at 6s 8d per pound[65] — though the metal was not specified; a knife could cost 20s;[66] a 'hanging' lock 24s;[66] a pan 55s[66] and a roasting jack, £10.[66] An unknown number of green horn spoons cost £12[66] but silver spoons were sold by weight.[21]

Not all merchants, however, operated from booths. Forty carried on their commercial activities presumably from their homes since only two had chambers, one in Edinburgh,[65] the other in Dumfries.[60] Several clearly were dealers in skins[61] and hides[27] and others in cattle and sheep. As the many farmers with whom merchants grazed their animals do not appear as creditors, they evidently were not paid to look after their animals. Very occasionally they appear as debtors. Thus three of the twenty-five farmers with whom William Fareis[35] grazed his animals owed him money, one for the steelbow mail of sheep. Clearly, he was leasing the sheep on the understanding that the sheep would be returned to the merchant at the end of the lease. The other two farmers' debts were unexplained. Perhaps they were looking after the animals as a form of paying interest on an unpaid debt due to the merchant. If the farmer had no liquid capital, the merchant would at least be getting some return, as well as spreading his assets to avoid such risks as exposing all his stock to raiders. It is possible that the farmer may have pledged the animal in return for some goods purchased but not paid for. Alternatively the farmer may have looked after the animal in return for a guarantee that the merchant would buy his animal skins. There are many debts recorded — one specifically for skins — to William Farrie by other merchants, ranging from £283 to 112 merks, as well as two, of 100 merks and £107 respectively, by cordiners. These merchants thus controlled the supply both of animals and skins and acted as wholesalers to other merchants in Dumfries.

Others without booths functioned as general merchants,[7] concentrating mainly on cloth[23] or dealing in malt[28] or in tanning.[72] Matthew Forsyth seems to have acted as a wholesaler in linen to other merchants, being owed £572 8s 2d by five Dumfries merchants.[52] Nevertheless there are countless examples which cannot be interpreted as a wholesaler dealing with a retailer. Thus John Black merchant was owed for scythes by Martin Parker merchant;[51] James Tait merchant owed one merchant for cards, tobacco and needles and four others for 'merchandise'.[53] Chapmen too, bought their stock in trade from merchants. In all thirty-two chapmen, two tinkers and one traveller owed debts for wares to ten different merchants, buying lint,[56] linen,[52] 'medhop' dye,[56] belts, girths, saddles, buckles, thread, thimbles,[78] gloves[60] and plaids.[52]

The bulk of trade was wholly local, selling to indwellers in Dumfries and the nearby villages. Some merchants ventured further afield to Edinburgh and thence to the Low Countries and France, or west to Ireland and south to England. Most of the evidence for trade with Edinburgh occurs, however, in the period before 1610 and was connected with the trade abroad in skins and cloth. There are few details of how commodities were transported to and from the capital but certainly cows were driven up. Thus Michael Dougal, merchant in Sanquhar, was owed by Lyon Thomson in Musselburgh for 'slaughter ky' and he was owed debts by two 'nolt drivers'.[79] There is no evidence of which routes were followed, though communications between north and south were along the broad valleys of Nithsdale and Annandale and along the narrow valleys of Eskdale and Ewes.

The scale and the range of trade between Dumfries and the continent was typical of a small provincial town. In 1600, John Kirkpatrick had in the hands of his factor in Veere, 1,050 exported sheep skins valued at £15 12s 8d per score and a further 400 at £6 5s per score. In his chamber in Edinburgh there were a further 300 sheep skins at £13 the score and in his loft in Dumfries 540 sheep skins at £16 the score. Doubtless the different pricing largely reflects the quality but the difference in price between the skins in Edinburgh and Veere probably reflected the costs of transport. In his booth in Dumfries were found the articles which had been imported — fabrics like Ypres grosgrain, fustian, bombasine, taffeta, silk, Holland cloth, silk threads and buttons, tallow, wax, brimstone, alum, Swedish iron and spices like ginger and mace.[65]

Much the same impression can be gathered from the testament of William Irving who, at the time of his wife's death in 1607, had in his loft in Edinburgh 760 sheep skins 'of the best sort' at £100 per hundred; 650 skins of poorer quality destined for France at £40 the hundred; 260 goat skins at £10 the score; two webs of walked cloth and twenty ounces of 'broken' silver at 52s the ounce. In his cellar were piled ten daker (groups of ten) of hides at £40 the daker, seven otter skins at £3 10s each, five tod (fox) skins at 40s each and twenty-one fowmart (polecat) worth £6. In Dieppe, in the hands of the factor Thomas Foulis, there were 1,900 francs, 1,000 of which had been 'sold' to Harry Hope, an Edinburgh merchant. In the hands of James Maill, factor to Matthew Puill burgess of Edinburgh, there were 1,354 ells of kersey cloth at 16s 8d the ell. By the time of his own death two months later it is clear that he had omitted to declare his interests in Veere at the time of his wife's death. He had £1,500 in cash with his factor in Dieppe and a further £1,000 in Veere. There were goods imported from the Low Countries in his loft in Dumfries — forty-seven stones of hemp at £3 the stone and fourteen stone of lint 'of the best sort' at £5 the stone and five and a half stones of lint 'of the worst sort' at £3 the stone. Goods from both the Low Countries and France were for sale in his booth — raw materials like hemp and lint, Danish and Swedish iron, each costing 30s a stone, and fir deals at 20s each; fabrics — grosgrain, figured velvet, fine dornick, lawn, buckram; silver belts, bracelets, spoons and a toothpick, gold tablets and rings; and foods like great salt, presumably from La Rochelle at £6 for a hogshead and sugar at two merks for a pound.[81]

The extent of the trade which passed through the hands of Edinburgh merchants is difficult to assess but can be seen in the debts owed by Edinburgh burgesses to Dumfries merchants. At the time of his wife's death, William Irving was owed £800 by Patrick Primrose, £375 by Harry Hope and 80 merks by James Rae, all burgesses in Edinburgh.[21] He himself owed Patrick Ellis, burgess in Edinburgh, £36 for iron.[81] William Williamson of Dumfries was owed £290 by Patrick Primrose while he himself owed James Thomson, merchant in Edinburgh, £180 for lint and Nicol Edgar, merchant in Edinburgh, £600 'of borrowed money'.[56] Three Edinburgh burgesses owed debts to Matthew Forsyth, merchant in Dumfries.[52] It is clear that Edinburgh burgesses acted as middlemen for Dumfries merchants in a network of trade which extended from England to the Low Countries and France. It involved the exporting of the raw materials, skins — in which Scotland had comparative advantage — and the importing of a wide range of commodities: manufactured cloth like Spanish taffeta,[64] foods like salt,[47] oil, vinegar,[52] spices,[65] chemicals like alum,[47] brimstone and dyes,[50] raw materials like iron and pewter,[55] and large quantities of hemp and lint.[56] The pattern is echoed in the trade of Michael Dougal, merchant in Sanquhar (the only other town in the commissariot with non-local trade). He had a store of 700 skins in Sanquhar and owed William Carruthers, burgess of Edinburgh, £29 for hemp, lint and iron and Gavin Carmichael, merchant of Edinburgh, £9 16s for iron.[79] The commodities which passed in both directions — usually through Edinburgh — in the overseas trade were extensive in range, if modest in volume. They indicate a taste for minor luxuries as well as the predictable demands of a market town with an agricultural hinterland devoted to mixed farming. Dumfries, despite its distance from east-coast ports, still provides in the early seventeenth century a typical profile of Scottish overseas trade of the period, still largely based on the North Sea routes — with one surprising omission. There is no evidence in the commissariot record for the wine trade, other than a single reference to a debt for sack.[61]

Trade with the Low Countries clearly continued after 1610, but evidence for it is less detailed. Thomas McMullen had sheep skins in Flanders worth 600 merks in 1627,[38] and James Maxwell also had sheep skins in Flanders at an estimated worth of 1,000 merks in 1629;[31] in 1638 Thomas Goldie, merchant in Dumfries, was owed 'by Robert Grierson, factor in Flanders, conform to his missive, £117 16s Flemish, extending in Scots to 1,178 merks';[34] also in 1638 Hugh Costein, merchant in Dumfries, had an unspecified amount of Flemish money in his booth.[82] Thereafter, the foreign trade was disrupted by the Wars of the Covenant.

There was an upsurge in unpaid and unspecified debts owed by Dumfries merchants to Edinburgh ones between 1637 and 1641. For example Thomas Armstrong, merchant in Edinburgh, was owed a total of £391 by four Dumfries merchants;[82, 83, 84] in 1640, William Smetoune, merchant in Leith, was owed 300 merks by bond;[51] in 1641, James Ramsay, merchant in Edinburgh, was owed £200 by David Frissell of Dumfries.[46] There was no corresponding indebtedness to merchants in Dumfries by merchants in Edinburgh, which suggests that Dumfries merchants were continuing to get goods from Edinburgh but were doing so as a simple transaction, not as part of a two-way trade passing through Edinburgh as an entrepôt. The trade in skins, however, may have been following a different pattern. Certainly James Maxwell, who had skins to the value of 1,000 merks in Flanders in 1629, owned the third part of a boat,[31] though this does not necessarily mean that it sailed from Dumfries.

There is evidence of a specific and limited pattern of trade with England, for a surprisingly large amount of it was carried not by sea but by packhorse overland, even by Edinburgh merchants.[85] The main elements involving Dumfries in the early years of the seventeenth century lay in skins and cloth, although by 1640, shortly before the trade ground to a halt, it had begun to include animals. Much of the evidence is fairly vague. In 1600 a chapman traveller in England was owed £248 by John Kirkpatrick, a Dumfries merchant.[65] Most Dumfries merchants dealt in cloth, like Matthew McBurnie, who had Yorkshire cloth in stock in 1603.[70] Others dealt in grain; in 1629 two Englishmen bought corn to the value of £120 Scots from John Carlisle.[31] A widow claimed 'her proper part and portion' of debts owed to her dead husband in England and Scotland in 1639; they included debts for oxen and mares owed by farmers in Derby, Peterborough and Norfolk as well as near Dumfries itself.[20] The fullest evidence of the nature of the two-way trade with England comes again in the testament of William Irving, who died in 1607. He was trading English kersey in Dieppe; he was owed 16s sterling (clearly by an Englishman); he owed £48 sterling to William Mathew, Englishman, and £3 sterling to John Rume for sheep skins bought from them 'of which one part received and another part in their hands'; he was selling English cloth locally, as debts to him in Scots currency show, as well as soap and unspecified goods to Englishmen such as John Riddick in Preston, as debts expressed in sterling prove; he was using a merchant in Cockermouth as a middleman, owing him £10 sterling for English wares; his trade extended to Lancashire where he owed debts to two merchants in sterling and owed two 'clothears' in Wakefield £9 and £12 sterling; he even had a stock of ready money of £50 sterling.[56] If trade with England was well established and diversifying by 1640, it seems to have ground to a halt in the 1640s. There is little evidence that what has been called the 'shot-gun common market'[56] of 1654 to 1660 had much effect in restimulating trade but few merchants in fact left testaments in that period and the testaments dative are badly recorded.

There is little evidence of trade with Ireland, but this is not surprising: even in the eighteenth century the bulk of the burgh's overseas trade was concentrated elsewhere, except for imported horses and re-exported tobacco.[87] There are references to bad debts by people 'now in Ireland'; Hugh Costein was owed £32 'by William Mure, sometime in Cumbria, now in Ireland';[54] Mungo Geddes was owed £12 by a merchant in Mosryne, in Ireland, for green horn spoons and there was an unexplained debt amounting to £4 sterling owed to him by Robert Croydie in Ireland.[66] It is, however, possible that other unspecified debts which were expressed in sterling could have involved trade with Ireland.

The wealth of merchants who traded overseas or in England far surpassed that of the local traders. The wealthiest overseas merchant had free gear (moveable assets) worth £9,324 in 1607[21] and the wealthiest trader with England had assets of £8,651 in 1639.[20] Thirteen of the sixty-six recorded merchants had moveable estates worth more than £1,000 — in marked contrast to the remainder of Dumfries burgesses, whose activities, even if they indulged in merchandising, were wholly localised. Only one estate of a non-merchant exceeded £1,000 — that of a maltman who left £1,024 in 1609.[88]

Some merchants — but no other Dumfries burgesses — formed partnerships in an attempt to increase the initial capital available and to spread risks. There is evidence of such partnerships in animal farming as well as in trading ventures, though in south-west Scotland in the seventeenth century the two were so inextricably linked that partnerships involving the possession of animals were clearly formed with trade in view. William Irving was in a partnership of four, owing a quarter of '425 beasts pasturing upon the Borders'. His partners were not obvious relatives, although two were either father and son or brothers. Within this partnership there was a further partnership of two so that William Irving owned only half of a horse, a mare, two cows and two oxen. Although not necessarily permanent, this partnership of two lasted from 1636 to the time of his death in 1639. It seems to have been a formal agreement since his widow claimed half of the debts owed to her husband and his partner 'conform to a subscribed account made between them.' A partnership involving four had been made concurrently in 1636, involving three in 1637 and four in 1638. The members of the partnership varied. It made for complicated accounting but the clerk declared that 'after just and due calculations' the debts owed to him 'de claro' came to £3,977.19s.4d.[20] The temporary nature of partnerships is further confirmed by the debt of 100 merks to Mungo Geddes, merchant burgess of Dumfries, by James Horner, also a merchant 'resting of an account when they were lawfeirs' (lawful partners).[66] These arrangements were simple joint ventures in farming; if there were four partners credits and debits were divided into four. There were no examples in which one partner would appear to have contributed less than another and been proportionally liable.

It was in ventures upon the high seas that partnerships were particularly advisable. The capital outlay on and maintenance of a boat was prohibitively high, even for the merchant princes of Edinburgh, and the risks of a cargo at sea great. James Maxwell, who had skins in Flanders worth 1,000 merks in 1629, owned 'the third part of a bark and furniture thereof estimated to 300 merks'.[31] This implies that an estimate — conservative since quot was to be paid on it — of the value of a used trading vessel was 900 merks.

However the partnerships could also involve only the goods which were being traded. Thus William Irving, merchant in Dumfries, was in partnership with Matthew Puill, merchant in Edinburgh, over two consignments of kersey cloth amounting to 1,354 ells which were exported to Dieppe; William Irving's share was 677 ells.[21] A debt refers to £4 10s owed by Matthew Puill which

William Irving paid for him 'for the custom of Keithlaw claith'.[81] This is likely to have been Keighley, the woollen manufacturing town in Yorkshire. If so, William Irving was bringing to the partnership the benefit of his trading contracts in northern England; he had others in Wakefield. He in turn was able to use the services of Puill's own factor in Dieppe.

Town and country were intimately linked through the market place of Dumfries and the relationship between the two was, from the evidence of the commissariot record, subtly changing by the second quarter of the seventeenth century. Up until about 1627 many peasant farmers paid their dues in kind. The monetary value is always given so it must be borne in mind that the records may simply reflect the traditional way of expressing the dues. After 1627, however, the majority paid in money. The trend suggests a transition taking place from a traditional agricultural economy in which money was far less important than land, to an economy in which money transactions played a significant part.

The initial stimulus had clearly come from the activities of the merchants. Overseas trade had obviously flourished in the later years of the sixteenth century. The Edinburgh registers afford ample proof of the existence of enterprising men in Dumfries who were prepared to take risks — preferably shared — in the pursuit of profit, using the surplus products of the rural economy. They were prepared to supply the raw materials (skins) and manufactured materials (cloth) for which there was a demand in the Low Countries and in France. They could not have done this without the general improvement in Scottish agriculture suggested by the fall in grain imports from the Baltic.[89] Higher productivity brought a surplus. Nor could they have traded without the stability given by the Anglo-Scottish peace and the personal union which meant that the Borders increasingly became a reliable route for trading traffic. Accordingly under conditions very like a customs union, English woollen cloth was brought north[70] and Scottish linen and animals were traded south.[20]

It was the merchants who made money through their trade in France, the Low Countries and England who injected liquid capital into the Dumfries economy. Some of it was invested, on death, into the family itself: William Williamson stipulated that his daughter's share of his estate 'should be put to good avail with the profit thereof' for her eventual dowry.[56] Whatever form the investment of his daughter's capital took — whether in cattle, a house which could be rented out, land or a wadset on land or in money lent at interest — money was continuing to circulate. It also circulated as part of the normal process of trade. Manufactured goods like luxury fabrics and groceries like spices, prunes, oil and vinegar were largely bought by merchants' families or by local lairds on credit. Much of the raw materials, like the fir deals from the Baltic, would have been used in house building. The countless debts owed to merchants by farmers for iron suggests that local smiths did not have the capital to buy their supplies direct; they earned a return for their labour but not a margin of profit on the raw materials they used.

Economic horizons were still limited, for merchants as well as for craftsmen, even if there was a certain stimulus provided by them to the economy, both of the town and the countryside which surrounded it. The merchants' investment in farming was strictly limited in scope. There is no evidence that they sought calculated improvement of agricultural methods, although they did experiment to some degree with growing different crops. Nor is there evidence of the industrial production of linen from all the lint imported from the Low Countries or of any clear link — as had certainly developed between Aberdeen's merchants and the rural hinterland — with rural cottage industries.[90]

The bulk of merchant surplus capital in Dumfries was directed, not towards systematic investment, but into the provision of credit, in the form both of money and goods. Most debts to merchants were a simple extension of credit for specific or unexplained wares, but there are clear examples of the borrowing of money, such as that 'by John Scot beltmaker £21 8s of borrowed money and partly for the price of certain wares'.[61] More sophisticated arrangements existed with bonds[23] and obligations,[21] when cautioners were called for,[58] or when annual rent was owed, particularly over a period of years, as 'by the goodmen of Cliftoune, younger and older, £100 conform to their obligation with five years' annual rent thereof, estimated to £50'.[54] Although some may have represented more formal means of recording a debt for goods, many must have taken the form of a document drawn up in confirmation of money lent. This is most likely when the sums of money were in round figures, like the 800 merks owed by the laird of Dalbeattie 'conform to his obligation'.[54] Money was lent in large amounts both by merchants to merchants or other burgesses of Dumfries, and by craftsmen to merchants. Membership of the merchant guild or a craft incorporation, or even repeated business transactions between lenders and borrowers, would have provided a certain guarantee against risk. Hugh Costeine, merchant, was owed a total of 800 merks by four different local merchants and himself owed 400 merks to a merchant in Edinburgh.[83] There is no evidence of bills of exchange being used in the settlement of debts between merchants of Dumfries and the capital but Thomas McMullen of Dumfries did owe a local merchant £200 for iron 'conform to my merchant ticket made to him',[38] which probably represented an uncleared debt which had originally been recorded with the merchant guild.

Relatively few merchants left 'ready money', perhaps because many retailers of goods saw fit to remove their supply before it was assessed for quot. Only two merchant testaments reveal large reserves of cash — of 3,000[18] and 6,000 merks.[20] Few Dumfries merchants were thus in a position to lend large sums yet there is evidence that several specialised in money lending — as parliament suspected in 1625, when it condemned merchants who made vast profits in trade which they switched to usury.[91] This can be surmised when debts for wares were small but debts by obligation as great as 1,600 merks,[24] or where the value of goods in a booth was £40 but the debts owed to the merchant included round sums and amounted to over £1,460.[19] It is all the more likely when there is no mention of goods but where there was 3,000 merks of liquid assets and £714 of debts described as 'borrowed money' or by bond; this merchant himself owed 500 merks to two heritors and a further 300 merks to the wife of a minister, who may have advanced capital to him.[18] Alternatively, a merchant might move back and forth between concentrating on money lending or trading, as is revealed in the inventories of the two wives of Hugh Costeine. In 1629 he had a stock of skins worth £1,000 and was owed 1,000 merks for wares; in 1637 his account book revealed £800 of debts for wares but over £2,513 of separately listed debts in round sums. When he died fifteen months later a complete turnover had taken place in the names of his debtors and in the balance of his assets, caused partly, no doubt, by the division of the estate which took place after his wife's death: he was owed 1,200 merks for wares and £1,666 for different debts in round sums.[82] There were other sources of credit as well; landowners lent money,[92] as did some craftsmen, although few rivalled the flesher who was owed a total in excess of £2,300[93] in 1663.

Several merchants — and a few other inhabitants of the burgh — enjoyed other sources of income, principally from the renting out of houses, chambers and booths. For example, John Spens collected rents from five different houses, one of them outside the town, at yearly rents ranging from £9 to £30. Some let out land within the burgh; Mungo Geddes was owed twenty merks and three pecks of pease as the unpaid part of the duty on ten roods of land[66] and Thomas Goldie charged five merks for the rent of a yard.[51] It generally seems to have been the case that lesser merchants rented their houses and booths from greater. For instance, John Black, whose assets amounted to £441, paid £18 for house rent, £16 for his booth and five merks for a yard.[51]

There is typically a great deal in testaments to reveal the lifestyle of the testators as well as the manner in which they left it. A successful merchant like William Irving, who had assets in excess of £8,651, spent 300 merks at the 'time of his sickness and upon his funeral'.[20] A more usual sum was £40 for a merchant and £20 for an ordinary burgess such as a maltman.[95] Many merchants could afford to employ a domestic servant, of either sex, but only some could afford more than one.[82] Craftsmen also had servants,[96] but most were probably employed in the craft rather than the home; one servant of a skinner was left his master's alum tub provided that he 'remove himself from his house'.[97] Some merchants had family ties with the landed classes,[15] others were related by marriage to ministers.[98] Merchants[99] and a few craftsmen[100] apprenticed their sons to Edinburgh merchants or to a craft there.[101] There were dynasties of merchants — McBurnies,[70] Goldies,[34] Corbets,[19] Sharps[37] — just as there were of craftsmen. There was much intermarriage between the two. The social fabric was held together by kin as well as by privilege.

The striking difference in standard of living lay not so much between wealthy merchants and craftsmen but between them and the poor of Dumfries. A prosperous merchant's wife had gowns, cloaks, ruffs, kerchiefs and coats.[75] A merchant's household could have ten coverings, two feather beds, four bolsters, three cods, five pairs of blankets and sheets, four stands of curtains, two pots, one pan, a mashing vat, two ale bowls, eight pewter plates and two chamber pots.[102] It was a modest household by the standards of the capital but it was clearly one which could, like that of Helen Henry, afford the customary legacy of £20 or so 'to be given to the kirk session for the supply of the poor and other pious uses'.[54]

Notes

All CC references are taken from SRO, Commissary Court Records; the CC5 series is of the Dumfries court and CC8 of Edinburgh.

   1. Robert Cunningham (CC8/8/44, 12 Dec. 1608); John Crichton (CC5/6/2, fo.86v); Robert Gibson (CC5/6/2, fo.127r): Robert Rowell (CC5/6/3, fo.110).
   2. John Thomson (CC5/6/1, fo.35v).
   3. John Tait (CC5/6/3, fo.31); John Young (CC5/6/1, fo.161r).
   4. William Gibson (CC5/6/2, fo.26r); Elizabeth Maxwell (CC5/6/3, fo.83).
   5. John Hunter (CC5/6/2, fo.41v); William Kennedy (CC5/6/1, fo.153r).
   6. James Porter (CC8/8/45, 5 Feb. 1610); Adam Turner (CC8/8/35, 20 July 1601).
   7. Marion Beck (CC5/6/2, fo.5v).
   8. Lawrence Corsane (CC5/6/3, fo.579); James Robson (CC5/6/2, fo.116v).
   9. James Copland (CC8/8/41, 2 Jan. 1606).
  10. Thomas Scott (CC8/8/38, 30 Jan. 1604).
  11. James Herron (CC8/8/37, 2 June 1603).
  12. John Morrison (CC8/8/38, 23 Feb. 1604).
  13. James McGowan (CC8/8/-, 26 Jan. 1653).
  14. James Burgess (CC5/6/2, fo.88r); James Martin (CC5/6/2, fo.15v).
  15. Christian Morrison (CC5/6/2, fo.30v).
  16. Thomas McBriar (CC5/6/2, fo.114v).
  17. John Blackstock (CC5/6/2, fo.74r).
  18. Thomas Glencorse (CC5/6/1, fo.106v).
  19. John Corbett (CC5/6/1, fo.223r).
  20. William Irving (CC5/6/2, fo.55r).
  21. Agnes Batie (CC8/8/43, 22 July 1607).
  22. Margaret Sproat (CC5/6/1, fo.62v).
  23. Herbert Johnston (CC5/6/1, fo.81r).
  24. Roger Kirkpatrick (CC5/6/1, fo.102v).
  25. Agnes Haistie (CC5/6/3, fo.462).
  26. John Ranyng (CC5/6/2, fo.43v).
  27. Isobel Brown (CC5/6/1, fo.203v).
  28. Gilbert MacLean (CC5/6/1, fo.75r).
  29. George Rigg (CC5/6/2, fo.1v).
  30. Isobel Crosbie (CC5/6/1, fo.74r).
  31. Janet Mulligan (CC5/6/1, fo.201v).
  32. Margaret Davidson (CC5/6/2, fo.31r).
  33. John Maxwell (CC5/6/2, fo.70v).
  34. Thomas Goldie (CC5/6/2, fo.19v).
  35. William Farrie (CC8/8/45, 26 May, 4 Aug. and 15 Nov. 1609).
  36. William McBurnie (CC5/6/3, fo.497).
  37. George Sharp (CC5/6/2, fo.64r).
  38. Catherine Cunningham (CC5/6/1, fo.139v).

39. Robert Johnston (CC8/8/35, 27 July 1601).
40. Janet Froude (CC5/6/1, fo.147r).
41. James Wilson (CC5/6/3, fo.637).
42. James Rigg (CC8/8/37, 27 Nov. 1602).
43. Janet Ferguson (CC8/8/42, 16 Jan. 1607).
44. William Shortrig (CC8/8/35, 2 April 1601, 14 Feb. 1604).
45. Archibald Rae (CC5/6/4, fo.9v).
46. David Frizzell (CC5/6/2, fo.91r).
47. Thomas McBurnie (CC8/8/38, 26 July 1603).
48. Janet Gibson (CC5/6/1, fo.221r).
49. David Mckilwayll, (CC5/6/4, fo.6v).
50. Janet Neilson (CC8/8/40, 1 Aug. 1605).
51. Christian MacLean (CC5/6/2, fo.73v).
52. Matthew Forsyth (CC8/8/45, 21 April 1609).
53. Bessie Taylor (CC5/6/1, fo.201r).
54. Helen Hendry (CC5/6/1, fo.192r).
55. William Gladstone (CC8/8/37, 14 May 1603).
56. Katherine Patesoun (CC8/8/44, 9 Nov. 1608).
57. Bessie Paterson (CC5/6/3, fo.314).
58. Margaret Beck (CC5/6/1, fo.143r).
59. Agnes Lawrie (CC5/6/1, fo.229v).
60. Robert Ferguson (CC5/6/2, fo.46v).
61. John Rae (CC5/6/1, fo.122v).
62. James Russell (CC5/6/3, fo.696).
63. Ninian Russell (CC5/6/1, fo.217v).
64. Jane Welsh (CC8/8/37, 5 Nov. 1602).
65. John Kirkpatrick (CC8/8/35, 8 Nov. 1600).
66. Mungo Geddes (CC5/6/1, fo.252v).
67. Peter Bigholme (CC8/8/35, 26 Nov. 1600).
68. James Russell (8 May 1656).
69. William Neilson (CC5/6/3, fo.602).
70. Thomas McBurnie (CC8/8/38, 26 July 1603).
71. Malie Kirkpatrick (CC8/8/35, 26 June 1600).
72. John Rammeis (CC8/8/35, 13 Dec. 1600).
73. David Graham (CC5/6/3, fo.307).
74. Adam Corbett (CC5/6/3, fo.666).
75. Margaret Spence (CC5/6/2, fo.112v).
76. Adam Clark (CC5/6/2, fo.77r).
77. Janet Thomson (CC5/6/3, fo.679).
78. James Glendinning (CC5/6/2, fo.16v).
79. Michael Dougall (CC8/8/41, 17 March 1606).
80. Janet McBurnie (CC5/6/1, fo.212r).
81. William Irving (CC8/8/44, 13 Oct. 1608).
82. Hugh Couston (CC5/6/2, fo.51v).
83. Janet Corbett (CC5/6/2, fo.9v).
84. George Irving (CC5/6/2, fo.11r).
85. J. Brown, 'The Social, Political and Economic Influences of the Edinburgh Merchant Elite, 1600–38' (Edinburgh Univ. Ph.D., 1985), 160, 169.
86. S. G. E. Lythe and J. Butt, *An Economic History of Scotland,*

1100–1939 (Edinburgh, 1975), 56.

87. L. E. Cochran, *Scottish Trade with Ireland in the Eighteenth Century* (Edinburgh, 1985), 79, 120, 150.

88. John Mulligan (CC8/8/45, 21 April 1609).

89. G. Donaldson, *Scotland: James V to James VII* (Edinburgh, 1965), 242.

90. Alexander Skene, in a pamphlet written in 1685, stressed the dependence of the burgh of Aberdeen on rural industry, especially for the manufacture of stockings and plaiding; see *Memorialls for the Government of Royall Burghs in Scotland* (Aberdeen, 1685), 94–7, 102–3.

91. *APS*, v, 39, 176b, 184a. 187a.

92. Robert Maxwell (CC5/6/3, fo.677).

93. John Wallace (CC5/6/3, fo.763).

94. John Spence (CC5/6/2, fo.34r).

95. Robert Furmont (CC5/6/2, fo.14v).

96. John McClauchrie (CC8/8/45, 21 April 1609).

97. Richard Knowes (CC8/8/37, 7 Aug. 1602).

98. Mr James Brown (CC5/6/2, fo.76r).

99. Thomas Maxwell (*Register of Edinburgh Apprentices, 1583–1666* (Scot. Rec. Soc., 1906), 9 April 1645).

100. John Murdo (ibid., 16 Oct. 1605).

101. Edward Rigg (ibid., 26 Dec. 1655).

102. John Richardson (CC5/6/3, fo.560).

8

The Burghs and the Scottish Revolution

David Stevenson

The noise of the town of Edinburgh's being joined to the supplicants, had such influence upon the boroughs, that whereas the most part of them had formerly lain by, very shortly after, all of them (Aberdeen only excepted) came into the cause; and indeed, being once engaged, turned the most furious of any; so that neither their own ministers, nor any other that disliked the course, could be in safety among them.[1]

Henry Guthry is not the most reliable of historians, but his comments on the part played by the burghs in the Scottish Revolution accord well with other evidence and neatly sum up some major aspects of the burghs' behaviour. The royal burghs of Scotland hesitated at first to involve themselves in defiance of the crown; they showed a strong tendency to follow the lead of Edinburgh; and once they joined the opposition to Charles I they did so with zeal. Moreover, the burghs tended to act in concert in public affairs rather than as separate units. They were used to deliberating on matters concerning their welfare in the Convention of Royal Burghs and to playing a role in national affairs as one of the three estates; once they joined the opposition to the king they formed a distinct burgh interest within the covenanting movement. In this the Scottish burghs present a major contrast to their English counterparts. In England borough representation in parliament was largely in the hands of the gentry, and thus its history in the civil war period was 'more a part of the history of the county community than a separate urban element in itself'.[2] English boroughs had few real representatives in parliament; moreover they lacked any form of national organisation, and were generally 'too intent on their single advancement, too unaccustomed to cooperation, to assume an independent or initiating part in matters of general political import', and therefore proved 'incapable of leadership in the kingdom's affairs'.[3] Not surprisingly, therefore, an excellent recent survey of borough reactions to the English civil war has nothing to say of national politics, concentrating exclusively on the isolated reactions of individual boroughs.[4]

English boroughs as such thus played no distinct part in national politics. By contrast, the Scottish burghs were strongly represented in central government. In parliament their commissioners (the great majority of whom were genuine merchant burgesses) formed one of the three estates. On the Committee of Estates, and other committees through which the convenanters ruled between sessions of parliament, all three estates had equal representation. The burgh commissioners were, moreover, well enough organised to make their presence as a distinct element in politics felt. They frequently met (as was traditional) in 'particular conventions' or more informal meetings before sessions of parliament to discuss what attitudes to take on behalf of the burghs when the three estates met.[5] Even after parliament assembled under the covenanters 'the several bodies' or three estates regularly met separately to agree on how to conduct themselves in the full parliament. There is an isolated reference to the 'speaker' for the burghs presenting the views of the estate to parliament, and announcements of this sort were evidently part of the routine of parliamentary business. Once burgh commissioners meeting by themselves had reached a majority decision, all the commissioners were expected to vote in parliament in accordance with this decision, even if they had originally opposed it. This insistence on burgh solidarity seems sometimes to have been limited to matters regarded as being of particular and specific interest to the burgh estate — such as trade regulation, burgh privileges and taxation — but on other occasions it seems to have been wider. In November 1640 burghs were instructed to elect as commissioners to parliament only men 'who will abyid consteintlie at all such conclusiounes as sall be maid be the most pairt of the burrowes'.[6] An act of the Convention of Royal Burghs passed in about 1646 confirmed this 'unanimous voting of the haill burghs' in parliament and evidently extended it to committees.[7]

Self-conscious and well organised as the burghs were, however, it cannot be said that the estate played any dominant role in the leadership of the covenanting movement at a national level. The burghs were determined to maintain their position as one of the three estates, and now the estates were the real rulers of the country this gave them a much greater say in government than previously, but they were at the same time willing to accept traditional social values so far as to be content that ultimate leadership of the covenanting movement, at least up to 1648, lay in the hands of the nobility. The burgh commissioners would give enthusiastic support to the movement, perhaps often more unanimous and heartfelt support than that of the other estates, but none the less they knew their place. Therefore burgess initiatives and protests at the national level tended to be limited to spheres in which they traditionally claimed special interests. Outside these spheres the voices of the burgess commissioners were seldom heard. None the less, their opinions were being quietly expressed through their votes, and, as will be seen, their votes could on occasion be crucial on major issues.

Docile as the burgh commissioners usually proved to be in accepting that leadership and initiative lay with their betters, it seems that the wholehearted enthusiasm of the burghs for the covenanting movement may have alarmed some of the more conservative covenanting leaders. In 1639 the nobles and shire commissioners demanded that, as part of a peace settlement with the king, they be authorised to hold annual conventions, like the burgesses.[8] Primarily, no doubt, this was an attempt to provide for some sort of continuing national organisation for all the estates, to keep an eye on the king once peace was made; but it also suggests a realisation that the burghs were much better organised, through their convention, than the other estates. The proposal came to nothing, but one of the constitutional innovations the covenanters did make served to reduce significantly the proportionate voting strength of the burghs in parliament. Up to 1640 though most shires sent two commissioners to parliament, each shire had only one vote. In 1640 the shires, newly declared a separate estate, demanded that each of their commissioners have a vote, which would have almost doubled their voting strength. Edinburgh town council resolved that this tended to 'the overthrow of thair estaitt' and ordered its commissioners to vote against the change, rising and leaving parliament rather than let it pass — and it was presumably intended that the other burgh commissioners would follow suit. In the end, however, the shire commissioners got their votes, the burghs being persuaded in 1641 to give way 'for love of peace, in so dangerous ane tyme' — any evidence of discord among the covenanters at so critical a time would have encouraged their enemies.[9]

One way of looking at this episode is simply to see it as a sign of the increasing role in national affairs aspired to by the lairds — an equivalent to their pushing their way into the Reformation parliament in 1560. But there must be more to it than this. Individual votes for shire commissioners meant a proportionate diminution of noble as well as burgess voting strength; yet for the reform to be passed in the face of burgess opposition the lairds must have had noble support. Why should the nobles act in so seemingly altruistic a way? A look at the membership of the June 1640 parliament helps provide an answer. Only thirty-six nobles were present, as royalist inclined nobles would not sit in a parliament held in defiance of the king, and twenty-three shires were represented. But there were fifty-two burgh commissioners.[10] On the old voting system in the unicameral parliament, the burgh estate was almost as strong as the other two combined. The burgesses, with their tradition of 'unanimous' voting, would need only a handful of nobles or lairds to join with them to outvote the other estates. The burgesses might as yet show no signs of exploiting their voting strength in order to usurp leadership of the covenanting movement, but in the longer term it might tempt them to develop such ambitions. On this interpretation the two estates representing landed wealth took fright and hastily contrived a way of increasing the landed interest's voting strength, by converting twenty-three shire votes into forty-three shire commissioner votes. The burghs reluctantly accepted this, perhaps seeing the strength of the argument that they had previously been over-represented. Yet they remained determined not to let their position in parliament slip any further, protesting vigorously at the stewartry of Kirkcudbright being represented separately from the shire of Wigtown, thus giving the lairds two extra votes.[11]

In this, the first clash of the burgesses with the other estates under the covenanters, the burghs had in the end to climb down. The same is true of two later occasions. In January 1644 when excise duties were imposed by the Convention of Estates there were disturbances in Edinburgh. Burntisland had instructed its commissioner 'na vayis to concent' but he had to report back that the burghs 'culd navayis' get the excise rejected.[12] Money was again the cause of a burgess protest in August 1649. Parliament ordered a reduction in interest rates from 8 per cent to 6 per cent per annum. This was evidently intended to go some way to compensate for increased taxation and heavy losses suffered through civil war, but may also indicate a distaste for usury on the part of the extreme kirk party regime then in power. Burgess reaction indicates that they saw themselves as net receivers, rather than payers, of interest. The burgh commissioners in parliament protested furiously. Sir James Stewart, provost of Edinburgh as well as the covenanters' chief financial official (holding the offices of Collector General and Commissary General), led the burgh protest and then walked out of parliament, followed by all the burgh commissioners except 'two or three obscure ones'.[13] Obviously they hoped this would prevent parliament passing the act and generally bring the regime to a standstill. But parliament proceeded without them. The burghs then threatened to extend their boycott to the Committee of Estates, which would govern the country when parliament adjourned, but again their bluff was called. Parliament suspended the rule that the presence of members of all three estates was necessary to form a committee quorum. When the committee began to meet and transact business without them, the burgesses hastened to take their seats rather than abandon their right to share in government.[14]

Thus the other estates were ready to put the burgh estate firmly in its place when this was thought necessary; but the fact that the burghs could not dominate parliament does not mean that their role was only nominal. On matters recognised as mainly concerning the burghs the other estates were evidently usually willing to let the burgesses have their way, not just their say. Moreover, though information about the pattern of factional allegiances in the estates is very limited, the evidence does serve to confirm Guthry's opinion that the burghs were 'the most furious', the most strongly committed to the convenanting movement, of the three estates. It was thus highly appropriate that the first national body to approve the National Covenant was the Convention of the Royal Burghs; its meeting at Stirling in August 1638 not only approved the covenant but ordered that no man be admitted a burgess or be sent as a burgh commissioner to the convention unless he signed the covenant.[15]

The only surviving figures to give details of a vote in parliament relate to the Lords of the Articles (the committee which prepared business for parliament) in 1639, when a crucial vote was taken on whether to refer proposals for parliamentary reform to the king or vote on them in the full parliament. The result was a victory for the more determined of the covenanters over moderates and royalists, and the result was strongly influenced by the burgess vote:[16]

	Refer to the king	Vote in parliament	Absent
Officers of State	4	0	0
Nobles	5	3	0
Shire commissioners	2	5	1
Burgh commissioners	1	6	1
Totals	12	14	2

In the Convention of Estates in 1643–4 the decision to accept the Solemn League and Covenant and intervene in the English Civil War had strong support from the burgesses. Henry Guthry again sourly commented 'The burghs were all cordially for them, none excepted, yea, they were more furious than any other corporations'.[17] In 1647 when the covenanting movement was splitting between the duke of Hamilton's faction, allied with moderate royalists, and the marquis of Argyll's faction which was backed by the kirk, most nobles in parliament supported Hamilton, and the lairds were evenly divided; but it was estimated that three-quarters of the burgesses voted for Argyll and the kirk.[18] By March 1648 Hamilton had won control of parliament in spite of burgess opposition and was pushing through the Engagement treaty with the king. Burgess resistence continued, but it was crumbling; Hamilton had well over three-quarters of the nobles, more than half the lairds and nearly half the burghs behind him. Thus the Engagement controversy had temporarily destroyed the unanimity of the burghs. It was said that it was 'especiallie the greater tounes' (Edinburgh, Perth, Dundee, Aberdeen, St Andrews, Linlithgow) that had swung round to back Hamilton,[19] so although most burghs still supported Argyll, the great majority of burgh wealth and population was behind Hamilton. The example of Edinburgh may well have been a major influence in leading many burghs to support the Engagement. The previous year Argyll had sought to get his own candidate elected provost of the burgh, but without success; a supporter of Hamilton was re-elected.[20] Certainly in 1648 Hamilton feared that burgh support for him might be weakening as the kirk came out in open opposition to the Engagement. Some burghs frequently changed their commissioners between sessions of parliament, but when parliament rose for a short recess in May 1648 the Engager majority forbade any such changes.[21]

Once the Engagers were overthrown and the kirk party seized power in September 1648, strong support for the latter emerged. The exclusion of Engagers from parliament increased the proportionate voting strength of the burgesses significantly, for the number of nobles present declined rapidly. In March 1648 the Engagers' parliament was attended by fifty-six nobles, forty-seven shire and forty-eight burgh commissioners. Under the kirk party in January 1649 the strengths of the estates were fourteen, forty-six, and fifty-one.[22] There seems no doubt, though voting figures are entirely lacking, that burgess support in parliament was now strongly in favour of the kirk party's relatively radical policies.[23] It also seems likely that many of the burgh commissioners who now sat in parliament were men of somewhat lower status and lesser wealth than their predecessors in covenanting parliaments, the older leaders of burgh oligarchies having been purged from power during the troubles.[24] But this suggestion is based on impressionistic evidence and detailed study of individual burghs would be necessary to prove the point conclusively. It is notable that a similar interpretation concerning the English boroughs, arguing that 'radicals' and 'social upstarts' came to power in the later 1640s, has recently been rejected; changes in power were largely matters of struggles between rival groups within the old burgh elites.[25]

There are also indications that under the kirk party the burghs were less ready to defer to Edinburgh than previously, the leadership of the capital having been descredited by its support for the disastrous Engagement. The stent roll of the burghs, which laid down the proportion of total taxation imposed on burghs to be paid by each one, dated back to 1612. Charles I had ordered that it be updated in 1635,[26] but nothing had been done. Resistance to change evidently came from Edinburgh, as the burgh recognised it was undervalued. By the 1612 roll Edinburgh paid 28.75 per cent of the tax burden of the burghs, but when the covenanters carried out valuations for the Tenth Penny in 1639–40 Edinburgh's share of the burghs' total rose to 32.7 per cent,[27] and it is tempting to see Edinburgh's influence behind the covenanters' subsequent return to the 1612 roll as a basis for taxation. But once the kirk party came to power parliament ordered the Convention of Royal Burghs, which was due to meet in July 1649, to revise the 1612 roll, as some burghs were heavily disstressed through it not being altered according to their 'Trade, estate and strength'. To ensure that action was taken, burghs which were overburdened were authorised to change the roll for themselves if the convention failed to act.[28] None the less, Edinburgh attempted to prevent change. Pretexts were found to persuade other burghs to consent to the convention being postponed, though the real reason was that Edinburgh 'feared for the stent roll'. The other burghs realised this, and quickly overthrew the decision to delay the convention.[29] 'Sundry of the burrowes had been long grudging that Edinburgh should bear so small a proportion of the common burden, judging that for their trade and their wealth, the one-half of the whole burrowes burden might be laid on them'. In practice the convention did not go so far as that; but the new 1649 stent roll it produced raised Edinburgh's share of burgh taxation to 36 per cent. 'This the Provost and Counsell of Edinburgh took in ane exceeding evill part, and stormed much at it, yet could not remeed it'.[30] It is tempting to see this disciplining of Edinburgh by the other burghs as a punishment for its support of the Engagement; the grievances over the stent roll might be old ones, but it was only in 1649 that something effective was done about them.

As the row over the stent roll indicates, the burghs on occasion squabbled among themselves, but generally they succeeded in presenting a fairly united front; from 1637 to the great royalist revival of 1650–1 this relative unity was used to support the covenanters; and even when this unity was temporarily broken in 1647–8 the split was over how best to advance the cause of the covenants.

How can the 'furious' support of the burghs for the covenanters be explained? Did the burghs have specific sectional grievances against Charles I to add to wider Scottish grievances? Some such sectional grievances can be identified, but it may be a mistake to look too hard for burgesses motives differing from those of other Scots. Burgesses doubtless shared in the general rising discontent at an absentee, anglicising king, determined to enforce his will without consultation or regard for vested interests or long-established beliefs and prejudices. In most burghs the relations of burgh council and kirk session were close, and fears about the king's ultimate intentions regarding religion were strong and genuine. Edinburgh emerged as a focus of opposition to the Five Articles of Perth and for the holding of conventicles in the last years of James VI's reign.[31] In the first year of his reign Charles I felt it necessary to intervene in the election of magistrates and council there, ordering that none be elected who were not willing to 'conforme themselffis to the ordour estaiblished in the churche'.[32] No direct connection between religious dissent in the burgh in the 1620s and the riots of July 1637 which began the troubles has been traced; but it would be surprising if no such connection existed.

In interfering in burgh elections Charles was doing no more than his father had often done in the past; none the less such actions were unpopular, leading burghs to worry about their liberties. In 1634 Charles again intervened in Edinburgh, nominating the provost and bailies.[33] His motives are unknown, but he had visited Scotland the previous year and had perhaps detected some lack of enthusiasm for his religious policies in Edinburgh as elsewhere. The only indication of any attempt to defy royal intervention in elections came from Aberdeen. The burgh had named three alternative commissioners to represent it in the 1633 parliament.[34] The senior of them, Provost Paul Menzies, took his seat and was elected to sit on the Lords of the Articles. But subsequently, in Menzies' absence, Bailie Patrick Leslie replaced him in the articles and voted against measures Menzies had supported. Motivation here is obscure. Leslie was to become a leading Aberdeen covenanter, so he may have voted against official religious policy, but the incident may equally well have arisen from factional disputes within Aberdeen's ruling elite. In the sixteenth century the Menzies family, acting as agents for the earls of Huntly, had dominated the burgh. Their power had since crumbled and Leslie may have been the ringleader of an anti-Menzies faction strongly represented on the town council. Menzies was re-elected provost for 1633–4, but at the election for 1634–5 he was replaced by Leslie. This brought down on the burgh the wrath of the king, who was informed that 'seditious convocatiounes' had brought about the election of Leslie, a man not fit to serve the burgh as he had betrayed it in the 1633 parliament. The burgh hastily replaced Leslie with Menzies as ordered, but the row flared up again at the 1635–6 election. Patrick Leslie tried to take part in the election, arguing that he had been deposed as provost but not as a councillor. He was supported by two bailies (one being Robert Farquhar, subsequently another local covenanting leader) and seven councillors, but eventually they withdrew, leaving Menzies, two bailies and six councillors to carry out the election. Protests to the king and privy council led to the election being annulled, and a new provost and compromise council was imposed on the burgh, including both Menzies and Leslie.[35] Any defiance of the king here evidently arose almost accidentally from a bitter local faction fight, but the way in which one faction in the dispute later became committed to the covenanters illustrates how the divisions over local disputes could be a major influence in determining allegiances once a national conflict broke out. Yet this clash of factions in

Aberdeen on the eve of the troubles did not immediately merge with the national quarrel; the burgh was at first seemingly united in opposition to the covenanters, and Leslie and Farquhar at first emerged as those least unwilling to submit to them rather than as positive supporters of the cause.

To occasional interference in elections Charles I added plans to alter the constitutions of the royal burghs. The idea of 'settling companies in trade' in Edinburgh, probably on the lines of the great trading companies of London, was said by Charles in 1634 to have first been raised by the burgh itself.[36] But by 1636 he was recommending the establishment of such companies, and the policy certainly fits in with his well-known tendency to seek wholesale anglicisation. At the same time the king ordered the adoption, in Edinburgh and other burghs, of 'a constant council', on the grounds that 'frequent chainge of persounes in publict effaires does breid inconstancie in government'.[37] During Charles' reign 'the most excessive demands and attacks, unprecedented in scale' were made on the privileges of the city of London,[38] and knowledge of this must have added to the fears of Scottish burgesses as to the intentions of the crown. The matter was put on the agenda for the 1637 meeting of the Convention of Royal Burghs, and Glasgow instructed its commissioner to 'voit and consent in name of this brughe that thair be ane constant counsell in ilk brughe of this kingdome'; but the outbreak of the troubles prevented the matter proceeding further. The attraction of a constant council to those already in office are clear, but even so the prospect of such a drastic constitutional change must have been unsettling, and it may have been that Glasgow's seemingly spontaneous support was the result of intervention by the archbishop of Glasgow, who still held the right of appointing the provost and bailies.[39]

The main specifically burgh grievances against the king were, however, economic and financial. There was an undercurrent of grumbling about patents and monopolies,[40] and taxation had increased greatly since the 1620s. The formerly intermittent land tax had become a regular annual imposition, but this development was recent enough for it still to be regarded as a grievance. At the normal rate of 30s per poundland per year its yield, if fully collected, was about £115,000 a year, according to the 1633 tax roll. From 1621 there was added to this a tax of 5 per cent on annualrents or interest payments, which it was claimed should bring in twice as much as that land tax — £230,000. It had been promised that this was only a temporary tax, but it became permanent, and in 1633 was raised to 6¼ per cent, to bring in £287,000 a year. Finally in 1633 the 'two of Ten' was introduced; it was announced that interest rates would be lowered from 10 per cent to 8 per cent but that this would be delayed for three years and in the interim the 2 per cent difference between the old and new rates would be payable to the crown as a tax. Working from the estimated yield of the 5 per cent of annualrents cited above, this new levy of 20 per cent of annualrents should have yielded about £920,000, making the theoretical total burden of the three taxes on the country in the years immediately after 1633 about £1,300,000 a year.[41] It seems likely that the estimates for yields of the taxes on annualrents are exaggerated, but none the less there is no doubt that the burden of taxation on the country rose very sharply. Moreover most of the extra burden came through taxes on interest payments, and these were regarded as hitting the burgesses much harder than the other estates — as the reactions to the covenanters' reduction of interest rates in 1649 indicates. The burgesses joined the other estates in protesting at the introduction of the tax on annualrents in 1621.[42] There is no evidence of any burgh protest in 1633 — perhaps not surprisingly as the king made it clear that he regarded petitioning about grievances as seditious — but it would be surprising if the burghs did not feel that they were being singled out for extra burdens. So far as Edinburgh was concerned, rising national taxation was only one of the burdens Charles I inflicted on her; the burgh was to have to pay for the privilege of being capital. Two new churches, the conversion of St Giles' into a cathedral for a new bishopric, increased stipends for burgh ministers and the building of a new parliament house were among the prices Edinburgh had to pay for continuing royal favour. Favour was only to be granted in return for obedience given, an attitude of cold calculation which roused resentment and could be contrasted with James VI's more gracious response, at least in his later years, to requests from his capital.[43]

None the less, when the Edinburgh riots of 23 July 1637 began the troubles the burgh authorities reacted with genuine horror and outrage. Resistance to the new prayer book which occasioned the riots had substantial popular support, and some of the magistrates and council might have had some private sympathy for the cause, but publicly they condemned the disorders and apologised fulsomely for them. But as disturbances and petitioning against the prayer book spread and the extent of support for the resistance from nobles, lairds and ministers began to emerge, the burgh found itself under pressure to side with the dissidents. Most burghs hung back, waiting for a lead from the capital, but a few ventured to act on their own. Among the local petitions presented to the privy council on 20 September were ones from the burghs of Ayr, Cupar, Dumbarton, Glasgow, Irvine and Stirling.[44]

Charles I realised the importance of maintaining the loyalty of Edinburgh, and the opportune death of the provost gave him an opportunity to strengthen his hold on the burgh by ordering it to elect Sir John Hay as provost. In some ways this was an astute move. Hay had frequently acted as agent for the affairs of Edinburgh and other burghs at court, and as clerk register had proved himself capable and trustworthy. But Hay was one of the staunchest supporters of the king's religious policies and he was certainly not qualified for election as provost as he was not a practising merchant burgess. Thus Charles' intervention may have hastened instead of preventing Edinburgh's defection. On 19 September the burgh council elected him provost, but they elected him from a leet including other candidates as an assertion of the burgh's rights, and three days later the bailies and council, in the absence of the new provost, decided to petition against the prayer book.[45]

As Henry Guthry indicated, the trickle of burghs opposing the king turned into a flood once Edinburgh declared itself. Just a few weeks later the great supplication to the king of 18 October bore the signatures of commissioners from thirty-six royal burghs along with those of nobles, lairds and ministers. Of the more important burghs only Aberdeen and St Andrews failed to sign, though it is noticeable that Banff was the only burgh north of Montrose to be represented.[46]

At the beginning of April 1638 it was reported that the National Covenant, only a month old, had already been signed by commissioners of all burghs except Aberdeen, St Andrews and Crail.[47] This appears to have been something of an exaggeration, for delegations of covenanters were dispatched not only to Aberdeen (where they met with almost no success) and St Andrews (where many were persuaded to sign), but to Inverness, Forres and Elgin. In Inverness the provost and two councillors argued against signing for politic reasons; 'their toune lay invyroned amidst the Hielands' and they dared not sign until neighbouring clans had done so. That such sensitivity to the susceptibilities of neighbours was necessary was to be proved some year later; one motive for the seizure of the burgh by royalist rebels in 1649 was that the

covenanters had begun fortifying it, and local clans were determined not to let any regime establish a permanent garrison
there.[48] However, one of the Inverness bailies successfully
organised signing of the covenant, and in Forres 'all the bodie of
the toune subscryvit most cheirfullie'. At Elgin a good deal of
pressure had to be applied before a similar result was achieved.[49]
Thus only Aberdeen held out. As a result, it became the first of the
burghs to experience the disasters which were to become almost
universal in urban Scotland by the end of the 1640s — civil war,
occupation and free quartering by rival armies which either
plundered or exacted money and supplies, the destruction of
property and goods, decay of trade, flight of citizens and their conscription or deaths in battle or by disease.

Any burgesses whose opposition to Charles I was influenced by
resentment at growing tax burdens on the burghs soon made the
discovery that rebellion and revolution were expensive commodities and that revolutionary regimes fighting for survival demanded
more from subjects and were more arbitrary in their exactions
than even ambitious and innovating rulers like Charles I. At first,
it is true, national taxation by the new regime was intermittent.
The Tenth Penny of 1639 eventually raised nearly £400,000, and
the burghs could congratulate themselves that the new valuations
meant that they were only assessed to pay just under one tenth of
the national total, instead of their traditional one sixth. The
Twentieth Penny was intended to raise half as much as the Tenth,
but in practice brought in little more than a quarter. The Loan
and Tax of 1643 totalled about £990,000.[50] But alongside these
national taxes the period of the Bishops' Wars of 1639–41 saw
desperate attempts to raise money through supposedly voluntary
loans, orders to surrender all gold and silver work and local
military exactions. Moreover the worst was yet to come. From
1644 excise duties, especially hated by the burghs, were imposed
and from 1645 the Monthly Maintenance was added to it, regularly levied at £1,296,000 a year[51] — ironically, this single tax
yielded (or should have yielded) almost exactly the same amount as
all three of the taxes imposed in 1633 and then complained of as
oppressive. And in the years of division and disaster for the
covenanting movement, which began in 1644, the maintenance
and excise were only the tip of the iceberg of demands made on the
country by war and the revolutionary regime, ranging from forced
loans, fines and quartering to hand-to-mouth exactions of money
and supplies wherever they could be found. In these years burgh

records throughout the country become clogged with endless complaints about misery, losses and impending ruin. Though doubtless some of these were exaggerated it is notable that the covenanting regime, though desperate for money, sometimes confirmed how bad things were by accepting the complaints and estimates of losses and granting exemptions from taxes and quarterings.

As already noted, Aberdeen was the first to suffer. In 1639 the burgh was occupied by five armies in turn, and each army, royalist or covenanter, had its own demands to make for supplies, levies, quarters and work on fortifications. In April the townsmen 'for the most pairt' reluctantly signed the covenant, but the few who had voluntarily signed earlier demanded that they be exempt from the extra burdens brought on the burgh by their neighbours' stubbornness.[52] Finally submission of the burgh to the covenanters came in May 1640, when it was forced to accept the cynically named 'Articles of Bonaccord' agreeing to supply Major General Robert Munro's army, supposedly out of 'thankfulness to the soldatista for keiping of good ordor and eschewing of plundering'.[53]

With the royalist rising of the marquis of Montrose in 1644, Aberdeen's earlier experiences — and much worse — became general for burghs north of the Tay. None escaped occupation by rival armies — at best exacting free quarter and supplies, at worst plundering, killing and burning. In and after the battle of Aberdeen in September 1644 about 160 inhabitants of the burgh were killed, including two bailies, the master of kirkworks and the master of hospitals, 'for the enemie, entring the toune immediatlie, did kill all, old and young, whome they fand on streittes'. The royalists also plundered widely, 'killing sic men as they fand within' the houses in some cases. The burgh's losses were calculated as £135,000; plundering by the Gordons in 1648 added a further £40,000 of losses.[54] In 1646 it was reported that free quartering had reduced some families to begging, and Aberdeen's total losses due to the troubles of 1639–48 were accepted by the regime as being £1,582,910 — though this includes some ships lost through bad weather rather than enemy action.[55]

There was widespread disruption of trade. Aberdeen complained in 1646 that trade in her main export — plaiding — had collapsed. One fair at which 200 horse packs of plaiding had normally been offered for sale now produced only one web.[56] From Banff came the despairing conclusion that after plundering by Montrose and other losses 'now our condition is so miserable that we have nothing whereby either to labor our land or use our trade'.[57] South of the Tay burghs generally escaped the most direct horrors of war, but they still suffered disruption of trade, taxation and other exactions, quarterings and levies. Losses in battle sustained by units recruited locally could have devastating effects. The battle of Kilsyth in 1645 is said to have left 200 widows in Kirkcaldy.[58] Dysart claimed that it had been flourishing until the Montrose campaigns of 1644–5 'where the most pairt of the skippers and traffiquers were killed and destroyed'.[59]

English conquest in 1650–1 brought further losses. English troops were usually reasonably well disciplined and behaved, but their conduct at Dundee formed a major exception. It was the one burgh that the English had to take by storm. The fighting and the indiscriminate killing that followed left hundreds dead, though the figure of 800 soldiers and townsmen and 200 women and children killed was probably exaggerated, as were the claims that the townsmen were too drunk to defend themselves. General Monck authorised twenty-four hours of plundering after the storming, and this is said to have produced booty worth £2.5 million Scots, including many ships.[60]

In 1648 Glasgow found itself in the position Aberdeen had been in nearly ten years before — that of being forced into political conformity by disciplinary military quartering. As the one leading burgh to oppose the Engagement, Glasgow was singled out for special treatment, her magistrates and council being deposed for their defiance and imprisoned in Edinburgh.[61] Major James Turner, a mercenary whose continental experience had doubtless given him a good training as to how to bring civilians to heel, led troops into the burgh. He later recorded:

At my comeing there I found my worke not very difficill; for I shortlie learnd to know, that the quartering two or three troopers, and halfe a dozen musketeers, was ane argument strong enough, in two or three nights time, to make the hardest headed Covenanter in the toune to forsake the kirk.

The Glasgow men, 'groune prettie tame' as their persecutor contemptuously reported, hastened to sign 'Turner's Covenant' submitting to parliament and the Engagement.[62] Glasgow magistrates were not alone in sampling the hospitality of Edinburgh Tolbooth or lighter forms of restraint in the capital. The provost of Dumfries was arrested in 1644 after Montrose had briefly occupied the burgh.[63] Patrick Leslie, former provost of Aberdeen, and a bailie of Lauder were imprisoned under the kirk party for their support for the Engagers.[64] Earlier, in 1644, Leslie had been kidnapped by royalists, along with Aberdeen's dean of guild; and the same fate had befallen the provost of Forfar in 1645.[65] But at least they were better off than the bailie of Montrose killed by royalists in 1644,[66] or the two Aberdeen bailies killed at the battle of Aberdeen.

To the exactions of a revolutionary regime, its soldiery and its enemies, were added the disaster of bubonic plague. The last major outbreak in Scotland affected all the major burghs and many minor ones to varying degrees between 1644 and 1649, though those north of Aberdeen escaped. Edinburgh, Stirling, Perth and Brechin suffered most. Brechin lost perhaps two-thirds of its population, South Leith between a half and two-thirds. Aberdeen and Lanark also suffered badly, but Glasgow escaped comparatively lightly. To add to the misery, part of Montrose and most of Kelso were burnt down as a result of over-zealous attempts to disinfect buildings; in the latter case seven or eight hundred people were left in midwinter without food or shelter, but soldiers were stationed round the burgh with orders to shoot any inhabitant trying to leave for fear that the infection spread. It has been estimated that burghs responsible for paying two-thirds of the burghs' share of taxation were severely affected; perhaps a fifth of the country's total urban population died of plague.[67]

In this period of continuous and deepening crises the pressure of public responsibilities on the ruling elites in the burghs grew enormously and, especially in the smaller burghs, reluctance to hold office emerged. In 1645 the elected magistrates of Montrose had to be ordered to accept office by the Committee of Estates.[68] The provost and bailies elected in Forres in 1647 refused office because of the burdens on the 'poore decayed toune' and obstruction by the former magistrates and town clerk, who refused to hand over the burgh charter chest and zeal.[69] About the same time the magistrates of Inverness appealed to parliament to 'gett them frie of ther Magistracie',[70] and in Stirling in 1649 the magistrates complained that they were being ruined by being forced to continue in office.[71] The regime not only added greatly to the work of holders of traditional offices, they created new ones and forced prominent citizens to accept them if necessary. Robert Farquhar, provost of Aberdeen, refused at first to become collector of the excise for the north of Scotland but was ordered to accept. The bailies and council of Burntisland reported, doubtless with satisfaction, that no one would become collector of the hated excise, so were ordered to do the collection themselves.[72]

At the centre as well as in the localities the covenanting regime made heavy demands on the time of leading burgesses. Government by the three estates and their committees was labour intensive. Complaints from burghs at having to pay the expenses of their commissioners to parliament, the General Assembly and the Convention of Royal Burghs were widespread. Before the troubles sessions of parliament were matters of a few days; under the covenanters they often lasted months. This posed problems for the commissioners sent as well as for the burghs paying them, for they might be forced to neglect their mercantile activities for long periods. Moreover sitting in parliament often led to election to the Committee of Estates or to financial or other committees, leaving unfortunate burgesses with a choice between not attending meetings and getting into trouble for that, or almost permanent absence from home. Attempts were made to deal with the problem by reducing committee quorums and by accepting that not all members would attend all the time; in 1644 the Committee of Estates suggested that the Convention of Royal Burghs draw up a rota of burgesses to attend meetings for a month at a time.[73] The naming of alternative burgh commissioners in commissions to members of parliament also helped spread the burden. Glasgow in 1643 told its commissioner to the Convention of Estates that he would be replaced if the session lasted more than twenty days;[74] Forres in 1650 authorised its commissioner simply to leave if the parliamentary session exceeded that period.[75] Forres' representative was luckier than that of Inverness. John Forbes of Culloden first asked to be relieved of having to attend parliament in 1648, but was still complaining unsuccessfully in 1650. He was told that no one was willing to replace him.[76] As these examples indicate, the problems of finding representatives willing to serve grew as the years passed and disillusionment with the regime increased. Elgin council debated in 1650 whether to bother sending a commissioner to parliament. It was decided to do so on the casting vote of the provost, whereupon the council turned on him and insisted that he go to Edinburgh, in spite of his furious protests that he had often been sent before.[77]

Some, however, were probably keen to serve and in time virtually built new careers for themselves out of service in parliament, on its committees, and as commissioners appointed to negotiate with the king or the English parliament. The financial administration of the covenanters was heavily dependent on the expertise of burgesses. Sir John Smith, Sir James Murray, William Thomson, James Jossie, John Denholm, John Campbell and John Drummond all served in leading offices concerned with raising taxes and supplying the armies, and all were burgesses of Edinburgh.[78]

It was not only magistrates and councillors who sometimes found the pressures on them intolerable and sought to escape them. Orders to inhabitants of burghs not to leave, or to return to, burghs are frequent, for flight was a common reaction to plague, persecution, taxation, quartering, levying or threat of attack. In Kirkcudbright in 1639 and Aberdeen in 1640 people fled to avoid conscription.[79] Kirkcaldy sought to counter fear of levying by offering rewards. Seventy-eight men willing to serve in the 1644 invasion of England were made burgesses. That only nine men were granted burgess-ship in 1648 for similar reasons presumably reflected a growing disillusionment and opposition to the Engagement.[80] After the battle of Aberdeen it was probably fear of further attack and inability to make a living in the plundered burgh that induced inhabitants to depart, 'leaving nothing behind them but emptie walles. So that be all appearances this town will altogether decay.'[81] In 1646 Aberdeen listed twenty-five substantial citizens who had emigrated to France, Poland, Norway or Flanders since the troubles began out of opposition to the covenanters, fear of royalist armies and desire to escape taxation and other burdens. Many others had left to settle elsewhere in Scotland, and the burgh was concerned that the more that fled, the fewer there were left to share public burdens.[82] The same point worried Glasgow council in 1648: 'the maist part of people wha is able to beire burdeine in the toune hes now left', voting with their feet against attempts to impose the Engagement and raising problems in collecting money to support the poor. Three years before, Glaswegians had been forbidden to flee by Montrose, who realised this was likely to be their reaction to the approach of his army.[83] Those leaving Edinburgh in 1645 must have been seeking to escape plague and taxes, while those deserting Inverness in 1647 presumably feared plundering and taxes.[84] Stirling evidently found inhabitants were still leaving even after the plague epidemic had ended, suggesting continuing disruption of the burgh's economic life.[85] Inhabitants who left Elgin in 1651 were ordered to return on threat of being treated as runaways (or deserters),[86] but the usual threat was of loss of rights and privileges.

The role of central government in burgh affairs increased greatly during the troubles, imposing new burdens and responsibilities on magistrates and councils. Central intervention in burgh elections also became common. At the start of the troubles most burghs had joined the covenanting movement voluntarily, though a few burghs, especially in the north, had needed to be leant on — and Aberdeen had been stamped on — to produce conformity. But on two occasions in the years that followed political and military developments led the regime to issue instructions as to the qualifications required of men to be elected magistrates or councillors or to hold office in burghs. Both crises occurred just before the annual Michaelmas elections, as they followed the defeat of Montrose in September 1645 and the overthrow of the Engagers in September 1648, and this contributed to the confusion surrounding some elections.

In 1645 orders were given that all who were guilty of 'complying' with the royalist rebels should be excluded from power; in 1648 it was Engagers who were purged from power. In Glasgow the two crises are closely linked. In the weeks before Montrose's defeat at Philiphaugh the burgh had submitted unwillingly to him; as there was no covenanting army in Scotland at this point, the burgh had had no choice if it was to avoid occupation and plundering. None the less Glasgow's magistrates and councillors were declared to be disqualified from office, with the sole exception of Councillor George Porterfield, who had been serving as captain of a company of Glasgow men in the Scottish army in England. He was now brought back and imposed on the burgh as provost. Not surprisingly those who had been purged protested vigorously that they were good covenanters who had been forced to comply with the enemy, but the regime, supported by a large discontented faction in the burgh, felt it necessary to make an example of them to discourage compliance elsewhere.[87] Yet the purge was counterproductive in that it led to prolonged and bitter divisions in the burgh. In the 1646 election those excluded the previous year carried out a coup and had themselves re-elected, but parliament intervened to restore the Porterfield faction.[88] In 1648 it was this faction which was itself purged, for the Engagers deposed Porterfield and his council for refusing to raise levies for the army of the Engagement; in their place the old deposed magistrates and council of 1644–5 were imposed on the burgh. But their triumph was short-lived; within a few months the kirk party seized power and the restored 1644–5 administration was again deposed, and

Porterfield and his anti-Engager council re-established.[89]

In Aberdeen the picture is confused by the fact that the royalists of the north-east were not finally subdued until 1647. Thus in September 1645 when Glasgow was being purged for compliance with the royalists, in Aberdeen the royalist Lord Aboyne appeared and insisted on a purge of leading covenanters in the burgh election.[90] There is confusion as to what happened in the next election, of 1646, but it seems that Aboyne's purge was not reversed, for early in 1647 parliament declared the election illegal and imposed a new council.[91] At the 1648 election the administration which had supported the Engagement managed to retain power, but Provost Leslie was soon detained in Edinburgh and late in 1649 a new council was again imposed.[92] Aberdeen's relative remoteness, in an area where central government had difficulty in asserting itself, was thus reflected in the fact that the purges following the 1645 and 1648 crises were delayed until 1647 and 1649.

The fact that Edinburgh was suffering severely from plague in 1645 spared the burgh from most of Montrose's demands which got Glasgow into trouble, as he was terrified of plague spreading to his army. But the burgh did obey his orders to release royalist prisoners. The burgh was influential enough to escape formal purging for this compliance, but when parliament met in November the commissioners from Edinburgh, along with those from Linlithgow, St Andrews and Jedburgh, were not allowed to take their seats until their conduct had been investigated; and Provost Sir John Smith was later forced to do public penance by the kirk.[93] Edinburgh did not escape so lightly in 1648; in the election that year the administration was thoroughly purged for supporting the Engagement.[94]

Such purges created intense local bitterness and even incidents of violence. In Ayr in 1645 the new, non-complying provost imprisoned his predecessor and the dean of guild, deprived the bailies of power and was evidently himself soon deposed.[95] Lauder defiantly re-elected Engagers as bailies in 1648; one of them was denounced to the Committee of Estates for enforcing the Engagement by beating his father with a staff in the street — and treating a councillor similarly during a meeting of the burgh court.[96] In Banff the deposed Engager provost took the provost's seat at a council meeting in defiance of his successor.[97] What precisely was going on in these burgh purges and feuds cannot be fully understood without detailed study of the individual burghs, for it is clear that, though purging was imposed from the centre, local actions and reactions reflected local rivalries and tensions. Unfortunately no such burgh studies have been undertaken for this period. The historian of the English boroughs in the civil war period who laments having 'all too few' studies of this sort to use should think himself lucky to have any.[98]

In 1650–1, as the English tide swept up from the south and drowned the last hopes of covenanting burgesses in the great cause of the covenants, foreign conquest must have seemed merely a crowning disaster to burgh communities already torn apart by war, plague and internal dissension. The extent of economic damage to the burghs and its long-term significance is hard to assess. If the complaints of some burghs and the descriptions of their plights are taken literally it is astonishing that they survived at all. Such complaints were often written to try to gain help and obviously tended to exaggerate, and even when not deliberately exaggerated they often reflect despair immediately after disasters, when a prognosis of impending total ruin is understandable. But soon the burgh communities began to pick themselves up and rebuild their lives. Under English rule in the 1650s there were clear signs of recovery in some burghs at least. Glasgow and Dumbarton trade began to recover. Aberdeen shipping movement increased sharply, as did exports of plaiding, and even during the troubles there had been temporary recovery when circumstances allowed.[99]

Such signs of a remarkable resilience in recovering from the disasters of war and plague should not, however, lead to under-estimating the suffering and losses of the Scottish burghs in the 1640s. Thousands of townsmen who had had a good expectation of surviving into the 1650s were rotting in mass graves after death in battle or from plague; and many of those who survived did so 'in reduced circumstances', struggling to restore shattered fortunes. Sir William Dick of Braid can hardly be said to be a typical burgess, for at the beginning of the troubles he was the richest Scottish merchant of the age. Yet his fate can be seen as symbolic of a traumatic age for his estate; he died in a debtors' prison in England in the 1650s.

Notes

1. H. Guthry, *Memoirs* (2nd edition, Glasgow, 1748), 29.
2. R. Howell, 'Neutralism, conservatism and political alignment in the

English Revolution: the case of the towns, 1642–9', in *Reactions to the English Civil War, 1642–1649*, ed. J. Morrill (London, 1982), 67.

3. P. Zagorin, *The Court and the Country. The Beginning of the English Revolution* (London, 1969), 131.

4. Howell, 'Neutralism', 67–87.

5. R. S. Rait, *The Parliaments of Scotland* (Glasgow, 1924), 13–15; J. D. Mackie and G. S. Pryde, *The Estate of the Burgesses in the Scots Parliament . . .* (St Andrews, 1923), *passim*; D. Stevenson, *The Scottish Revolution, 1637–44. The Triumph of the Covenanters* (Newton Abbot, 1973), 167, 190.

6. *The Government of Scotland under the Covenanters, 1637–1651*, ed. D. Stevenson (SHS, 1982), p. xxxvi; J. Balfour, *Historical Works*, 4 vols. (Edinburgh, 1824–5), iii, 277; *Abdn. Recs., 1625–42*, 246.

7. *Burghs Conv. Recs.*, iv, 533.

8. Stevenson, *Scottish Revolution*, 172.

9. *Edin. Recs., 1626–1641*, pp. xxii, 241–2; Stevenson, *Scottish Revolution*, 194; SRO, GD 112/40/2, Breadalbane Muniments, 8 June 1640; R. Baillie, *Letters and Journals*, ed. D. Laing, 3 vols. (Bannatyne Club, 1841–2), i, 389.

10. *APS*, v, 258–9.

11. Ibid., VI, i, 286, 614.

12. Ibid., VI, i, 61, 76–7; Guthry, *Memoirs*, 144–5; SRO, B 9/12/8, Burntisland Council Minutes, 1643–6, fos. 11r, 11v.

13. D. Stevenson, 'The financing of the cause of the covenants, 1638–51', *SHR*, 51 (1972), 118; Baillie, *Letters*, iii, 99; Balfour, *Historical Works*, iii, 422–3.

14. SRO, PA 11/8, Register of the Committee of Estates, fos. 99r, 102r, 102v; Stevenson, *Government*, p. xlii.

15. Historical Manuscripts Commission 8: *9th Report*, ii, 254; J. Spalding, *Memorials of the Trubles*, ed. J. Stuart, 2 vols. (Spalding Club, 1850–1), i, 106; *Burghs Conv. Recs.*, iv, 543.

16. Stevenson, *Scottish Revolution*, 174. The Lords of the Articles were abolished in 1640.

17. Guthry, *Memoirs*, 146.

18. D. Stevenson, *Revolution and Counter-Revolution in Scotland, 1644–1651* (London, 1977), 87; *The Diplomatic Correspondence of Jean de Montereul* [*Montereul Corres.*], ed. J. G. Fotheringham, 2 vols. (SHS, 1898–9), ii, 83.

19. Stevenson, *Revolution and Counter-Revolution*, 100; Baillie, *Letters*, iii, 35.

20. *Montereul Corres.*, ii, 288.

21. *APS*, VI, ii, 71.

22. Ibid., VI, ii, 3–4, 124–6.

23. See Stevenson, *Revolution and Counter-Revolution*, 134–45.

24. As suggested in ibid., 135–6, 213, and D. Stevenson, 'Church and Society under the covenanters', *Scotia: American-Canadian Journal of Scottish Studies*, 1 (1977), 33.

25. Howell, 'Neutralism', 76–7, 85–7.

26. *The Earl of Stirling's Register of Royal Letters*, ed. C. Rogers, 2 vols. (Edinburgh, 1885), ii, 859.

27. Not 34.1 per cent, as erroneously stated in Stevenson, 'Financing',

93. For a convenient summary of the stent rolls see T. C. Smout, *Scottish Trade on the Eve of the Union, 1660–1707* (Edinburgh, 1963), 282–3.

28. *APS*, VI, ii, 240.

29. *ACL*, iii, 151, 152, 154.

30. Baillie, *Letters*, iii, 98; *Edin. Recs., 1642–55*, 205; *Burghs Conv. Recs.*, iii, 332–3, 336–8.

31. See D. Stevenson, 'Conventicles and the kirk, 1619–27', *Records of the Scottish Church History Society*, 18 (1972–4), 101–5.

32. *Edin. Recs., 1604–26*, 275–6.

33. *Edin. Recs., 1625–41*, pp. xiv, 149–50; *Stirling's Register*, ii, 774, 786.

34. *ACL*, i, 384.

35. *Abdn. Recs., 1625–42*, 70–4, 80–95, 102–4; *ACL*, ii, 28–31, 63–4; *Stirling's Register*, ii, 812, 833. The uneasiness of the relationship between noble patrons and the Menzies provosts of Aberdeen in the sixteenth century is a recurrent theme, however, in A. White, 'Religion, Politics and Society in Aberdeen, 1543–1593' (Aberdeen Univ. Ph.D., 1985); see 16–17, 35, 44–6, 58–66, 187–96, 304–5, 310–16.

36. *Stirling's Register*, ii, 754.

37. *Edin. Recs., 1626–41*, pp. xv, 179, 180, 185.

38. V. Pearl, *London and the Outbreak of the Puritan Revolution* (Oxford, 1961), 71.

39. *Glasgow Recs., 1573–1642*, 381–2; W. S. Shepherd, 'The Politics and Society of Glasgow, 1648–74' (Glasgow Univ. Ph.D., 1978), 7–8, 215.

40. E.g., *Edin. Recs., 1626–1641*, pp. xxx–xxxi.

41. *APS*, v, 13–16, 39–40; Rait, *Parliaments*, 494; Sir William Purves, *Revenue of the Scottish Crown, 1681*, ed. D. M. Rose (Edinburgh, 1897), 183–200.

42. *State Papers and Miscellaneous Correspondence of Thomas, Earl of Melros*, ed. J. Maidment, 2 vols. (Abbotsford Club, 1837), ii, 423–4.

43. *Edin. Recs., 1626–41*, pp. vii–x, xiii, xv–xvi, xliii–xliv, xlvii–xlviii; R. K. Hannay and G. P. H. Watson, 'The building of the Parliament House', *Book of the Old Edinburgh Club*, 13 (1924), 1–78. It was said that one of Charles' reasons for founding the bishopric of Edinburgh was to remove from the burgh authorities control over the appointment of burgh ministers (E. Hyde, Earl of Clarendon, *The history of the rebellion and civil wars in England*, ed. W. D. Macray, 6 vols. (Oxford, 1888), i, 115).

44. J. Leslie, Earl of Rothes, *A Relation of Proceedings concerning the Affairs of the Kirk*, ed. D. Laing (Bannatyne Club, 1830), 48; *RPC, 1635–1637*, 700–1; The Stirling petition was not in fact approved by the town council until 25 September (*Stirling Recs., 1519–1666*, 177–8).

45. *Edin. Recs., 1626–41*, pp. xvii, 194–5; *RPC, 1635–7*, 534.

46. D. H. Fleming, 'Scotland's supplication and complaint against the Book of Common Prayer', *Proceedings of the Society of Antiquaries of Scotland*, 60 (1925–6), 374–5.

47. Baillie, *Letters*, i, 62.

48. Stevenson, *Revolution and Counter-Revolution*, 146.

49. Stevenson, *Scottish Revolution*, 86, 91–7; Leslie, *Relation*, 107–9.

50. Stevenson, 'Financing', 98–102.

51. Ibid., 107.

52. *ACL*, ii, 269; *Abdn. Recs., 1625–42*, 157, 158, 285; Stevenson, *Scottish Revolution*, 138, 140, 148.

53. *ACL*, ii, 205–7.

54. *Abdn. Recs., 1643–1747*, 29–30; *ACL*, iii, 115, 116.

55. *ACL*, iii, 117–24.

56. *ACL*, iii, 43.

57. W. Cramond, *The annals of Banff*, 2 vols (New Spalding Club, 1891–3), i, 44–6.

58. L. Macbean, *Kirkcaldy Burgh Records* (Kirkcaldy 1908), 43.

59. T. M. Devine, 'The Cromwellian Union and the Scottish burghs: the case of Aberdeen and Glasgow, 1652–60', in *Scottish Themes. Essays in honour of S. G. E. Lythe* (Edinburgh, 1976), 13–14.

60. S. G. E. Lythe, *Life and labour in Dundee from the Reformation to the Civil War* (Abertay Historical Society, 1958), 28–30; Balfour, *Historical Works*, iv, 315–16.

61. Stevenson, *Government*, 71, 79–80; *Glasgow Recs., 1630–62*, 134–7; *APS*, VI, ii, 91–2, 93.

62. J. Turner, *Memoirs*, ed. T. Thomson (Bannatyne Club, 1829), 53, 54; *APS*, VI, ii, 91.

63. *APS*, VI, i, 238.

64. SRO, PA 11/7, fo. 20v; PA 11/8, fos. 89v, 91r–92r.

65. *Abdn. Recs., 1643–1747*, 17–18; Stevenson, *Government*, 50–1, 52.

66. Spalding, *Memorialls*, ii, 347, 348.

67. *Scottish Population History from the Seventeenth Century to the 1930s*, ed. M. Flinn (Cambridge, 1977), 133–49.

68. Stevenson, *Government*, 6–7.

69. SRO, PA 11/5, fos. 56r–v; R. Douglas, *Annals of the Royal Burgh of Forres* (Elgin, 1934), 49.

70. *More Culloden Papers*, ed. D. Warrand, i (Inverness, 1923), 41–3.

71. *Stirling Recs., 1519–1666*, 197.

72. Stevenson, 'Financing', 104–5.

73. Stevenson, *Government*, p. xlii.

74. *Glasgow Recs., 1630–62*, 59.

75. Douglas, *Annals of Forres*, 52.

76. Warrand, *More Culloden Papers*, i, 79, 85, 87, 110.

77. W. Cramond, *The Records of Elgin, 1234–1800*, 2 vols. (New Spalding Club, 1903–8), i, 287.

78. Stevenson, *Government*, 193–8.

79. *Kirkcudbright Town Council Records, 1606–1658*, ed. John, Marquis of Bute and C. M. Armet, 2 vols. (Edinburgh, 1908), ii, 598; *Abdn. Recs., 1625–42*, 233–4, 238.

80. Macbean, *Kirkcaldy Burgh Recs.*, 164, 165. In 1642 Kirkcudbright admitted two men as burgesses gratis as they had willingly served in England in 1640 (Bute and Armet, *Kirkcudbright*, ii, 680, 681).

81. SRO, PA 11/3, fos.72v, 145v. See also *ACL*, ii, 381, 383.

82. *ACL*, iii, 43–4.

83. *Glasgow Recs., 1630–32*, 146; SRO, PA 11/6, fo. 30v.

84. *Edin. Recs., 1642–55*, 63–4, 71, 77; SRO, PA 11/5, fo. 113r; J. Burns, 'Memoirs', 10, in *Historical Fragments*, ed. J. Maidment

(Edinburgh, 1833).

85. *Stirling Recs., 1519–1666*, 192.

86. Cramond, *Records of Elgin*, i, 289.

87. *Glasgow Recs., 1630–62*, 80–7. There was evidently strong opposition in parliament to the purge of Glasgow magistrates, which nearly led to the restoration of those deposed; see J. Spreul, 'Some remarkable passages of the Lord's providence', 7–8, in Maidment (ed.), *Historical Fragments*. For the interrogation of former provost James Bell as to his dealings with Montrose, see SRO, PA 7/7/47.

88. *Glasgow Recs., 1630–62*, 97, 99–100, 102–7, 109; *APS*, VI, i, 625–7, 629; Spreul, 'Some remarkable passages', 8, misdates the restoration of the Porterfield faction to early 1648 instead of early 1647 and says the 'malignants' willingly resigned as they could not cope with the 'pestilence' in the burgh; once the 'godly' were back in office the epidemic ended!

89. *Glasgow Recs., 1630–62*, 137–41, 149–50; *APS*, VI, ii, 93; SRO, PA 11/6, fo. 66v; PA 11/7, fos. 2v–3r.

90. *Abdn. Recs., 1642–1747*, 57–8.

91. Ibid., 73–5; *ACL*, iii, 58–9, 70, 76–7.

92. *Abdn. Recs;. 1642–1747*, 103–5.

93. *APS*, VI, i, 476, 494; *Edin. Recs., 1642–55*, pp. xiv–xv, 72–6, and see ibid., 102, 103–4, for the 1646 election.

94. Ibid., pp. xxi, 170–2, 174, 210–11.

95. SRO, PA 12/10, Warrants of the Committee of Estates, undated.

96. SRO, PA 11/7, fo. 20v; PA 11/8, fos. 91r–92r.

97. SRO, PA 11/7, fos. 149r–150r.

98. Howell, 'Neutralism', 71. A partial exception to the lack of studies Scottish burghs is provided by Shepherd's thesis on Glasgow; see n. 39 above.

99. Devine, 'Cromwellian Union', 1–16.

9

Edinburgh in Mid-Seventeenth Century

Walter Makey

Thomas Tucker was a Cromwellian customs official concerned to increase the revenues of the ports of Scotland. In 1656 he submitted a report which was interesting in itself and particularly interesting in its remarks about the port of Leith. It was not merely that Leith was more important than the other ports; there was something odd about it that tempted the stranger to muse. Leith was a great port with all the advantages of a fine commercial site, but it was a place of little consequence dominated by the merchants of the city of Edinburgh: '. . . did not that city . . . obstruct and impede the growing of the place [Leith], it would, from being her slave, become her rival . . .'. The 'castle of Edinburgh' had once given 'both rise and growth to that city by inviting people to plant and settle there for sheltering themselves under the strength and security thereof'. But now, 'in times of peace', the advantages of Leith should 'soon invite the inhabitants . . . to descend from their proud hill into the more fruitful plain to be filled with the fullness and the fatness thereof'. The seventeenth century, Tucker thought, was different from the sixth or the twelfth; Edinburgh should start again.[1]

This was perhaps another way of saying that Edinburgh was uncommonly durable. It had survived not merely a decade of revolution and another of military occupation but also centuries of economic change. The constants were the castle on the crag, the burgh on the upper half of the tail and, some little distance away at the mouth of the Water of Leith, the port which aroused the eloquent curiosity of Thomas Tucker. The road from Leith, as ancient perhaps as the place itself, climbed gently through a rich arable landscape before negotiating its first natural obstacle in the narrow defile between Calton Hill and the New Town plateau. But, if this was the first, it was not the last. The road must still find its way across the broad marshland below the Nor' Loch; it must still climb the side, here steep though not impossibly so, of the tail to the Netherbow; it must still descend the other side into the narrow Cowgate valley and then it must climb the even steeper ascent to the St Leonard's plateau to find easier ground on its way to Dere Street.

This was the road which had once, in the distant days of the twelfth century, joined Leith to its wool producing hinterland and which had passed, almost incidentally, along the eastern boundary of the burgh of Edinburgh. There had been a castle burgh on its lofty ridge and a seaport town by the Firth of Forth. But now, in the seventeenth century, much had changed and more was changing. Edinburgh, as a royal burgh, had acquired a monopoly of foreign trade. Goods inevitably came and went through Leith, but, for most commodities at least, the market was a couple of miles away on the proud ridge of Edinburgh. The ways of commerce were littered with obstacles, artificial and natural alike. In the meantime the castle of Edinburgh had become the capital of the kingdom. It was the seat of government, whether by parliament or privy council; it had the national courts, whether civil or criminal. The General Assembly usually met there; Charles I had given it a cathedral and called it a city. Population grew and manufacture thrived. The fruitful plain might have its advantages; but old Edinburgh, whether Canterburian or Presbyterian, Cromwellian or royalist, pro-English, pro-French or just plain Scottish, just went on and on. It was, as David Calderwood aptly said always mindful of its 'particular'.[2] It had the momentum of the centuries behind it.

Like most capitals, Edinburgh had gradually been developing a voracious appetite for imports. The details are beyond the limited scope of this article, but the outlines are obvious enough. We know, from the dues paid in the haven at Leith, the ports of origin of most of these shipments.[3] Many of them still came from the ports of the Netherlands: they came from Amsterdam, Rotterdam, the staple port of Veere, Ostend and Dunkirk. But others came from London, Lynn and the ports of Tyne and Wear. A series of cargoes from Rouen, Dieppe, St Malo, La Rochelle, Bourdeaux and Cadiz suggest a flourishing trade with France and Iberia. A further series from Hamburg, Lübeck, Danzig, Stockholm, Gothenburg and the ports of Norway as convincingly indicates a busy traffic with North Germany, the Baltic and Scandinavia. These voyages satisfied a need for high grade iron from Sweden, for timber boards and planks from Norway and the other Baltic ports, for grain from the natural granaries of the North German plain and northern France and a taste, almost a need, for claret from Galicia. But we should perhaps resist the temptation to attach particular commodities to particular ports. A considerable proportion, of the imports consisted of a bewildering variety of mixed manufactures which could be obtained in any of the entrepôts of Atlantic Europe. Again it was possible to buy not only claret but all the more exotic products of the East and Latin America in London or any one of two or three ports in the Netherlands. Indeed it might often be convenient to do so.

Some of the ships involved in the trade were registered in foreign ports but most of them came either from Leith itself or from other Scottish ports. Once more the list is both long and revealing. In 1640–1 it included Kirkwall, Irvine and Glasgow, but most of the ports were nearer home. There was Prestonpans on one side of Leith and South Queensferry on the other; there was Bo'ness a little further up the Forth. And, on the opposite shore, in Fife, there were Kinghorn, Kirkcaldy, Easter Wemyss, Dysart, Elie, Easter and Wester Anstruther, Pittenweem and Crail, with St Andrews only a little further away. Different years would yield slightly different lists, but it is perhaps sufficiently obvious that Edinburgh–Leith was itself an entrepôt for south-east Scotland and Fife and that it was joined, by bands of silver and gold, with the other entrepôts of the North Sea.

The weighhouse (or Tron) was definitely situated in the burgh and its records, which survive from 1613–17, look at the trade patterns from a different perspective.[4] They mention butter and cheese, both of which were domestic products carried overland into the burgh; but they also mention iron, which must have come from Sweden, raisins, which did not come from Scotland, as well as a fine assortment of spices and dyestuffs most of which can only have come from abroad. For the most part these can only have come into the burgh from Leith. Again it may be admitted that hemp and tow could have been used within the burgh for building purposes, but both suggest shipbuilding and thus the port of Leith.

Perhaps the burgh should have been at Leith, as Tucker suggested. Manufactured imports must be unloaded at Leith, hauled wearily to a distant market in Edinburgh, unloaded there, loaded up again and sent back to Leith for shipment to their eventual destination. This was of course rather absurd, but it is fair to add that many of these imports were neither heavy nor bulky and that most of them were used either in Edinburgh itself or in its hinterland. To this extent at least, Edinburgh was nearly was well situated as Leith. Again, Edinburgh was a regional as well as an international market. Dairy produce or grain from all over southern Scotland could be exchanged there for manufactures, whether locally produced or imported. The trade in staple goods makes most of these points the other way round. Some four-fifths of Scottish exports of hides left through the capital and its port;[5] but this trade, important though it was, was only the by-product of a cattle trade primarily concerned to supply meat to the inhabitants of Edinburgh. The cattle ambled into the burgh from near and far, finding their own fodder as they came; transport costs were low. A high proportion of their hides were treated and used within the burgh and only a residue was shipped from Leith. Again, the wool which had once gone straight to Leith now turned left at the Netherbow into Edinburgh's broad market street; some of it went to the looms of the burgh, some of it to the clothmakers down by the Water of Leith; the rest went to exporters who sent it back to the Netherbow and down the road to Leith. These last added half a mile and extra trans-shipment to their costs; the clothmakers lost virtually nothing unless their cloth was exported. A market by the sea would only have yielded a small saving in total costs. In this respect Tucker's argument was less than compelling.

For this reason among others, the privilege of buying and selling remained with Edinburgh. The middle years of the seventeenth century still saw Edinburgh as a merchant's city and Leith as a seaman's town. To oversimplify a little, goods were loaded and unloaded on the right bank of the Water of Leith while ships were built and repaired on the left bank; the former, called South Leith, had carters and sledders busily conveying goods to and from the capital; the latter had ropemakers, shipwrights and the like. Both sides had petty craftsmen, all relatively poor and, in any case, hugely outnumbered by the horde of labourers necessary to the life of any seaport. A town without natural leaders found an aristocracy of skippers, who were by definition often away from home.[6] It was not too difficult to dominate Leith. The same was true of the pigmy suburbs which were growing up beyond the gates of the capital. The Cowgate port had a craft settlement straggling up the steep road that went to St Leonards. Potterow port and the Society port led out into the small triangular suburb of Bristo, the West port of the Grassmarket into the linear suburb of Westport. These were tiny groups of craftsmen who waylaid the traveller as he approached the burgh and tempted him with cheap goods. Canongate had a much longer history; it had once been the abbey's burgh and it was now the emporium of a court centred on the palace of Holyrood. Essentially it was a small but prosperous town of vintners and skilled craftsmen. It competed with Edinburgh on quality rather than price.

Edinburgh, challenged in different ways from all directions, responded resourcefully enough. In effect the fathers of the burgh used the concept of superiority to enhance their political power. Most of South Leith had been captured during the reign of Mary. The two plateaus, one on each side of Edinburgh's slender tail, came with the bequest made by George Heriot, goldsmith to James VI, in 1623; so too did Canongate, North Leith and Pleasance. The conquest of South Leith was completed by the acquisition of the King's Wark in 1647. Finally, Westport and Bristo, now united into the barony of Portsburgh, were purchased in 1648. Edinburgh still had its rivals but they were all under control.

The Heriot bequest has a particular interest. The new school would be run by the ministers and town council of Edinburgh acting as trustees. It seems to have been assumed that the ministers would supervise the school and that the council would manage the estates and thus appoint the bailies. But the council then bought Canongate, North Leith and Pleasance from the trust, that is from itself. Valuation must have been a delicate matter, but the priorities are surely evident enough. Rural revenues would pay the expenses of the school and they were obviously welcome; but rural power was less important than urban power. The council wanted Canongate and Leith. Edinburgh was always careful of its particular; merchants and craftsmen might sometimes squabble among themselves, but they were united in defence of their common monopolies.[7]

These manufacturing monopolies were far from complete. The suburbs continued to exist and perhaps to prosper. They were controlled rather than destroyed. More important perhaps, Edinburgh merchants regularly imported goods which might have been made in the burgh. Again, there were other industries which could not possibly have been sited there. Ships were necessarily repaired in Leith; the repairer used ropes that were either imported or manufactured in Leith. Salt offers an almost exact parallel; in so far as it was home produced, it was made from coal-fuelled pans inevitably situated on the shoreline of the Forth. Leith may have had its share of these and it certainly took salt from various ports on both sides of the Forth, notably those with local outcrops of coal. Herring caught in the Forth were cured with local salt in similar localities before being sent to Edinburgh. If these were industries that demanded a coastal location, there were others that were drawn almost as compulsively to the mills along the Water of Leith. Paper making needed clean water, water power and a large market; the river provided the first two and the capital the other. Dalry, a paper mill since the 1590s, was an appropriate site and there would eventually be more. There had been fulling mills along the Water of Leith for two centuries or more and, to some extent at least, the rest of the industry was following them. As a further development a much more ambitious manufacturing complex was established at Haddington, on the River Tyne, in the 1640s. These movements are doubly significant. Weaving and fulling were among the ancient crafts of Edinburgh; they were now, apart from those using the burgh's mills at Dean, beyond its bonds. But, if this was so, clothmaking had long been financed by merchants from Edinburgh; so indeed was the new enterprise at Haddington and so, as we shall see, were some of the shoreline industries of the Forth. Manufacture, like commerce, was largely conducted by men who satisfied the necessities of the burgess system by residing in Edinburgh. From time to time individual merchants were tempted by the fat plain by the sea; but the fathers of the burgh always brought them back.[8]

This affluent, bustling burgh was obviously quite different in most ways from its thirteenth-century predecessor, but in one respect at least it was strikingly similar. It had not grown very much. It is true that it had gained the anomalous oblong that extended eastwards from the Netherbow down the south side of the Canongate and that the Flodden Wall had added bits and pieces here and there. But the additions were small and partly consisted of open space. The total area of the extended burgh was only 160 acres and the area actually inhabited was substantially smaller.[9]

Edinburgh was important, small and very crowded. The foreign travellers, to whom Edinburgh offered endless fascination, all agreed that this was so. Henri, duc de Rohan was a Huguenot who visited Edinburgh in 1600. He did not like it very much. 'It had', he thought, 'no beauty except that of its great street [now the Royal Mile] which stretches from one end of the town to the other and is both wide and straight as well as of great length'; but it was 'so stocked with inmates that there can hardly be another town so populous for its size'. He courteously refrained from mentioning the smell and he paid tribute to its fertile hinterland and its flourishing commerce before leaving hurriedly for the sunnier south. Sir William Brereton, an English puritan who came in 1636, stayed longer and was more perceptive. Edinburgh was the seat of government, the centre of church and state; its castle, 'very high and sufficiently commanding', could batter the town. From this vantage point, you may take a full view of the whole — built upon a hill nothing oversteep but suffiently sloping . . . to give a graceful ascent to the great street . . . an English mile long and . . . the best paved I have ever seen'. The houses were 'substantially built of stone' and 'some [were] five, some six storeys high'. Edinburgh was impressive, but its indewellers were 'most sluttish, nasty and slothful people'. He could never enter a house 'but [he] was constrained to hold his nose'. None the less Edinburgh was a place of consequence and its great market street was 'always thronged with people'. A few days later an 'intelligent, understanding man' told him more. There were some sixty narrow and inconvenient 'back lanes', all of them inhabited, leaving the broad High Street on either side. He also learned that the burgh was divided into four parishes each with 'no more than about 4,000 communicants'. This part of Brereton's account is somewhat muddled but, however his words are construed, he plainly thought that Edinburgh had a total population of over 20,000.[10] We might add that they all lived in an area of very approximately 100 acres.

Travellers' impressions are translated into a semblance of reality in the plan so carefully drawn by Gordon of Rothiemay in 1647. Like all its predecessors, this is strictly speaking a view rather than a map. In effect — though not in fact — Gordon suspended himself from a balloon moored at the eastern end of the Meadows; but Gordon had, on the authority of the town council, surveyed the burgh and, unlike all his predecessors, he drew to scale.[11] His east-west distances were almost right; north-south distances were, if we allow this was a perspective drawing, at least right enough. He inevitably made Edinburgh-Canongate look even narrower than it actually was but Gordon plainly went to a lot of trouble over his public buildings; his portrayals of St Giles, the Parliament House, the Tron Kirk and the weighhouse at the head of West Bow are interesting and, at least in so far as they can still

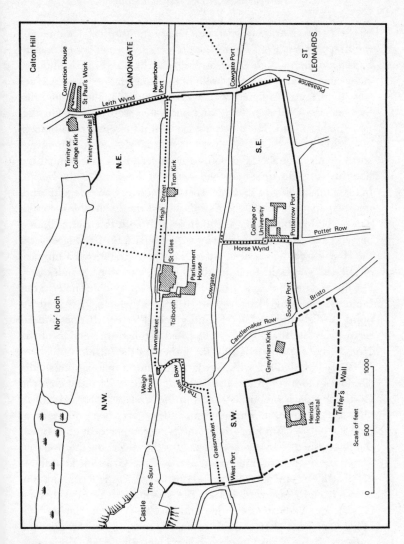

Figure 9.1: Edinburgh in the mid-seventeenth century

Calton Hill
Correction House
St Paul's Work
CANONGATE
Netherbow Port
Cowgate Port
ST LEONARDS
Leith Wynd
Trinity or College Kirk
Trinity Hospital
N.E.
Pleasance
High Street
Tron Kirk
S.E.
College or University
Potterrow Port
Potter Row
Horse Wynd
St Giles
Nor' Loch
Parliament House
Tolbooth
Cowgate
Society Port
Bristo
Lawnmarket
Candlemaker Row
Greyfriars Kirk
Weigh House
The West Bow
Telfer's Wall
N.W.
Grassmarket
S.W.
Heriot's Hospital
Castle
The Spur
West Port

Scale of feet
0   500   1000

199

be checked, remarkably accurate. This is an historical document of the first importance. One of the defects of Gordon's view is perhaps apparent enough. The south side of the burgh, nearest to the camera as it were, shows up well; open space on the outskirts gives way to the crowded tenements of the interior; the boundaries between the two are clearly and accurately shown. But Gordon fails further north. He shows a mass of undifferentiated buildings extending from the High Street to the Nor' Loch. This is not entirely unreasonable. Gordon would indeed have seen something like this from his imaginary viewpoint to the south of the burgh, but it is misleading in several respects. There are no closes; there is no open space between the buildings and the Loch; the northern rim of the inhabited area is shown as a straight line rather than a jagged edge. Gordon was more successful with the frontages along the High Street which he could actually see. He showed a mixture of tall and very tall stone buildings some with stone arcades very like the one in Gladstone's Land. This was reasonable enough; but there was nothing like the 'face of boards' which, in Brereton's opinion, disfigured a 'stately and graceful' street. It does indeed seem probable that Gordon presented a tidied-up version of the High Street for the delight of the fathers of the burgh.

The real difficulties with Gordon are more subtle than this. The site takes the form of a ridge declining relatively gently from the Castle approach (about 350 feet) in the west to Holyrood Abbey (120 feet) in the east. The adjacent valleys carry two tiny streams, both called the Tumble, which find a confluence near the abbey; the watershed between them is not however at the western extremity of the crag but at the head of the Grassmarket (about 230 feet). The one, curving round the base of Castle Rock, into the broad trough, occupied during the seventeenth century by the Nor' Loch, between the ridge and the New Town plateau; the other took the shorter and rather steeper route through the narrower defile of the Cowgate valley which divided the ridge from the St Leonards plateau.[12] Gordon, perhaps because he wanted to show detail clearly, flattened the landscape; Brereton, perhaps because he hesitated to venture into stinking closes, failed to notice how steep they were.

This is vitally important, for the problems of old Edinburgh all derived from its crags, its ridge, its valleys and its plateaus. The catchment area of the two tiny Tumbles was defined by the crest-lines of the two plateaus; the Old Town of Edinburgh thus depended entirely on local rainfall for its water supply. This had been sufficient in the distant days of David I, but the springs trapped in the sandstones of the ridge were now, in the first half of the seventeenth century, barely capable of meeting the demand of a much larger city even in a wet year. In a dry season, its wells ran dry and its inhabitants did not often wash. Rather similarly its valleys and their tiny streams were quite unable to carry its excrement out to sea. The Nor' Loch was a stagnant cesspool that tended to evaporate in a hot summer; the elaborate sewer, recently excavated in Marlin's Wynd, merely conveyed the problem a few yards down the slope into the bottom of the Cowgate valley.[13] In fact a lot of miscellaneous muck was just left lying about. The scavengers made special efforts in times of pestilence but, for the most part, failed miserably. From time to time, the farmers of the landward area were invited into the burgh to remove the muck and to deposit it as manure on their fields. The resulting increase in crop yields was spectacular, but the problem must have been reimported into the burgh through its food supply.[14] Edinburgh, alone among Scotland's major towns, had no great river and it was inevitably a public health nightmare. Everybody seemed concerned but nobody really knew what to do. A scheme devised in 1598 proposed to bring water from the Burgh Loch, half a mile away to the south; nothing more was heard of it, presumably because the source was lower than the upper wells of the High Street. The parliament of 1621, meeting in the New Tolbooth and plainly offended by the smell, voiced its disquiet but achieved nothing. A solution of a kind was eventually found in 1681 when a long lead pipe introduced a limited supply of fresh water brought by gravity feed from the distant springs of Comiston on the other side of the Braid Hills. The wells of the burgh were rejuvenated but the burns stayed foul. In the meantime, the brewers found a simpler answer to their own somewhat easier problem. In 1636 Brereton had noticed and admired 'a common brewhouse' which supplied 'the whole city with beer and ale'; it had the 'greatest, vastest leads, boiling keeves, cisterns and combs' that he had ever seen.[15] This can only have been the building shown on Gordon's plan just inside the Society Port and it must have tapped the still undeveloped springs beneath the St Leonards plateau. Old Edinburgh was not the healthiest city in Europe, but at least the beer was good.

Out of squalor and difficulty, true magnificence rose. Brereton's stately street ran down the crest of a ridge which declined from west to east more steeply than the valleys on either side. The sides of the ridge thus became progressively less steep as the ridge itself descended; on the south side the slope was a precipitous 1 in 3 at Castlehill, 1 in 4 at St Giles, 1 in 12 at the Netherbow, and so on down to the approaches to Holyrood where there was virtually no slope at all. The upper half of the ridge, attached as it was to the Castle on the crag, had become the royal burgh; the lower half, adjacent to the abbey, had become the abbot's burgh. Over the centuries the one had developed rapidly, the other relatively slowly and in the seventeenth century, as both tax rolls and Gordon's plan testify, the one was crowded, the other spacious. There was perhaps a real irony here. In the Canongate, where building conditions were fairly easy, there was still plenty of room; in Edinburgh, where slopes were almost cliffs and conditions fantastically difficult, there were so many buildings that its people seldom saw the sun. The mason has been a significant figure in the history of Edinburgh.

All this had been a gradual process. The Edinburgh of David I had had a long and possibly discontinuous line of timber dwellings straggling down its crestline street and each dwelling its narrow toft or close tumbling down the cliff behind. Now, in the seventeenth century, the tofts were built up and the word close had acquired its modern meaning. Edinburgh, as one contemporary put it, was like a 'double wooden comb, the great street the wood in the middle and the teeth of each side the lanes'.[16] The process of expansion had pushed the builder down the steep slopes towards the Nor' Loch on the one side and all the way down to the Cowgate and up the opposite slope on the other. The closes and wynds carried not only muck but a teeming population of lesser craftsmen and labourers passing to and from their homes. The seventeenth century was very different from the twelfth, but the old property lines were still respected. Each close still served an area corresponding to an ancient toft with a frontage of one, two, three or more roods on the High Street or the Cowgate. But, however many the roods, the tofts were always longer than they were broad; building patterns tended to be confined in narrow rectangular boxes trending down a slope varying from 1 in 3 to 1 in 12. Inconvenient kailyards were now building sites that were perhaps more than merely inconvenient.

The well-known surviving tenement in the High Street, Gladstone's Land, with its narrow frontage of 23ft 5ins, illustrates this tendency and at least two others. The building, as it has survived, has a backland and a foreland. The former was built during

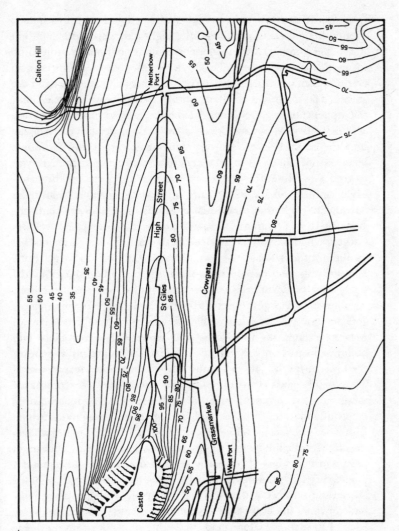

Figure 9.2: The contours of the site of Edinburgh

203

the sixteenth century as a single whole complete with basement, ground floor, four upper floors, the highest of which had an attic; it also had wooden balconies supported on timber pillars projecting forwards into the street. The foreland was a seventeenth-century addition containing the same basic elements and completed in two stages. The main body of the addition was finished by c1620, but the upper floors were further extended a few years later and supported by a stone arcade. The two stages together carried the building some twenty feet out into the street. There is surely evidence of three stages of encroachment here: the timber balconies of sometime in the sixteenth century, the extension of c1620 and the arcade of c1630.[17] But encroachment may usually have been less blatant than this. Towards the end of the century, James VII was to imply, in a charter granted in 1688, that the burgesses had burrowed their cellars under the street, claimed the ground thus gained as their own and then built on top of it.[18] But, however this may exactly have been, there can be no doubt that the growth of Edinburgh was assisted by the simple expedient of stealing the edges of the High Street.

Gladstone's Land surely tells us even more than this. It was, with its cellars, its five floors and its attic, an extremely tall building erected on very narrow foundations on ground which, at the back of the site at least, must have fallen quite steeply away. That it still stands is a tribute to those who built it. That it was so tall is surely a comment on Edinburgh's growing population and its confined site. We should not perhaps exaggerate this. Moubray's House and the adjacent Knox's Land, both just above the Netherbow, are both of approximately the same shape but both have two floors less.[19] None the less Gordon's plan shows a long line of very tall buildings; it may be inexact in detail, but it was for the most part accurate in essence. After all, Robertson's Land, built towards the end of the seventeenth century on the southern edge of Parliament Close, had something like a dozen storeys; its feet were somewhere down in the Cowgate valley; its head was roughly level with the roof of St Giles.[20]

Robertson's Land really belongs to a different era. Its mansion flats were piled in layers one on top of the other and, to this extent, they belong to the past rather than the future. But they were large, luxurious and dignified; they looked forward into a more spacious age. The seventeenth century had long been attempting to create dignity out of chaos. In 1644 the magistrates and Council acquired the power to buy up dilapidated dwellings with a view to their redevelopment on modern lines. The uniformity of the frontages shown on Gordon's plan of 1647 may well be spurious, but it surely reflected the north side of the High Street as it ought to have been. The shape of the future was specified in some detail by the town council after a serious fire in 1674. New tenements must be built with uniform stone frontages supported where necessary with arches or pillars; timber frontages, at once dangerous and undignified, were forbidden. It was intended, though not insisted, that the owners of existing timber tenements should follow suit. Robert Milne, king's master mason, continued the process. Milne's Court, which still survives, swept medieval closes aside and built all over them. Old Edinburgh, he seemed to be saying, was almost dead.[21] But the search for a New Town within the narrow confines of the old one, which went on for almost a century, was surely bound to fail. Edinburgh must leave its lofty ridge and seek the broader expanses of its plateaus. It would follow the brewers.

It is obvious that seventeenth-century Edinburgh suffered a crisis of overpopulation. Edinburgh had probably been growing appreciably since the middle years of the fifteenth century; but no satisfactory estimate of its population is possible before the Reformation and even then the task is difficult. There are now surviving lists of voluntary contributions, in effect of taxation, from 1565 onwards as well as muster rolls, the earliest of 1558, which give the numbers of merchants, craftsmen and their servants liable for military service. These lists, it has been concluded, indicate a population of about 12,000 in 1560. There is little doubt that this estimate is very close to the truth. The tax rolls improve in quality and quantity in the 1580s and there is a rather equivocal, yet still valuable, estimate, made by the presbytery, of the number of communicants in the parish, then somewhat smaller than the burgh, of Edinburgh in 1592. The total was 8,000 living in 2,239 households and this, it has been argued, may represent a population of something less than 15,000 for the burgh. The pressure was growing and it continued to grow.[22] In 1636 Brereton was told by his 'intelligent' informant that the parish, which had by now expanded to coincide with the burgh, had about 16,000 communicants. Using a multiplier of 1.7 to include children, this would represent a total population of some 27,000 — perhaps too many.[23] But the 1630s produced another sort of tax, incidentally for the payment of ministers' stipends, and the tax roll actually gave a name and address for every householder. It is plainly accurate within the limits of seventeenth-century bureaucracy and it is obviously entitled to more respect than either of our estimates of communicants. It shows 3,901 inhabited houses and 903 business premises of various sorts. There is perhaps only one significant defect in the roll. It is extremely difficult to be certain whether booths, which varied considerably in value, were also houses or not. Usually they were not, but it seems reasonable to conclude that the real total was rather more than 4,000, perhaps 4,100, recorded households together with an unknowable number of tiny houses which escaped the vigilance of the burgh's officers.[24]

It is always difficult to translate households into population: large houses had many servants and possibly apprentices too, very small houses had none of either. The problems are numerous and it is quite impossible to quantify any of them. Estimates from other towns and other periods suggest an average of between rather more than four and rather less than five. The writer, who has little faith in seventeenth-century bureaucracies, has preferred the higher figure because of the danger of omissions. This would suggest a regular population of rather less than 20,000 to which one further allowance must obviously be added.[25] Edinburgh was at once plagued by and dependent on the hordes of 'sturdy beggars' who were at worst the raw material of the Edinburgh mob and at best an invaluable supply of cheap labour. To take only one example, the building miracles performed on Edinburgh's slopes required a lot of excavation and earth did not move itself. No doubt the number of vagrants varied considerably; but it is surely likely that they pushed the population well above 20,000. However these figures are construed, it is evident that the population of Edinburgh grew very considerably during the first three decades of the seventeenth century and that it went on growing, perhaps less rapidly, thereafter.

The annuity tax roll of 1635 naturally shows a huge preponderance of very small houses. Out of 3,901, 829 paid less than £5 per year in rent; another 855 paid £5–£9; not far short of half of the houses paid less than £10 per year; two-thirds paid less than £40. By contrast a tiny fraction (eleven out of 3,901) paid more than £400 and some at least of these represented whole tofts with frontages of several roods. But these were unusual; nearly all of the remaining third paid from £70 to £219 per year. This was plainly a burgh with considerable inequalities of wealth and these can be expressed geographically as well. In the burgh as a whole, the average house paid a rent of just over £40; in the two administrative districts immediately opposite St Giles, the averages were £68 and £57; across the road and immediately west of the church, the figure was £54. If all these areas were substantially above average, the two districts which encompassed the Grassmarket were, with £14 and £20, considerably below. These were extremes, but it is fair to add that the centre of the burgh was wealthier than its outskirts. The districts south of the Cowgate, the area between the High Street and Trinity College Kirk and the anomalous oblong in the Canongate were all below average. Old Edinburgh was very populous but very small and its internal variations were less significant than its similarities. It would be an exaggeration to suggest that everybody knew everybody else, but this was the most intimate of cities. Its vast inequalities of wealth were softened by propinquity. Seventeenth-century Edinburgh was affluent, bustling, riotous and insanitary; snobbish it was not.

The annuity tax roll tells us as much as we are entitled to expect about the population of this rumbustious capital and quite a lot, though less than we would wish, about its social structure. It sometimes, but by no means invariably, attaches an occupation to the names, so meticulously recorded, of the heritors or tenants concerned. This poses insoluble problems with common names. How many John Smiths were there in the Edinburgh of the 1630s? And, if there were many, what did they do? In theory at least, these questions are often unanswerable. The ordinary tax rolls of the burgh give occupations but, unlike the annuity roll, they tell of a tax paid only by the relatively wealthy. The burgess roll obviously has similar limitations but the apprentice register, merely because it includes people who did not become burgesses, identified some journeymen as well. But some journeymen left the burgh as soon as they had qualified and these present a problem which even the surviving records of the craft incorporations themselves fail satisfactorily to solve. Again the records of testaments yield a vast amount of detail about important people and a few that were less important; but they relate neither to the whole of the population of the burgh nor to a statistically valid sample of it. Even the marriage register, extraordinarily comprehensive though it is, relates only to those who got married.[26] The virtue of the annuity roll is quite simply that it gives an approximate indication not only of the presence but of the wealth of everybody in the burgh; it includes the poor as well as the wealthy; it includes all the wealthy whether they paid ordinary taxation or not. The calculations in Table 9.1 are based on a large, if arbitrarily chosen, sample drawn

Table 9.1: *Edinburgh householders, 1635 (A, B, C, D surnames only)*

Occupation	Annual Rent Payable (£ Scots)						Total
	0–9	10–19	20–39	40–69	70–199	200+	
Merchants	0	7	28	48	52	12	147
Craftsmen	5	30	66	45	20	1	167
Other Trades	7	12	12	7	3	1	42
Professional	0	4	9	30	37	8	88
Journeymen	16	44	11	1	0	0	72
Labourers	7	6	0	1	1	0	15
Unknown	115	53	34	26	6	0	234
Women	74	66	41	31	19	3	234
Non-Edinburgh	0	2	7	14	20	0	43
All Householders	224	224	208	203	158	25	1042

Note: Most of those without a known occupation were either journeymen or servants. Many of the women paying a low rent also worked for a wage.
Source: ECA, MS Annuity Tax.

from the annuity roll. They are included in the full knowledge that they are less than exact; it is only claimed that they are not essentially misleading.

To begin with the top end of the list, the merchants tended to pay very high rents. There were none in the lowest category but the proportion grew steadily until the highest in which they provided almost half of the total. The professional group, consisting mainly of lawyers of one kind or another, displayed a rather similar curve. It is reasonable to conclude that the two groups, seen as groups rather than as individuals, were about as wealthy as each other and that the craftsmen, with a peak in the 20–39 category, were poorer. The journeymen's peak is one category lower at 10–19 and the 'labourers', perhaps better described as skilled workers unattached to any of the traditional incorporations, are concentrated almost entirely in the two lowest categories. The 'unknown' largely consist of the unskilled and, scarcely surprisingly, they show a definite peak in the lowest category. It is interesting that women heads of household display a rather similar trend. Those in the lowest categories were, if guesses as yet unsubstantiated can be allowed, largely unmarried women or perhaps widows engaged in unskilled work of some kind; those in the higher groups were, on much better evidence, widows of burgesses carrying on the businesses of their dead husbands. In most cases these had been merchants; but a few had probably been craftsmen who had foresworn the actual practice of their crafts. It is at least extremely unlikely that any woman, or at least any tolerably wealthy woman, actually worked with her hands.

We can refine some of these distinctions through the ordinary tax rolls of the burgh. These are a useful guide to the wealth of the merchants and craftsmen who, apart from the office of provost, monopolised the government of the burgh. Thus, while eighty-seven merchants and 308 craftsmen paid less than £5 per year in 1634, fifty-five merchants and no craftsmen paid more than £80. The typical merchant paid between £10 and £39 per year, the typical craftsman less than £10. But there were merchants and merchants, craftsmen and craftsmen. A merchant living in a house worth £20, £30 or £40 a year and paying perhaps £5 to £15 in taxes may well have earned his fairly ordinary living by selling goods that others had brought into the burgh. In effect he was a shop-keeper, but the seventeenth century called him a merchant. Thomas Gladstaines once owned the whole of the fine house which still bears his name and was then worth more than £500 per year; he was essentially an export-import man, a merchant in the true sense of the term. His tax payments had been well above average in the early 1620s; but, probably because of commercial misfor-tune, they declined later in the decade. In 1634 he only paid £3; well before 1635, he had sold the best part of his house and was living in the top floor flat. The purchaser was David Jenkin another export-import man who, by the 1640s at least, had come to specialise in the arms trade. In 1635 he lived in one of the middle flats, assessed at £150, in his own part of Gladstone's Land; but he rented out the rest of it and he had property else-where in the burgh as well in Leith. He probably speculated in building land at a time when it was almost certain to increase in value. The value of his dwelling was comfortably rather than spec-tacularly above average; his tax payments, no less than £100 in 1634, were always very high. His activities were various, but the period called him a merchant.[27] It also called William Dick a merchant, but his activities were much more various still. legend insists that great cartloads of bullion followed each other out of his courtyard into the High Street to pay the armies of the Covenant and that he could ride from Linlithgow through Leith to North Berwick without leaving his own land. The legend, whether literally true or not, accurately suggests that William Dick was more than a little larger than life. The facts, as we know them, are eloquent. He was, of course, an export-import man who had once chartered a Yarmouth vessel to hawk Scottish goods round the ports of northern Italy. He lived in a counting-house complex embracing a frontage of about three roods and extending from the High Street just opposite St Giles down to the Nor' Loch. With the exception of a few ground floor booths, he had the whole of one of the larger medieval tofts; in 1635 it was assessed at £500 per year. In 1634, his tax payment was £1,200 and he paid nearly three times as much as anybody else in the burgh. In 1642 he had a country residence at Braid, the nearby Grange of St Giles and the lands of North Berwick. And he held more as a mortgagee. He had herring works in North Berwick and he held others on wadset; he owned ships; he owned coal and salt works probably in the region of Prestonpans and Joppa; he had granaries in Leith; he was a customs farmer; he lent money to private individuals and to the government of the day. To oversimplify a complicated process, he advanced money to needy rulers on the security of taxation; the taxes came in slowly but they eventually came; in the end William Dick got his money back with the interest. This proved a fairly safe process during the personal reign of Charles I; it worked well enough during the Bishops' Wars; it survived the perils of the 1640s; it failed during the 1650s when the Cromwellian governments neither used his services nor enforced debts left behind by their predecessors. In 1655 William Dick died in a debtors' prison in London because Oliver Cromwell refused to save him. But we should perhaps remember him as once he had been. In the 1630s the young Montrose toured France on credit provided by William Dick. He had a factor in Paris; indeed his reputation had travelled along the sea lanes to the ports, the entrepôts and the banking centres of Europe. Everybody knew that his credit was good. He was a moneylender in the grand manner; but the period called him a merchant.[28]

The tax payments of William Dick were about eighty times the burgess norm of £15 per year; a typical merchant paid somewhat more than the norm and a typical craftsman substantially less. Indeed just over 80 per cent of Edinburgh's craftsmen paid less than £10 per year.[29] These, like the lesser merchants, were small business men who lived comfortably without aspiring to real wealth. There was of course another 20 per cent, but none of these paid more than £67 and only a few more than £40. There were none of the stature of William Dick or David Jenkin. These figures cover a large number of different occupations and to this extent they are slightly misleading. In fact each occupation had its own structure, it own character and its own impact on the economy of the burgh. There were only seven bonnetmakers concentrated in a small area on the west side of Leith Wynd; the typical bonnetmaker paid only £2 in tax and all of them were poor. They suffered from the competition of ten hatmakers who were concentrated only less closely in the same quarter of the burgh. To judge from the tax rolls, the hatmakers, with an average of £6, were winning.[30] These two crafts, both small and both closely grouped, were not entirely dissimilar; but the tailors offered a complete contrast. There were no less than 134 of them scattered all round the town. Their average was only £6 but this masked huge differences. The vast majority were rather poor but some, including several in the relatively fashionable area opposite St Giles, paid as much as £40 or even £60. These obviously had larger establishments selling superior clothes to a wealthier clientele but all of them surely reflected a burgh increasingly conscious of the niceties of life. They, perhaps more than any of the other crafts, illustrate Edinburgh as a centre of consumption. The dyers, though they too worked on cloth, were different again. Perhaps because of the smell, they belonged to the fringes of the burgh. Their vats were situated in poor areas but they themselves were far from poor; two of them paid £33 and another £27; the average was £12. This was indeed a capital intensive industry using expensive raw materials and it employed a fair number of skilled journeymen. The local clothmakers were by contrast in obvious decline. Nine weavers (average £3) and four waulkers (average £7) survived, but their industry had already found a better home among the waulkmills of the Water of Leith.[31] The skinners and furriers would eventually follow the weavers down to the river but, for the time being, most of them still lived and worked in the burgh. Their business was to convert hides and skins into leather and leather into saleable goods, notably gloves. Their numbers, no less than forty-six, and their tax payments, which averaged £8 and included one of £53, suggest affluence. The cordiners (shoemakers) had thirty-one members scattered throughout the burgh. They lived very close to their usually fairly humble customers and they were mainly concerned to supply a basic commodity for which there was a reasonably steady demand. Theirs was a small scale operation; their average was about £3 per year and only two of them significantly exceeded it. The cordiners of Edinburgh were neither rich nor poor.

The incorporation of hammermen was an umbrella organisation embracing the metalworkers and associated trades of the burgh. It had forty-two members making an average tax payment of £5. In a sense this is unremarkable but the details are interesting. The basic metalworker was obviously the blacksmith; but there were only ten and their average (less than £2) was the lowest in the town. They were perhaps more vulnerable than most to cheap competition from the suburbs that straggled along all the main roads into Edinburgh. Again Edinburgh had once been a centre of weapon manufacture; now, in 1634, it had only two taxpaying armourers with an average of under £5 and it is natural to suspect competition from the Canongate. Half a dozen cutlers with an average of £13 suggest a healthier industry; but, if this was so, there was only one lorimer, who paid £12, and only two saddlers with the tiny average of £3. The pewterers were relatively numerous but eleven of them only yielded £42 in tax; while the locksmiths, though reasonably prosperous (average £10) only numbered five; one — but only one — shearsmith paid £40. The hammermen show evidence of economic decline in total contrast to their considerable political influence.[32] The goldsmiths, once hammermen but separately incorporated since 1525, were more prosperous; fourteen of them contributed a total of £182; one paid £40 and two more £27 each. Their booths were concentrated, as though to remember George Heriot, in the immediate vicinity of St Giles; but none of them seem to have aspired to the moneylending function which had made George Heriot wealthy. They were highly skilled craftsmen with low labour costs and a very valuable product. They were affluent, but they left greatness to William Dick, whom the period called a merchant.

The food processing trades were different again. In the thirteenth century these trades had been dominated by capitalist victuallers who had controlled supplies and regulated the prices of the finished products. The baxters and the fleshers had been rather more than wage earners but rather less than independent businessmen. The victuallers had been *probi homines* of a kind that continued to dominate the town council. The seals of cause, granted to the fleshers in 1488 and to the baxters in 1523, had brought a measure of freedom. But traces of the old subordination survived into the seventeenth century. The council was always preoccupied with the increasing appetite of its growing burgh and displayed its concern by controlling prices. Bread was normally put on a sliding scale based on the cost of wheat. The baxter pursued his complicated calling under constraints that were not of his making. He bought his wheat in the Grassmarket, took it to be ground in the town's mills at Dean, carried it back to his bakehouse, made it into bread and sold it at a price determined by his usually fairly affluent customers. His ovens were expensive and, in some cases at least, his labour costs substantial. In 1634 there were thirty-eight master bakers distributed fairly evenly across the burgh. The average tax payment was, at £6 per year, quite high and two paid as much as £30. The flesher bought cattle and sheep at the far end of the Grassmarket, he slaughtered them, possibly on the edge of the Nor' Loch, but more often in his own yard if he had one or the open street if he had not. His contribution to the smells of a crowded burgh can only be described as distinguished. There were no fleshers north of the High Street and twenty-four between the High Street and the Flodden Wall. He needed more space than the burgh could easily afford; but his equipment was as simple as his turnover was rapid; he needed very little capital. His average was only £3 and few individuals significantly departed from it.[33] The candlemakers were among his best customers and their distribution closely followed his. Theirs was an ancient if underprivileged trade, but its importance in a city of narrow alleys and tall buildings is obvious. The candlemakers of Edinburgh could not fail and their average, at £7 per year, was strikingly high. One shining example paid £40.

If the candlemakers were underprivileged, the surgeons emphatically were not. They had led the opposition to the merchants during the early 1580s and they had emerged from the resulting settlement, the decreet arbitral of 1583, as an influential craft with a permanent place on the town council. And yet the tax rolls of the 1630s record twelve surgeons with an average payment of only £8 per year, very little more than a candlemaker. Political influence did not necessarily reflect wealth; but, at first glance at least, this does seem odd. The explanation probably resides in the peculiarities of a system of taxation which taxed profits — whether from trade, moneylending or the ownership of landed property — and ignored wages, salaries and fees. If the remuneration of a surgeon was regarded, like that of a lawyer, as a fee, it would not have been taxed.

The doubts which surround the surgeons may seem to be dispelled by the very low averages yielded by the building trades. According to the tax rolls, the town had twenty-nine wrights with an average of £6 per year and twelve masons with an average of £3. These figures may seem absurd in a burgh with a building boom, but they surely were not. The masons and wrights, who built the Tron Kirk and the Parliament House during the 1630s, worked for a very high wage; they were not working for themselves. These were of course public projects, but there is no reason to think that the private sector was essentially different. Thomas Gladstaines financed the development of his famous tenement in the Lawnmarket; later in the century, Robertson developed his tower block in Parliament Square. The one was a merchant, the other a brewer who called himself a merchant; both employed masons, neither was a mason himself. A little later still the king's master mason developed Milne's Square and Milne's Court; he was part owner of both and he designed both. He was at once a speculative builder and an architect; like Gladstaines and Robertson, he employed masons and wrights for wages which did not show up in the tax rolls.

The valuation made for the annuity tax offers some support for this thesis. The examples which follow are confined within the limits of our A, B, C, D sample, but they are revealing. Three surgeons and the widow of a recently deceased fourth lived in houses worth £100, £100, £110 and £40 respectively. One of them paid tax at the modest rate of £15, the others much less; but their houses suggest a standard of living comparable with that of a fairly successful lawyer. The masons and wrights lived less well than this; but, if their house rents are any guide, they were not poor. Half a dozen masons, all paying little or no tax, lived in houses with annual values of £10, £16, £16, £20, £24 and £27. These were all on the small side of a burgh average of £40, but none of them fell within the smallest category and all of them were within the craft norm of £10 to £39 per year. The wrights were a little wealthier, perhaps because more of them supplemented their wages with repair work done on their own account. One lived in a tiny house worth only £7 per year, but the others included three in the £10–£39 category and three more paying £40, £40 and £53 respectively. Andrew Hastie, who received a £4 per week wage for his work on the Parliament House, lived in a house worth £40 per year and he paid no tax at all.[34]

This burgh of nearly 4,000 houses was governed by a town council consisting of twenty-five full members. These were the Lord Provost, four bailies, the treasurer, the dean of guild, ten merchants including previous magistrates or their substitutes, two craft councillors and six council deacons always drawn from the same crafts. The remaining eight deacons, usually called extraordinary deacons, were entitled to attend on certain specified occasions. It follows from this that the merchants always had a majority over the crafts and that some crafts, those represented by the council deacons, were politically more influential than others. These were the hammermen, surgeons, goldsmiths, tailors, skinners and, during this period, the cordiners. These, with some reservations about the last, were the crafts which had led the revolt of the early 1580s and forced their way into the burgh oligarchy. The tax roll of 1634 and the annuity tax roll of 1635 offer two separate assessments of the wealth of the council and its component parts. These calculations rest on a large sample consisting of all those mentioned in either roll who had served at any time between the elections of Michaelmas 1626 and Michaelmas 1641. The average councillor paid £53 in tax (or about 3½ times the average for the burgh) and lived in a house worth £102 a year (about 2½ times the burgh average). The equivalent figures for magistrates were £131 and £150, for other merchant councillors £69 and £144, for a rather small sample of craft councillors £10 and £89, for the council deacons £16 and £55 and for the extraordinary deacons £5 and £36. There is a comforting similarity between the two curves thus implied. Both show that the magistrates were richer than other merchant councillors, that the two together were much wealthier than the rest of the council and that, within the craft element, the council deacons were wealthier than the extraordinary deacons. Above all they reveal an oligarchy of wealth dominated by men who, whatever they actually were, called themselves merchants.[35]

This then was Edinburgh in mid-century. It was still tied to the castle on the crag which had first been fortified in the sixth century; it had been a royal burgh since the twelfth century and a capital since the fifteenth; by then it had the weight of the centuries behind it. The burgesses of Edinburgh were perched on their lofty ridge and they had forgotten how to get off. They were tied to a cramped site, tormented by steep slopes and cursed with a poor natural water supply. Their port was two crooked miles away at Leith; their mills, on which they were only less dependent, were down on the Water of Leith at Dean. As population grew, all these problems came together to produce a crisis. Everything was wrong; but Edinburgh, not for the first time or the last, somehow contrived not merely to survive but to triumph. Suburbs were swallowed up; industries migrated to the outskirts; pure spring water eventually came from afar; little new towns began to appear within the narrow confines of the old one. The resources of seventeenth-century Edinburgh were stretched, but they did not actually burst; the poor jostled the rich in an atmosphere of riotous conviviality. After all, the site, however impossible it might be, was truly magnificent. The Castle, the broad High Street and even the narrow closes had blended into their setting to produce a landscape of staggering beauty. Small wonder that it puzzled visitors from distant parts. Tucker was perplexed and thought that it ought to have been somewhere else; Brereton admired the dignity of its High Street but was appalled by the squalor of its closes. But everybody agreed that it was unique and that it was too crowded. David Buchanan was a well-travelled Scot who composed a convincing description of Edinburgh as a companion to Gordon's plan of 1647: 'I am not sure,' he said, 'that you will find anywhere so many dwellings and such a multitude in so small a space as in this city of ours.'[36]

Notes

The map of the contours (Figure 9.2) of the site shows rockhead contours, expressed in metres, that is, the land surface as it actually was without the glacial drift, which on the ridge was seldom more than two metres deep.

1. 'Report by Thomas Tucker . . .', in *SBRS Misc.* (1881), 17.
2. D. Calderwood, *History of the Kirk of Scotland* (Wodrow Soc., 1842–9), v, 177–8.
3. ECA, MS Accounts for Building and Repairing Churches, 1635–47; this volume includes the Book for the Merk per Tun, 1636–48.
4. ECA, MS Account of Goods in Edinburgh Weighhouse, 1613–17.
5. I. Guy, 'The Scottish export trade, 1460–1599, from the Exchequer Rolls' (Unpublished St Andrews M.Phil., 1982), 94.
6. 167 Leith skippers are given in a list of 1643; see J. Brown, 'The Social, Political and Economic Influences of the Edinburgh Merchant Elite, 1600–38' (Edinburgh Univ. Ph.D., 1985), 14.
7. F. W. Bedford, *History of George Heriot's Hospital* (Edinburgh, 1872), 31–73, 291–328; *Charters and Documents relating to the City of Edinburgh* (Edinburgh, 1871), 82–3; *Edin. Recs., 1626–41*, 328–34; ECA, MSS Historical Charters, 98; ECA, MS Inventory of City Muniments, iv, 109; v, 425–36.
8. P. Cadell, 'Industrial archaeology of the Water of Leith', in *The Water of Leith*, ed. S. Jamieson (Edinburgh, 1984), 38–54. See G. Marshall, *Presbyteries and Profits* (Oxford, 1980), 140–2, for the Haddington enterprise.
9. Brown, 'Thesis', 10.
10. *Early Travellers in Scotland*, ed. P. H. Brown (Edinburgh, 1891), 92–5, 136–47.
11. *Edin. Recs., 1641–55*, 116; *The Plan of Edinburgh Exactly Done . . .* (1647).

12. *Edinburgh, 1329–1929* (Edinburgh, 1932), 353–68; B. Sissons, 'Geomorphology of central Edinburgh', *Scot. Geog. Mag.*, 87 (1971), 185–96.

13. N. M. M. Holmes, 'Excavations within the Tron Kirk, Edinburgh, 1974', *Post Medieval Archaeology*, 9 (1975), 160–3.

14. ECA, MSS Moses Bundles, 197, no. 7103.

15. J. Colston, *The Edinburgh and District Water Supply* (Edinburgh, 1890), 8–18; *APS*, iv, 632; *Early Travellers*, 141–2; *Edin. Recs., 1589–1603*, 75.

16. *Early Travellers*, 67, 141.

17. *RCAHMS, Edinburgh* (Edinburgh, 1951), 74–8; J. Gifford, C. McWilliam and D. Walker (eds.), *The Buildings of Scotland, Edinburgh* (London, 1984), 59, 195–6.

18. ECA, MS Historical Charters, 104.

19. *RCAHMS, Edinburgh*, 94–9; *Buildings of Scotland, Edinburgh*, 205–8.

20. M. Wood, 'All the stately buildings of Thomas Robertson', *Bk. Old Edin. Club*, 24 (1942), 126–57; H. Armet, 'Notes on buildings in Edinburgh in the . . . 17th century', ibid., 29 (1956), 111.

21. *APS*, VI, pt. i, 227; *Edin. Recs., 1665–80*, 177–8; *Buildings of Scotland, Edinburgh*, 59, 194; *RCAHMS, Edinburgh*, pp. lxxii, 73.

22. M. Lynch, *Edinburgh and the Reformation* (Edinburgh, 1981), 9–14; *Edin. Recs., 1589–1603*, 68, 75; ECA, MSS Moses Bundles, 195, no. 7029; the details of the 1592 census are given in M. Lynch, 'Whatever happened to the medieval burgh?', *Scot. Econ. and Social History*, 4 (1984), 7.

23. *Early Travellers*, 141.

24. ECA, MS Extent Roll for the Annuity Tax, 1635; the property owners, but not the tenants, are listed by C. B. Boog Watson, in *Bk. Old Edin. Club*, 13 (1924), 93–146.

25. Lynch, *Edinburgh*, 9–11. The annuity tax roll also reveals that some 4 per cent of households were possessed by people such as landed proprietors, great and small, who did not permanently reside in Edinburgh and were exempt from the tax. These households have not been included in the given totals but some of their servants probably did actually live in the burgh for most of the time.

26. ECA, MS Extent Roll for National Taxation, 1634. The alphabetical lists, published by the Scottish Record Society, of the *Edinburgh Register of Testaments*, the *Edinburgh Register of Apprentices* and the *Edinburgh Marriage Register* have been used in these calculations.

27. ECA, MS Annuity Tax, 1635; Extent Roll for National Taxation, 1634. See Brown, 'Thesis', 470, 483, for further details of Gladstaines and Jenkin.

28. ECA, MS Annuity Tax, 1635; Extent Roll for National Taxation, 1634; J. S. Smith, *The Grange of St Giles* (Edinburgh, 1898), 46–56, 385–7; S. G. E. Lythe, *The Economy of Scotland in its European Setting* (Edinburgh, 1960), 139–62; C. B. Boog Watson, *Names of Edinburgh Closes and Wynds* (Edinburgh, 1923), 22–6; see also Brown, 'Thesis', 459; D. Stevenson, 'The financing of the cause of the Covenants', *SHR*, 51 (1972), 89–123.

29. ECA, MS Extent Roll for National Taxation, 1634.

30. Only eight Edinburgh bonnetmakers and hatmakers are listed in the poll tax of 1694, with a further three in Leith; see Whyte, Chapter 10, this volume, Table 10.4.

31. By the 1690s 10.9 per cent of the adult male workforce in Leith was engaged in textile trades, but Edinburgh still retained as much as 16.6 per cent of its workforce in textiles; see Whyte, Chapter 10, this volume, Table 10.2.

32. ECA, MS Minute Books of the Incorporation of Hammermen, vol. iii, 1628–83; *Edin. Recs., 1403–1528*, 47.

33. *Edin. Recs. 1403–1528*, 54, 214; *1603–25*, 409.

34. ECA, MSS Accounts for Building and Repairing Churches, Accounts for Building Parliament House, 1633–40; R. K. Hannay and G. P. H. Watson, 'The building of Parliament House', *Bk. Old Edin. Club*, 13 (1924), 1–78; R. S. Mylne, *The Master Masons* (Edinburgh, 1893), 213–48.

35. *Edin. Recs., 1573–89*, 250–8, 265–71; see n27, above.

36. David Buchanan, 'Description of Edinburgh, 1647–52', in P. H. Brown (ed.), *Scotland before 1700* (Edinburgh, 1893), 313–18.

I should like to thank Dr James Brown, Dr Joyce McMillan and Dr Helen Bennett, all of whom have regularly used the Edinburgh City Archives, for helpful conversations on the subjects covered in this paper. I gratefully acknowledge their assistance. The conclusions reached are, of course, my own.

10

The Occupational Structure of Scottish Burghs in the Late Seventeenth Century

Ian D. Whyte

In recent years urban historians have shown considerable interest in the social and economic structure of early-modern European towns.[1] An important aspect of this work has been the study of urban occupations as a means of shedding light on the character of individual towns. Much of this work has concentrated on larger towns possessing wide ranges of specialist occupations. Nevertheless, smaller centres were more important numerically and, though modest in size and limited in the variety of their activities, they constituted most rural dwellers' experience of urban life. In addition there has been a lack of comparative studies of the occupational structures of towns, whether at different levels of the urban hierarchy within a country or region or between similar-sized towns in different areas.[2]

Scotland, though not as well documented as some European nations during early-modern times, is particularly interesting as regards urban occupational structures for several reasons. First, the relatively small size of both Scotland and of most Scottish burghs, facilitates a comparative approach. Second, Scottish urban development during the seventeenth century differed in some important respects from that of England where much recent work on urban occupations has been concentrated. Burgh foundation was still proceeding vigorously in Scotland during the seventeenth century[3] and the urban hierarchy was less fixed than that of England, which remained remarkably stable between 1500 and 1700.[4] Third, while the proportion of Scotland's population living in towns, however defined, was certainly smaller than in England or the Low Countries, the level of urbanisation, especially in Lowland Scotland and most notably in Fife and Lothian, was probably quite high compared with many parts of Europe. As a rough measure, the proportion of Scotland's population living in the four largest towns in the later seventeenth century was probably greater than in Ireland, the Scandinavian countries or France, and possibly similar to Spain or Italy.[5] Such comparisons must be treated with care but they may indicate that urban development in late seventeenth-century Scotland was not as backward as has sometimes been supposed. Lastly, the contrasting legal status and trading position of royal burghs on the one hand and burghs of barony and regality on the other, makes a comparative study of the occupational structures of towns from each group of especial interest, particularly during the later seventeenth century when royal burghs were facing increasing competition from the upstart unfree centres.[6]

Studies of the role and functions of burghs in early-modern Scotland have concentrated on their institutional frameworks rather than on their societies and economies,[7] but from what is known of these it is possible to pose some questions about the occupational structure of Scottish burghs. To what extent were the burghs homogenous in their social and economic characteristics? One would expect there to have been major differences in levels and distribution of urban wealth between the capital, the larger regional centres and smaller burghs, whether royal or baronial. One would also expect variations in the relative importance of different occupational groups between the larger burghs with administrative functions and substantial overseas trade, and smaller local centres. Equally, one could postulate contrasts in the occupational structure and distribution of wealth between royal and baronial burghs as a result of their contrasting legal status and trading privileges. Any such differences which can be identified should help to clarify the relationships between royal and baronial burghs at this time and determine the extent to which their economic activities were in competition or co-operation as well as adding to our general understanding of how towns functioned in the Scottish economy.

Looking more closely at manufacturing one might ask to what extent individual burghs specialised in the production of particular commodities. Work on early-modern towns in England has suggested that the general level of urban specialisation was low.[8] Most towns had a similar spread of employment in trading, retailing, and basic industries such as textiles, clothing, leather making, metal working, building, and food and drink. Deviations from this basic pattern, representing elements of functional specialisation, were not very marked.[9] Was this the case in Scotland? One would expect there to have been some variation at least in the activities which were carried on in Scottish burghs not only due to differences in their size and status but also to variations in the physical character and economic resources of their hinterlands.

A number of sources provide information on burgh occupations. Burgess registers can be used to chart the changing fortunes of individual merchant and trades incorporations. Such men and their families, however, only formed about a third of the population in many burghs.[10] Some urban marriage registers for the later seventeenth and early eighteenth centuries provide the occupations of husbands, but the best source for an introductory survey of burgh occupations is the poll tax records of the 1690s. Data have survived for burghs in three main areas: Aberdeenshire, the Lothians and Renfrewshire.[11] Information has also been obtained for individual burghs elsewhere. Thirty-seven centres were analysed ranging from Edinburgh and regional centres like Aberdeen and Perth through smaller royal and baronial burghs to non-burghal market centres. In addition, partial information was available for Dumfries, Glasgow and Inverness.[12] The poll tax lists are by no means perfect for this purpose; there are indications that the occupational classification used by the tax collectors was a simplified one.[13] Nevertheless, the records provide a fairly standardised basis for comparing broad categories of occupation between a number of centres.

Urban occupations can be classified by two principal methods: by type of activity and type of product.[14] Both systems have advantages in different contexts. A type-of-activity classification has been employed here initially to explore the broader functional differences between burghs while a type-of-product classification has been used for the main kinds of manufacture to highlight particular specialisations. It must, however, be emphasised that within the occupational categories which have been used people may have carried out a variety of functions. For instance, a craftsman listed as a tailor may have bought and processed the cloth for his workshop, manufactured garments himself, supervised the work of his journeymen and apprentices and handled the sale and distribution of the finished products. Many people may have had more than one occupation but this is rarely indicated in the poll tax records. The type-of-product classification involved little ambiguity or overlap except between the leather and clothing trades. Cordiners and shoemakers have been assigned to the leather trades and glovers to clothing.

A type-of-activity classification of occupations

Table 10.1 shows a breakdown of the male pollable workforce of the thirty-seven centres using a type-of-activity classification. The manufacturing category equates with what Patten has termed 'artisan-retailing' and does not assume that all tradesmen were solely engaged in manufacture.[15] Otherwise, the divisions are reasonably clear-cut and should be adequate to bring out general trends.

Edinburgh was clearly distinguished from other large burghs by the prominence of the professions. Much of this was due to the law, which accounted for 62 per cent of this group, and medicine, which made up a further 22 per cent. The remainder included those in the church, education and army officers. This group substantially outnumbered the Edinburgh merchants. In addition, landowners formed a smaller but still significant group in the capital, including those who owned town houses and those occupying rented accommodation at the time of the survey. Almost certainly the size and importance of this group in the capital is underestimated, as many of the nobility probably occupied their town residences for only part of the year and were polled on their country estates.[16] Many men listed as advocates and merchants would also have been heritors. The landowners would have helped to maintain the demand for high-level services which supported the professions as well as stimulating the city's luxury trades. The many domestic servants in their households were also an important element in the city's population. There was, however, considerable variation within the landowning group. At one extreme were the earl of Crawford and the duke of Gordon who maintained large retinues including private tutors and chaplains.[17] At a lower level were men like Robert Hamilton, 'heritor at Newbattle and frequently resident in Edinburgh' with two men-servants.[18] At the bottom there was a good deal of genteel poverty — for example Patrick Inglis, gentleman 'now denuded and out of possession' with only a single servant woman.[19]

Aberdeen, as the northern capital, also had an important professional group, proportionally the largest after Edinburgh. Landowners and gentry formed a slightly larger proportion of the population than in Edinburgh but Aberdeen did not function as a social centre for the nobility in the same way as the capital. The resident heritors were mainly small lairds, many of them from cadet branches of ubiquitous north-eastern noble families like Forbes and Gordon, living off rents of under £500 Scots per year.

Of the larger burghs those which were heads of sheriffdoms and regalities — Perth, Paisley and St Andrews — had higher proportions in the professions, again mainly in law. Selkirk, centre of a remote and sparsely-populated sheriffdom, had a smaller professional elite. In the case of Paisley and St Andrews the proportion of resident heritors was also comparatively large but the men classified in this group were usually mere bonnet lairds and portioners. A group of larger baronial burghs — Bo'ness, Dalkeith, Leith and Musselburgh — were all deficient in professional employment. This was not entirely due to their less exalted status as baronial burghs for Peterhead — and to a lesser extent Fraserburgh — had professional groups more comparable in importance with those of the larger royal burghs. It is probable that the professions were better represented in Peterhead and Fraserburgh due to their comparative isolation from Aberdeen and the proximity of a fairly densely populated rural hinterland which may have enhanced their importance locally and increased their provision of high-level services. In the case of the first group of baronial burghs their nearness to Edinburgh may have diminished the need for a wide range of professional services. In the smallest burghs, whether royal or baronial, one or two ministers, a notary and a schoolmaster comprised the professional element. Centres below about 180 pollable persons did not possess a full range of the main professional groups.

Given the importance of the merchant guilds in the larger royal burghs, the strength of the merchant community might be expected to provide an indication of urban prosperity, although within this group in particular great contrasts in wealth and status occurred. The merchant class in Edinburgh was not as large in relation to the male pollable population as in some other burghs. There were barely twice as many men styled 'merchant' as in Aberdeen. To balance this, the Edinburgh merchant elite was far more wealthy[20] and may have contained a larger proportion of men engaged in overseas trade than in Aberdeen. Many of the wealthier Edinburgh tradesmen may have handled the distribution within Scotland of the products of their workshops. Among the larger burghs a clear group is formed by those with an important

Table 10.1: Type-of-activity classification: percentages of male pollable population

Pollable Population		Landowners and Gentlemen	Professional Services	Services, Trade			Services: Male Domestic Servants	Manufacturing	Labourers	Agriculture	Female Servants per Male Servant
				Merchants	Shipping and Transport	Total Trade					
Edinburgh	14,088	3.4	15.3	9.0	1.3	10.3	24.1	36.0	7.1	3.8	2.4
Aberdeen	3,740	3.9	9.9	22.0	4.5	26.5	13.7	28.7	15.3	2.0	5.5
Musselburgh	1,800	1.5	1.7	1.8	2.7	4.5	13.8	49.0	10.1	19.4	1.4
Leith	1,700	3.1	1.7	2.0	13.5	15.5	11.3	43.1	23.0	2.3	2.9
Perth	1,695	0.5	8.0	10.9	3.0	14.0	10.0	63.5	4.0	0	5.1
Bo'ness	1,417	0.9	1.6	5.7	28.8	34.5	6.1	27.5	10.4	19.0	3.8
Dalkeith	1,180	1.8	2.5	5.8	0.5	6.3	12.6	59.2	4.8	12.8	2.3
Paisley	1,141	5.2	8.3	9.8	1.2	10.9	5.9	60.2	4.6	4.8	4.5
Greenock	754	0	3.0	12.8	38.0	50.8	2.6	35.3	5.6	2.6	11.3
Selkirk	724	1.1	3.3	10.1	1.5	11.6	14.6	45.4	9.4	14.6	1.1
St Andrews	702	5.1	8.7	3.1	0.8	3.9	18.9	39.0	5.5	18.9	1.9
Grangepans	487	0	0.6	1.2	23.8	25.0	4.8	26.2	20.8	22.6	6.3
Fraserburgh	323	2.8	3.7	23.4	20.5	43.9	6.5	27.2	9.3	6.5	7.1
Peterhead	314	1.0	6.3	9.5	17.9	27.4	5.3	28.4	26.3	5.3	8.2
Newark	236	1.3	0	6.7	26.8	33.3	9.4	25.0	13.3	9.3	3.6
Eyemouth	218	4.5	1.1	3.4	3.4	6.8	17.0	20.6	9.1	41.0	2.5
Cartsdyke	207	0	1.1	3.3	41.8	45.1	3.4	37.4	12.1	1.1	5.7
Bathgate	202	1.1	5.8	3.5	0	3.5	5.9	31.3	7.0	45.3	2.4
Old Meldrum	190	0	5.6	22.5	0	22.5	7.0	33.9	22.5	8.5	1.8
Inverurie	187	2.6	6.5	3.9	0	3.9	19.5	28.6	22.1	16.9	1.3

Table 10.1 — continued

Pollable Population		Landowners and Gentlemen	Professional Services	Services, Trade			Services: Male Domestic Servants	Manufacturing	Labourers	Agriculture	Female Servants per Male Servant
				Merchants	Shipping and Transport	Total Trade					
Turriff	176	0	5.8	8.6	0	8.6	20.3	24.6	18.8	21.7	1.5
Mid Calder	160	1.5	4.7	3.1	0	3.1	10.7	40.0	24.6	15.4	1.6
Anstruther Wester	152	3.4	3.4	3.4	10.3	13.8	13.8	43.2	22.4	0	0.8
Rosehearty	121	2.0	4.0	8.0	49.0	57.0	2.0	20.0	10.0	6.0	11.0
Newburgh	117	0	0	0	50.9	50.9	7.3	9.1	12.7	20.0	1.8
Kincardine O'Neill	114	2.6	0	10.5	0	10.5	7.9	26.3	7.9	44.8	5.0
Greenlaw	114	1.8	1.8	0	0	0	16.0	28.6	14.3	37.5	1.2
Huntly	98	0	0	20.0	0	20.0	27.0	33.0	12.0	8.0	1.1
Ellon	95	0	0	1.9	0	1.9	15.1	29.3	46.2	7.5	0.9
Eaglesham	92	0	4.3	8.6	0	8.6	4.3	65.4	10.9	6.5	1.0
Kilbarchan	79	3.4	3.4	17.2	0	17.2	13.9	17.2	34.6	10.3	1.5
Deer	64	0	3.8	3.8	0	3.8	15.4	30.8	3.8	42.3	2.0
Tarves	61	0	10.7	17.9	0	17.9	17.9	17.9	24.9	10.7	2.0
Aboyne	59	3.7	0	3.7	0	3.7	11.1	44.5	14.8	22.2	2.7
Insch	59	0	8.0	4.0	0	4.0	13.0	25.0	25.0	25.0	3.7
Port Glasgow	58	4.8	0	14.3	4.8	19.0	4.8	23.8	3.8	14.2	15.0
Kilmacolm	43	0	0	21.1	0	21.1	15.7	26.4	21.1	15.7	1.7

Source: SRO, MSS Poll Tax Returns

regional trading role and large merchant communities. Aberdeen, Paisley, Perth and Selkirk fall into this group while the incomplete data for Dumfries, Glasgow and Inverness indicate that they were similar. St Andrews was the only larger royal burgh which had a relatively small merchant community. Of the baronial burghs Fraserburgh, Peterhead and Greenock had large merchant communities. By contrast, Bo'ness, Dalkeith, Grangepans, Leith and Musselburgh had small merchant groups. All these burghs were close to the capital and there is evidence that their trade was dominated by Edinburgh merchants and also, in the case of Bo'ness, by those from other royal burghs including Glasgow, Linlithgow and Stirling.[21] The profits from trading tended to by-pass the inhabitants of Bo'ness itself.[22] Grangepans was even more dependent and had only two resident merchants. Although shipping was the most important single occupational category in Grangepans the shipowners were merchants from other burghs.[23] The contrast with Greenock, which one might have expected to have been similarly dependent on Glasgow, is striking.

The designation 'merchant' was almost universal, suggesting that trading was still unspecialised. Only twenty-two men in Edinburgh were listed as 'shopkeeper' and outside the capital this term was used infrequently. Other sources indicate, however, that craftsmen such as the Edinburgh candlemakers had their own shops and handled at least some of the distribution of their own goods,[24] so that people polling as shopkeepers may have specialised in the sale of imported items. Clearly production, wholesaling and retailing were not yet distinctly separated.

There was, naturally, a marked contrast in the transport and shipping sector between coastal and inland burghs. Within this category have been included men listed as mariner, seaman, skipper, fisherman, boatman, carrier and carter. The number of people in this grouping in Aberdeen is suspiciously low, especially in view of the importance of the fishing industry in the town in the early eighteenth century[25] but the coastal quarter of Footdee is missing from the records. The low figures for Perth confirm the evidence of the customs records that the upper Tay was too shallow for effective navigation at this time and that most of the burgh's trade went through ports lower down the Firth.[26] The importance of transport and shipping was marked in Greenock, which was a major centre of the herring fishery,[27] and only slightly less so at Bo'ness, Fraserburgh, Leith, Newark and Peterhead. Greenock, Fraserburgh and Peterhead had substantial percentages both in shipping and the merchant class, suggesting a measure of independent trading activity, but in the case of Bo'ness, Grangepans, Newark and Leith the concentration of employment in shipping, with the smallness of the professional and merchant groups, strengthens the impression that such centres were closely tied in with the activities of the major royal burghs which traded through them. Specialisation in fishing was extreme in some smaller centres, accounting for 52 per cent and 50 per cent of the recorded male population in the east coast ports of Rosehearty and Newburgh respectively, the highest level of specialisation in any function for any centre.

Overland communication employed few people full time, even in the largest burghs. Edinburgh and Aberdeen had some stablers and horse hirers but specialist freight carriers were as likely to be found in surrounding rural areas. Among the smaller centres Old Meldrum and Huntly had unexpectedly large numbers of merchants in relation to their size, suggesting that they had important subregional roles in trading and distribution. Minor local traders with little stock, including itinerant chapmen, were found in even the smallest centres.

Male domestic servants were particularly numerous in Edinburgh and other large royal burghs, where they made up a substantial proportion of the male pollable population. The significance of this group has often been underestimated in previous studies of urban occupations, possibly because many sources fail to record them. Nevertheless, they made up nearly a quarter of the male workforce of Edinburgh, reflecting the greater wealth of the capital for only St Andrews, of the other larger burghs, approached this figure. Details of female employment are generally lacking in the poll tax records except for female domestic servants. These formed a large and well-defined group outnumbering male servants in all the major burghs studied. Table 10.1 shows the ratio of female to male servants and there is a distinct tendency for the figures to fall in step with the sizes of the burghs. Male servants generally outnumbered female ones in rural areas[28] and the smaller burghs, themselves semi-rural in character, reflected this.

Manufacturing was the largest single type-of-activity group in many burghs, as one would have expected, employing around half the recorded male workforce in many cases. Edinburgh and Aberdeen had proportionally smaller manufacturing sectors due to the importance of other groups, but in the case of Edinburgh much craft activity probably went on in the suburbs beyond the burgh limits. The highest percentage in manufacturing was recorded by Perth but most of the towns in which manufacturing dominated were baronial burghs with correspondingly small merchant communities and professional classes.

It is hard to be precise about employment in agriculture in Scottish burghs at this time. It is likely to have engaged a sizeable proportion of the population of many burghs on a part-time basis. Many merchants and tradesmen, even in the largest towns, would, as burgesses, have possessed shares in the arable lands and common grazings of their burghs. An uncertain proportion, particularly significant in Edinburgh, Glasgow, Aberdeen and Dundee, would also have owned and leased land beyond the town limits. In smaller burghs where little infilling of burgage plots had occurred, a good deal of produce may have come from gardens and orchards actually within the burgh.[29] Even in Edinburgh a considerable proportion of the population obtained temporary employment in the surrounding countryside at harvest time.[30] The poll tax records, however, only identify those inhabitants who were engaged in agriculture as their primary occupation. Such people were not absent even in Edinburgh, though most of the people in this category were cottars and smallholders living in the suburbs. The existence of urban dairies in Edinburgh is suggested by a small number of 'cow feeders' in the less densely built-up Canongate, which also contained over thirty gardeners. The agricultural element in baronial burghs like Bo'ness and Dalkeith may be partly due to the difficulty of differentiating between burgh and rural populations in the poll tax returns. In the smaller centres, however, the agricultural element rose dramatically, accounting for over 40 per cent of the recorded male population in several cases.

The occupational groupings which have already been considered must have made up a substantial proportion of the workforce in the burghs concerned. One final, almost residual, group remains for consideration: the unskilled population of labourers and casual wage earners. This group may be equated in part, but by no means entirely, with the urban poor. It has been suggested that, in the sixteenth century at least, Scottish towns did not experience the large surges of poor, unskilled subsistence migrants from rural areas which were a feature of English towns[31] and which created problems of urban poverty on such a scale that it has been suggested that between 30 per cent and 40 per cent of the population of some larger English provincial towns may have been below the poverty line.[32] The situation in Scotland towards the end of the seventeenth century is not so clear. The problem of poverty and the size of the floating immigrant workforce in the burghs at this time deserves detailed study. Poverty could, of course, occur among burgesses and guild brethren, as is evidenced by the records of individual incorporations.[33] In addition, many people listed as tradesmen and indistinguishable in the poll tax records from guild brethren may have been poor immigrants trying to eke out a living on the fringes of burgh society with skills in textile, clothing, leather or metal manufacture learned in the countryside. A category of workmen and labourers, whether employed regularly or on a casual basis, has been identified and while such people were not necessarily all on or below the poverty line they clearly formed a comparatively low status group in burgh society. Even allowing for the likelihood that many casual workers escaped registration or were exempted from payment of the poll tax due to poverty, this group was a substantial one forming nearly a quarter of the recorded workforce in Bo'ness, Leith and Peterhead. Among the larger burghs the proportions in this group tended to be greatest in the ports where many men were probably employed in loading and unloading vessels. The high proportions in some smaller burghs may reflect concentrations of agricultural labourers serving surrounding ferm touns. The size of this group was small in Edinburgh compared with Aberdeen and it is likely that this group has been under-represented in the capital.

A type-of-product classification for manufacturing

The foregoing breakdown of the workforce by type of activity has demonstrated some important differences in the occupational and economic structure of the burghs studied. When the manufacturing sector is further broken down by type of product, as in Table 10.2, additional elements of specialisation emerge. The production of coarse woollen and linen cloth, while carried on in all centres, showed a marked concentration in some burghs. Among the larger towns, Edinburgh, Leith and Perth were relatively deficient in the textile trades, although there were many textile workers in the countryside around the first two.[34] Defoe's description of the linen industry as the mainstay of Perth's economy suggests that the importance of textiles grew rapidly there in the two decades

Table 10.2: Type-of-product classification: percentages of total manufacturing

	Textiles	Clothing	Leather	Metal	Wood and Construction	Food and Drink
Edinburgh	16.6	26.2	16.1	12.9	13.6	14.6
Aberdeen	20.3	21.6	17.2	9.3	21.4	10.2
Musselburgh	29.6	10.4	28.6	7.4	10.1	13.9
Leith	10.9	9.2	16.9	10.4	31.3	21.3
Perth	13.5	27.6	5.8	3.9	15.8	33.4
Bo'ness	11.9	12.6	5.4	4.0	19.3	33.8
Dalkeith	24.9	14.5	11.8	5.4	12.6	30.7
Paisley	42.0	14.3	15.5	5.0	9.7	13.5
Greenock	18.5	12.3	18.5	5.0	37.1	8.6
Selkirk	20.5	8.2	40.2	14.8	14.8	11.5
St Andrews	19.7	11.5	11.5	8.3	21.9	27.1
Grangepans	37.8	18.9	5.4	18.9	10.8	16.2
Fraserburgh	14.4	32.1	25.0	7.1	14.3	7.1
Peterhead	12.9	32.2	19.4	6.5	22.5	6.5
Newark	4.1	21.7	30.8	4.0	35.4	4.1
Eyemouth	5.6	33.3	11.1	5.6	33.3	11.1
Cartsdyke	8.9	11.8	8.8	11.7	55.9	2.9
Bathgate	34.0	19.0	12.0	4.0	19.0	12.0
Old Meldrum	17.0	4.0	49.0	13.0	17.0	0
Inverurie	32.0	14.0	32.0	14.0	8.0	0
Turriff	27.0	33.0	7.0	0	20.0	13.0
Mid Calder	21.0	21.0	13.0	8.0	24.0	13.0
Anstruther Wester	44.8	15.6	4.0	7.4	4.2	24.0
Rosehearty	22.3	22.3	22.3	11.1	22.0	0
Newburgh	33.4	33.4	16.6	0	16.6	0
Kincardine O'Neill	10.0	20.0	40.0	10.0	20.0	0
Greenlaw	29.0	4.0	12.0	12.0	29.0	4.0
Huntly	17.0	33.0	17.0	8.0	25.0	0
Ellon	26.6	20.0	26.6	6.6	20.0	0
Eaglesham	50.0	7.1	7.1	10.7	25.0	7.1
Kilbarchan	16.7	16.7	16.7	16.7	16.7	16.7
Deer	12.5	50.0	12.5	12.5	12.5	0
Tarves	0	20.0	40.0	40.0	0	0
Aboyne	60.0	10.0	30.0	0	10.0	0
Insch	0	17.0	17.0	0	49.0	17.0
Port Glasgow	0	20.0	0	80.0	0	0
Kilmacolm	29.0	29.0	14.0	0	0	28.0

Source: SRO, MSS Poll Tax Returns.

following the poll tax.[35] Aberdeen also had comparatively few textile workers. Before the 1670s the town had been a major exporter of woollen plaiding and knitted stockings,[36] but much of the actual production may have taken place in surrounding rural areas. On the other hand Musselburgh, and especially Paisley, had high proportions of their craftsmen in the textile trades though in the case of the former some may have lived outside the burgh limits. In 1703 it was recorded that a woollen manufactory had existed for some years in Musselburgh employing a large number of people.[37] Significantly, it had been financed by Edinburgh merchant capital. Defoe also testified to the importance of woollen manufacture in the town.[38] The importance of the textile industry as an employer is probably substantially underestimated in the poll tax records due to the lack of information on female and child labour. On the other hand textile production, even on a large, organised scale, was not necessarily urban-based as the establishment of woollen manufactories at Gordon's Mill, outside Aberdeen, and at Harcarse in rural Berwickshire, indicates.[39]

The high proportions of textile workers in Musselburgh and, to a lesser extent in Dalkeith, suggests that the industry in these towns may have been linked with Edinburgh, the cloth being woven in and around the baronial burghs and sent to the capital for dyeing and making up by the city's tailors. Edinburgh certainly had one of the highest levels of specialisation in clothing, as one might have expected given the concentration of wealth in the capital. Edinburgh had nearly seven times as many clothiers polling in the three highest wealth categories as Glasgow and twenty-one times as many as Aberdeen. Paisley may have been linked with Glasgow in a similar manner, though the high proportion of textile workers in smaller centres like Eaglesham may indicate that a regional specialisation in textiles was already developing in Renfrewshire. Other regional centres like Aberdeen and Perth come out relatively strongly in the clothing trades. In Perth this was due to the strength of glovemaking, which accounted for 6.3 per cent of the recorded male workforce. Situated on the edge of the Highlands, where goat keeping was more general than in the Lowlands,[40] Perth was well located to obtain supplies of high-quality kid.

Leather manufacture seems to have occupied about 15 – 18 per cent of the tradesmen in many burghs but Musselburgh had a high degree of concentration on this activity and Selkirk was very specialised indeed, the leather trades being by far the most important sector of the town's economy, accounting for over 40 per cent of the tradesmen. As the centre for an upland area with an emphasis on cattle as well as sheep rearing this is understandable; the textile trades were also fairly strong in Selkirk suggesting local linkages with sheep farming too. The souters of Selkirk were famed in Border song[41] and it is interesting to note that the poll tax records confirm the old tradition. Other towns with concentrations in this industry were Paisley and Newark in the more pastoral west. Edinburgh and Aberdeen had lower percentages in leather manufacture, but they did have more workers in the higher-class branches of the trade: beltmakers, lorimers and saddlers. In smaller centres like Old Meldrum a local specialisation closely related to the products of the immediate rural hinterland is suggested by the high degree of specialisation.

There was less absolute variation in the metalworking sector largely because this was not such an important group of trades numerically but the figures for Edinburgh are swelled by workers in high-class occupations; armourers, gold and silver smiths, pewterers and gunsmiths, who are less frequent in other large burghs and rare elsewhere. Building and construction workers were also a relatively stable group. The proportion of craftsmen in these trades was, however, higher in ports due to shipping-related activities. Leith had as many coopers as Edinburgh, Cartsdyke as many as Paisley. Edinburgh, with more wealth, more stone-built tenements, and restrictions on the use of wood in house construction due to the fire hazard,[42] had a larger proportion of glaziers and slaters than smaller burghs such as Paisley where the preponderance of timber-framed housing swelled the numbers of wrights.

The food and drink sector consisted mainly of baxters, brewers and maltmen, and fleshers. The importance of these activities is probably under-represented to a greater degree than some others. In the smaller burghs much baking, brewing and fleshing may have been done as a part-time occupation, as well as on a purely domestic basis, and a good deal of it may have been done by women. Ale sellers are rarely mentioned in the poll tax returns. In 1693 the fourteen brewers of Leith (fifteen are listed in the poll tax returns of 1694) petitioned the town council of Edinburgh to require the licensing of ale sellers.[43] Subsequently, ninety-six ale sellers in South Leith parish applied.[44] Some of these would have lived outside the burgh itself, but only three are recorded in the poll lists. It is likely that ale selling was a widespread part-time occupation, particularly among women.

232

Considering the scale of the grain trade which focused on Edinburgh and the importance of brewing in the capital[45] the number of brewers there is surprisingly small but there are indications that much of the industry was located immediately around the capital rather than within it.[46] The high percentage in the food and drink group in Perth is mainly due to the importance of brewing in the town. Most of the maltmen were, however, small-scale operators. Perth had only three maltmen in the highest wealth categories against thirty-three in Glasgow. The provisioning of vessels for longer voyages may help to account for the importance of this group of activities in Bo'ness compared with smaller ports whose trade was mainly coastal.

Dalkeith had an unusually high number of fleshers. This may be explained in relation to Edinburgh's market for fresh meat. The slaughtering of animals was not allowed within Edinburgh itself,[47] and this encouraged fleshers from the surrounding area to compete with those of the capital. The Scotts of Buccleuch, who owned land in the vicinity of Dalkeith, brought livestock from their extensive Border estates to fatten them for the Edinburgh market.[48] The animals may have been slaughtered at Dalkeith and the meat delivered to the capital. A by-product, tallow, supplied a group of Dalkeith candlemakers who competed in the capital with the city's own tradesmen.[49] On the other hand the leather industries were not prominent in Dalkeith. The hides may have been sent elsewhere for processing, possibly to Musselburgh, which had a large concentration of leather workers.

Few burghs had many workers in industries whose location was linked to the distribution of a specific, limited resource. Bo'ness and Grangepans are unusual in the importance of the coal and salt industries. In Bo'ness, however, coal mining employed only 2.9 per cent of the male pollable population and salt production another 1.6 per cent, confirming the burgh's report of 1699 that outcrops of coal in the immediate vicinity of the town were becoming worked out and that, while the town exported coal and salt in large quantities, most of the production came from mines and saltpans further along the coast.[50]

In the late seventeenth century efforts had been made to establish 'manufactories' with government support to produce commodities which were normally imported at high cost.[51] Leith had soap, sugar and glass works by 1694[52] but it is impossible to estimate how many people were employed in them as their labour force was probably listed under general descriptions such as 'workman'.

The pattern of urban wealth

So far this study has considered what people did in the burghs rather than the rewards which they reaped for their activities. The poll tax records also provide data on the distribution of urban wealth. There are problems in using them as wealth may often have been under-assessed with people polling in lower categories than they should have done.[53] Analysis is also complicated by the modest lower limit of the highest wealth category, 10,000 merks. The value of trading stock above this level is rarely given. The records for Inverness credit some men with up to 50,000 merks of stock and in the largest burghs the wealthiest men must have possessed much more.

Table 10.3 shows the distribution of wealth in the burghs for which data are available. Merchants and tradesmen who were listed in the three highest categories — 500–4,999 merks, 5,000–9,999 merks and 10,000 merks and over — are included as are professional people polling at higher rates, heritors with over £300 Scots a year income from rents, and 'gentlemen'. The numbers in each of three groups — professional and landowning, merchants and tradesmen — are expressed as percentages of the total male pollable population. The overall tendency for the royal burghs to have higher proportions of wealthier inhabitants and the smaller to have very few or none is hardly surprising. It must, however, be remembered that many poor inhabitants may have been omitted from the poll lists and that the proportion of these is likely to have been higher in the larger towns. The contrast in wealth between Edinburgh on one hand and Leith and Mussel-burgh on the other is marked, although Dalkeith, whose trade was claimed in 1692 to have been far greater than that of Mussel-burgh,[54] seems more prosperous. Poorer still was Grangepans with only 6.1 per cent of its recorded male population in the three highest wealth categories, lending support to the burgh's pleas of poverty to parliament in 1699.[55] The high figure for St Andrews relates in part to the influence of the university. The large proportions of wealthy inhabitants in Paisley and Bo'ness are more surprising and suggest that even if many of the activities in such centres were controlled by other royal burghs some of the profits at least remained in local hands.

Glasgow, Aberdeen, Paisley and Greenock had large proportions of merchants in the wealthier category while in Edinburgh and St Andrews, professional and landed wealth was more

Table 10.3: The distribution of urban wealth

	% recorded male pop. with over 500 merks stock or in higher poll categories	Merchants	Tradesmen	Professional and Heritors
Edinburgh	18.1	3.5	5.3	9.2
Glasgow	11.3	6.0	2.7	2.0
Aberdeen	16.6	6.9	4.2	5.8
Musselburgh	6.3	0.6	3.5	2.2
Leith	7.5	0.2	4.5	2.7
Perth	14.0	3.7	8.1	3.6
Bo'ness	17.4	3.3	13.8	1.4
Dalkeith	11.1	1.8	7.1	2.1
Paisley	21.4	5.9	9.8	5.6
Greenock	13.3	5.7	6.4	1.2
St Andrews	38.0	1.8	25.9	11.1
Grangepans	6.1	1.1	5.0	0.6
Fraserburgh	15.7	11.4	0.6	3.6
Peterhead	11.8	4.8	3.5	3.4
Newark	6.9	2.5	3.4	0.8
Cartsdyke	7.8	2.6	4.4	0.9
Bathgate	1.8	0	0.9	0.9
Old Meldrum	5.0	5.0	0	0
Inverurie	0	0	0	0
Turriff	4.9	1.2	0	3.8
Mid Calder	3.9	1.3	1.3	1.3
Rosehearty	6.7	6.7	0	0
Newburgh	0	0	0	0
Kincardine O'Neill	3.7	3.7	0	0
Rawes of Huntly	0	0	0	0
Ellon	0	0	0	0
Eaglesham	0	0	0	0
Kilbarchan	2.6	2.6	0	0
Deer	0	0	0	0
Tarves	0	0	0	0
Aboyne	0	0	0	0
Insch	9.0	3.0	0	6.0
Port Glasgow	13.8	8.3	5.5	0
Kilmacolm	4.5	4.5	0	0

Source: SRO, MSS Poll Tax Returns.

significant. Bo'ness, by contrast, had a higher proportion of wealthy tradesmen than most towns, though Paisley and Perth also came out well in this respect.

Edinburgh might have been expected to have had the highest overall proportion of wealthy men but this was not the case. The far greater range of wealth in the capital must be remembered though; if the thresholds for stock among merchants and tradesmen had been 50,000 merks rather than 10,000 the picture would probably have been very different. People in the higher wealth categories occur only sporadically in the smallest burghs, being most commonly merchants with barely 500 merks of trading stock. Such centres contained few tradesmen of substance and few professional people.

The functions and regional impact of Edinburgh

It has already been suggested that the occupational classification used in the poll lists may under-emphasise specialist occupations. Nevertheless, Table 10.4 presents a list of some of these for the larger burghs. The presence of an array of luxury trades in the capital distinguishes it from regional centres such as Aberdeen and Perth, although it must be remembered that the data for Glasgow are incomplete, relating only to the higher wealth categories.

The strength of the printing, bookselling and wigmaking trades emphasises the capital's role as a centre of education, culture and fashion. It is not suggested that such activities were absent elsewhere, merely that they existed as small-scale adjuncts to more basic occupations. In Edinburgh, however, the level of demand was sufficient to sustain them as full-time occupations. Outside Edinburgh and, possibly, Glasgow, the occupations listed in Table 10.4 were represented only sporadically, if at all. Even Aberdeen had less than half the specialist occupations of Edinburgh and most other large burghs had only one or two. Leith, as Scotland's largest port and a satellite of Edinburgh, had more specialist functions than Perth.

Edinburgh also affected the occupational structures of other burghs within a radius of twenty miles or more. Leith, Musselburgh, Bo'ness, Dalkeith and Grangepans were deficient in professional occupations and merchants, had fewer people in the higher wealth categories, and had high proportions of their workforces in manufacturing. The control of the economies of Bo'ness and Grangepans by Edinburgh merchants is attested by other sources.[56] The importance of Dalkeith as a market centre depended largely on its proximity to Edinburgh.[57] The occupational structures of Dalkeith and Musselburgh suggest that their manufacturing activities were also closely tied to the Edinburgh market, furnishing products which were either consumed or finished there. Due to the dominance of the capital these towns had failed to develop regional or subregional roles involving the

Table 10.4: Employment in some specialist occupations

	Edinburgh	Glasgow[a]	Aberdeen	Musselburgh	Leith	Perth	Bo'ness	Dalkeith	Paisley	Greenock
Armourers	8	—	4	—	—	—	—	1	—	—
Bookbinders, booksellers, stationers, printers	40	2	7	—	—	—	—	—	—	—
Bonnet and hatmakers	8	—	1	—	3	—	1	1	4	—
Candlemakers	25	—	—	2	—	—	—	5	—	—
Clock and watchmakers	9	—	4	—	2	—	—	—	—	—
Coppersmiths	20	1	1	—	2	—	—	1	—	—
Feltmakers	31	—	—	1	—	—	—	—	—	—
Fletchers	2	—	—	—	—	—	—	—	—	—
Furriers	2	—	1	—	—	—	—	—	—	—
Goldsmiths	46	5	5	—	—	—	—	—	—	—
Gunsmiths	14	—	—	—	—	—	—	—	—	—
Jewellers	2	—	—	—	—	—	—	—	—	—
Mirrormakers	1	—	—	—	—	—	—	—	—	—
Perfumers	1	—	—	—	—	1	—	—	—	—
Pewterers	25	1	2	—	—	2	—	—	—	—
Seivewrights	2	—	—	14	—	—	—	—	—	—
Swordsmiths and cutlers	5	—	—	—	—	—	—	—	1	—
Tobacco cutters, spinners and sellers	2	—	1	—	6	—	—	4	—	—
Upholsterers	2	—	1	—	4	1	—	—	—	1
Vintners	24	—	—	2	—	—	3	—	—	1
Violers	8	—	2	—	—	—	—	—	—	—
Wigmakers	65	—	—	—	—	—	—	—	2	—

Note: a. Only data for higher wealth categories available for Glasgow.

Source: SRO, MSS Poll Tax Returns.

provision of higher-level services and manufactures. Unfortunately, data were not available for Linlithgow and Haddington to determine whether their balance of occupations was also influenced by Edinburgh. Only Bo'ness was, in some respects, different. While its economy was linked with Edinburgh, which provided an important market for its coal and salt, it had a considerable export trade in its own right, even if much of this was controlled by merchants from other royal burghs.[58] Bo'ness was an upstart baronial burgh which had grown through industry rather than by the provision of services for the surrounding countryside. Its success is shown by the large proportion of tradesmen in the higher wealth categories. Its economic base, along with that of Grangepans, differed from that of the other burghs studied but, were data available, it is probable that Prestonpans and some of the Fife and Ayrshire coal and salt burghs would have presented a similar picture.

The Scottish urban hierarchy

The centres studied here are selected by the chance survival of the evidence and do not form a random sample of the Scottish urban hierarchy in the late seventeenth century. Nevertheless, it is instructive to examine some of their hierarchical characteristics. A rank correlation of $+0.74$, significant at the 0.05 per cent probability level, exists between the pollable population of the burghs studied and their dates of foundation. The smallest centres were, by and large, latecomers — post-1660 burghs of barony and non-burghal market centres. The ancient royal burghs and pre-seventeenth century baronial burghs formed most of the large centres in this group.

The exceptions to this pattern were Bo'ness and, to a lesser extent, Greenock and Newark, all post-1660 foundations whose growth was based on new, dynamic elements in the Scottish economy: the coal and salt trade in the case of Bo'ness, the expanding west-coast and incipient trans-Atlantic trade in the case of the Clyde burghs. At the other end of the scale were declining royal burghs like Anstruther Wester, whose burgesses in the late 1680s were petitioning for a reduction in taxation as the burgh was 'past all hopes of having trade in tyme coming'.[59] The burgh was situated in an area where competition from other market centres was intense. Inverurie, dominated by Aberdeen, was in a similar position.

How many of these centres were truly urban? Too much attention has been paid in the past to institutional factors in the development of Scottish burghs. The present study indicates the importance of occupational characteristics in determining urban status. In assessing the functions performed by various centres a distinct break occurs at between 250 and 300 pollable persons, corresponding to a population of perhaps 450 or 500. Burghs at this level, such as Peterhead and Fraserburgh, had a complete range of professional services, a merchant community and all the major branches of manufacturing. Below this level the range of functions diminishes rapidly and the twenty-two smallest centres cannot be considered as urban, most of them performing functions which in areas of nucleated rural settlement would have been discharged by villages.[60]

Uniformity or diversity?

In summary, distinctive elements of specialisation within the Scottish urban hierarchy can be identified, even with the limited sample of burghs studied. These elements can be demonstrated at two levels — at a general one in terms of variations in the importance of different types of activity, and more specifically within the manufacturing sector. The most marked overall specialisation was that of Edinburgh in high-level professional services, indicating how profoundly its position as the capital differentiated it from other burghs. Aberdeen, and to a lesser extent other regional centres, were also relatively strong in these functions. Aside from the importance of the professional groups the larger royal burghs had, characteristically, a reasonable balance between trading, manufacturing and lower-level services. Merchants formed an important group not only in larger royal burghs like Aberdeen but also in some smaller baronial burghs like Fraserburgh and Greenock, though the contrasting roles of the two types of centre with regard to overseas and internal trade and the differences in the scale of operation of many of their traders should not be forgotten. High levels of specialisation in trading, including people involved in shipping as well as merchants, was a feature of rapidly-growing coastal baronial burghs like Bo'ness and Greenock. In older baronial burghs like Fraserburgh the concentration of merchants may relate to the town's distance from Aberdeen and point to its having had an important subregional role in distribution.

Greenock, with a lack of professional services and little manufacturing, appears to have had an unbalanced occupational structure with the expansion of shipping-related activities outstripping the growth of other sectors. There were no clear differences in the importance of manufacturing to distinguish the larger royal burghs from baronial burghs. Fishing could generate high levels of specialisation in smaller coastal centres.

At a lower level there were marked elements of specialisation within the manufacturing sector. Among the larger burghs this included textiles in Musselburgh and Paisley, leather in Sellkirk, glovemaking in Perth and food and drink in Perth and Bo'ness. Woodworking and construction was particularly significant in the ports. Burghs rarely showed a marked concentration in both trading and manufacturing, pointing to the home-based nature of the demand for most Scottish products. The industrial specialisations which have been identified in baronial burghs like Dalkeith, Musselburgh and Paisley also suggest that close economic ties existed between different types of burgh at regional and local levels and it may be a mistake to view the rise of some of the larger baronial burghs in the later seventeenth century as automatically posing a threat to the old-established royal burghs. The activities of the two types of centre may well have been more closely integrated and complementary than has sometimes been appreciated. At a smaller scale, elements of specialisation in the minor centres emphasise their purely local role as foci for making up raw materials derived from the surrounding area and in distributing goods produced or imported by larger centres.

The findings suggest that the general occupational structure of Scottish burghs at this time was similar to that of English towns. The primary function of most burghs was to act as generalised central places at different scales for their rural hinterlands. Elements of specialisation did exist but there were no one-industry towns. It has been suggested by Clarkson that half a dozen groups of crafts and manufactures — textiles, clothing, leather, metalworking, construction, food and drink — dominated the workforce of English towns.[61] Patten, following Hoskins, believed that these industries accounted for up to two-thirds of the urban workforce, leaving only a third for the professions and elements of specialisation, such as shipbuilding, which were grafted on to a basic superstructure of occupations which was common to all towns.[62] The present study suggests that the importance of these groups has been over-emphasised. Clarkson's categories, and those of Patten and Hoskins, conform closely to the manufacturing sector defined here. In the fifteen largest burghs studied this group made up on average only 40 per cent of the pollable male workforce and only approached two-thirds in Paisley and Perth. It is probable that previous studies have underestimated the importance of domestic servants and, secondly, of labourers and workmen, two groups which were numerous in many burghs. In addition, the dominance of port-related functions in coastal towns may not have been fully appreciated. While none of the burghs studied were one-industry or even one-activity towns there was greater scope for diversity and specialisation than might have been expected and this in turn argues for a higher degree of sophistication in the Scottish urban system than has sometimes been suggested.

Conclusion

This survey, based on a single source with manifest imperfections, serves only as an introduction to a complex topic. As such it perhaps poses more questions than it answers. Nevertheless, it has emphasised some important aspects of the occupational structure of Scottish burghs in the late seventeenth century. Marked differences between individual towns reflect important contrasts in function within the urban hierarchy. Some of these differences can be attributed to the dichotomy within the Scottish burghal system. Royal burghs still clearly exerted influence over the activities of baronial burghs. The nature of these controls, and the effects which they had on the burghs concerned, appear to have been articulated at a regional and local level between specific groups of centres rather than on a national scale. Thus the occupational characteristics of individual burghs can only be understood fully with reference to the regional economies within which they operated and the functions and activities of the other urban centres with which they interacted.

Other occupational differences between burghs of similar size and comparable status may be explained with reference to geographical location; the relative independence of baronial burghs like Fraserburgh and Peterhead stands in marked contrast to the dependent character of Grangepans, for example. Historical chance also played a part: the presence of the university in St Andrews made its occupational structure distinctly different from other medium-sized burghs which were studied.

It has not been possible to give more than fleeting consideration to the ways in which the economic resources and agrarian structures of landward areas affected activities within the burghs which served as their market centres, their export outlets and their sources of imports. Nevertheless, it is clear that such factors were important in explaining elements of specialisation particularly in manufacturing but also in other aspects of urban activity.

The research presented here has been based only on the recorded occupations of pollable men. It is uncertain what proportion evaded registration or were exempted from the tax. The occupations of the lowest levels of urban society are probably under-represented here and more research using a variety of burgh records is necessary to gain a better idea of the size of this group and its activities in different towns. Equally the activities of women, apart from domestic servants, have been neglected.

The picture which has been presented is merely a cross-section through time. It would be interesting to know more about how urban occupational structures evolved from the seventeenth to the later eighteenth century. Detailed study of burgh marriage registers, where these record occupations, in conjunction with other burgh records may help to show how the socio-economic structure of the early-modern Scottish town developed in the initial phases of the Industrial Revolution. Nevertheless, it is hoped that enough has been outlined here to demonstrate something of the complexity of activities within Scottish burghs during early-modern times and to suggest some fruitful directions for further research.

Notes

1. This can be seen in recent surveys such as J. Patten, *English Towns, 1500–1700* (London, 1978), P. Clark (ed.), *The Early Modern Town* (London, 1976), and P. Clark and P. Slack, *English Towns in Transition, 1500–1700* (London, 1976).

2. Patten, *English Towns*, 19–21.

3. J. W. R. Whitehead and K. Alauddin, 'The town plans of Scotland: some preliminary considerations', *Scot. Geog. Mag*, 85 (1969), 110. New foundations are listed in G. S. Pryde, *The Burghs of Scotland: a Critical List* (London, 1965), nos. 70–81, 265–443.

4. Patten, *English Towns*, 114–16.

5. The data on which these calculations have been based are contained in R. Mols, 'Population in Europe, 1500–1700' in C. Cipolla (ed.), *The Fontana Economic History of Europe*, vol. 2, *The sixteenth and seventeenth centuries*

(London, 1974), 41–3, and R. A. Butlin, 'Irish towns in the sixteenth and seventeenth centuries' in R. A. Butlin (ed.), *The Development of the Irish Town* (London, 1977), 92–7.

6. This is a recurring theme in a report to the Convention of Royal Burghs in 1692; see 'Register containeing the state and condition of every burgh within the kingdome of Scotland in the year 1692' in *SBRS, Misc.* (1881), 56–156.

7. E.g. A. Ballard, 'The theory of the Scottish burgh', *SHR*, 13 (1916), 16–29: D. Murray, *Early Burgh Organisation in Scotland* (Glasgow, 1924); W. Mackenzie, *The Scottish Burgh* (Edinburgh, 1949). For a recent survey see I. H. Adams, *The Making of Urban Scotland* (London, 1978).

8. Patten, *English Towns*, 168–9.

9. Ibid., 168–9.

10. M. Lynch, *Edinburgh and the Reformation* (Edinburgh, 1981), 10.

11. The returns for Aberdeenshire and Renfrewshire have been published: *List of pollable persons within the shire of Aberdeen, 1696*, ed. J. Stuart, 2 vols. (Spalding Club, 1844); D. Semple (ed.), *Renfrewshire Poll Tax returns* (Glasgow, 1864). Records of two of the urban parishes of Edinburgh have been published : *Edinburgh Poll Tax returns for 1694*, ed. M. Wood (Scot. Rec. Soc., 1951). The remaining returns are in MS in SRO, mainly in the E70 series, the catalogue for which lists the location of additional material scattered among sheriff court records and private papers.

12. SRO, E70 series.

13. The Edinburgh marriage registers, which begin to record occupations in the late seventeenth century have a greater diversity of occupational designations than the poll tax returns.

14. J. Patten, 'Urban occupations in pre-industrial England', *Trans. Inst. Brit. Geogr.*, new series, 2 (1977), 296–313.

15. Ibid., 310.

16. The annuity tax of 1635 shows that 4 per cent of households in Edinburgh proper were then occupied by nobles or lairds; see Makey, Chapter 9, this volume, n. 25.

17. *Edin. Poll Tax returns*, 11, 15.

18. Ibid., 17.

19. Ibid., 18.

20. T. M. Devine, 'The merchant class of the larger Scottish towns in the later seventeenth and early eighteenth centuries', in G. Gordon and B. Dicks (eds.), *Scottish Urban History* (Aberdeen, 1983), 99. The same was true a century earlier; see M. Lynch, 'Whatever happened to the medieval burgh', *Scot. Econ. and Soc. Hist.*, 4 (1984), 11.

21. T. C. Smout, *Scottish Trade on the eve of the Union, 1660–1707* (Edinburgh, 1963), 138–9.

22. *APS*, X (1699), 120–1.

23. Ibid., X (1699), 115.

24. Ibid., IX (1695), 513.

25. D. Defoe, *A tour through the whole island of Great Britain, 1724–6* (Penguin ed., 1971), 655.

26. Smout, *Scottish Trade*, 141.

27. Defoe, *Tour*, 603.

28. M. Flinn (ed.), *Scottish Population History* (Cambridge, 1976), 195.

29. The open nature of many burghs at this time is shown by the views of J. Slezer, *Theatrum Scotiae* (London, 1693).

30. T. C. Smout, *A History of the Scottish People, 1560–1830* (London, 1972 ed.), 167.

31. J. Wormald, *Court, Kirk and Community: Scotland 1470–1625* (London, 1981), 46. Cf. P. Clark (ed.), *Country Towns in Pre-Industrial England* (Leicester, 1981), 3–4.

32. Ibid., 10.

33. Smout, *Scottish People*, 163.

34. This is clear from the poll tax returns for the rural parishes immediately around the captial.

35. Defoe, *Tour*, 645.

36. Smout, *Scottish Trade*, 142.

37. *APS*, XI (1703), 82b.

38. Defoe, *Tour*, 573.

39. *APS*, XI, 81a, 82b.

40. T. C. Smout, 'Goat-keeping in the old Highland economy', *Scot. Studs.*, 9 (1965), 186–9.

41. W. Scott, *The Ministrelsy of the Scottish Border* (London, 1869 ed.), 77–82.

42. R. G. Rodger, 'The evolution of Scottish town planning', in Gordon and Dicks (eds.), *Scottish Urban History*, 77–8.

43. *Edin. Recs., 1689–1701*, 128.

44. Ibid., 131.

45. Smout, *Scottish Trade*, 132.

46. This is also indicated by the poll tax returns for the rural parishes immediately around the capital.

47. *APS*, IX (1695), 361.

48. SRO, Buccleuch Muniments, GD 224/3, 943/15.

49. *APS*, IX (1695), 513.

50. Ibid., X (1699), 120–1.

51. Ibid., VII (1661), 465.

52. Ibid., IX (1695), 491.

53. Flinn (ed.), *Scottish Population History*, 57.

54. 1692 Burgh Report in *SBRS Misc.* (1881), 58.

55. *APS*, X (1699), 115.

56. Ibid., X (1699), 115, 120–1.

57. Defoe, *Tour*, 628.

58. SRO, MS Customs accounts, E72/5.

59. *Burghs Conv. Recs.*, iv, 90.

60. J. Patten, 'Village and town: an occupational study', *Agric. Hist. Rev.*, 20 (1972), 1–16.

61. L. A. Clarkson, *The Pre-Industrial Economy in England, 1500–1750* (London, 1971), 78.

62. W. G. Hoskins, 'English provincial towns in the sixteenth century', *Trans. Royal Hist. Soc.*, 5th ser., 6 (1956), 15; Patten, *English Towns*, 151.

Select Bibliography

The bibliography is intended only as a guide to further reading and does not generally include primary sources unless they have useful commentary as well. Most burgh records were printed in extract form by, or in association with, the Scottish Burghs Records Society. All books were published in London unless otherwise stated.

Aberdeen Council Letters, ed. L. B. Taylor, 4 vols. (Oxford, 1942–54)

Adams, I. H. *The Making of Urban Scotland* (1978)

Adamson, D. 'The hearth tax', *Trans. Dumf. & Galloway Nat. Hist. & Antiq. Soc.*, 47 (1970), 144–77

Anonymous 'Mr Gross on Scottish guilds', *Scottish Review*, 32 (1898), 61–81

Ayr Burgh Records, 1534–1624, ed. G. S. Pryde (SHS, 1937)

Bain, E. *Merchant and Craft Guilds: a History of the Aberdeen Incorporated Trades* (Aberdeen, 1887)

Ballard, A. 'The theory of the Scottish burgh', *SHR*, 12 (1916), 16–27

Barbé, L. A. *Sidelights on the History, Industries and Social Life of Scotland* (1919)

Brown, J. M. (ed.) *Scottish Society in the Fifteenth Century* (1977)

Brown, P. H. (ed.) *Early Travellers in Scotland* (Edinburgh, 1891)

—— (ed.) *Scotland before 1700 from contemporary documents* (Edinburgh, 1893)

—— *Scotland in the Time of Queen Mary* (1904)

Burrell, S. A., 'Calvinism, capitalism and the middle classes: some afterthoughts on an old problem', *J. of Modern History*, 32 (1960), 129–41

Campbell, A. J. 'The burgh churches of Scotland', *Recs. Scot. Church Hist. Soc.*, 4 (1932), 185–94

The Compt Book of David Wedderburne, 1587–1630, ed. A. H. Millar (SHS, 1898)

Davidson, J. and Gray, A. *The Scottish Staple at Veere: A Study in the Economic History of Scotland* (1909)

Devine, T. M. 'The Cromwellian Union and the Scottish burghs: the case of Aberdeen and Glasgow, 1652–60', in *Scottish Themes*, ed. J. Butt (Edinburgh, 1976), 1–16

—— 'The Scottish merchant community, 1680–1740' in *The Origins and Nature of the Scottish Enlightenment*, eds. R. H. Campbell and A. S. Skinner (Edinburgh, 1982), 26–41

—— and Lythe, S. G. E. 'The economy of Scotland under James VI', *SHR*, 50 (1971), 91–106

Dickinson, W. C. 'Burgh life from burgh records', *Aberdeen Univ. Rev.*, 21 (1946), 214–26

—— and Duncan, A. A. M. *Scotland from the Earliest Times to 1603*

(rev. ed., Oxford, 1977)

di Folco, J. 'The Hopes of Craighall and land investment in the seventeenth century' in *Lairds and Improvement in the Scotland of the Enlightenment*, ed. T. M. Devine (Glasgow, 1978), 1–10

Dodd, W. 'Ayr: a study of urban growth', *Ayrshire Arch. & Nat. Hist. Colls.*, 10 (1972), 302–82

Donaldson, G. 'The legal profession in Scottish society in the sixteenth and seventeenth centuries', *Juridical Rev.*, 21 (1976), 1–19

—— 'James VI and vanishing frontiers' in *The Scottish Nation*, ed. G. Menzies (1972), 103–17

Dow, J. 'Scottish trade with Sweden, 1512–80', *SHR*, 48 (1969), 64–79

—— 'Scottish trade with Sweden, 1580–1622', *SHR*, 48 (1969), 124–50

Dunlop, A. I. (ed.) *The Royal Burgh of Ayr* (Edinburgh, 1953)

Durkan, J. (ed.) *Protocol Book of John Foular, 1528–1534* (SRS, 1985)

Dwyer, J., Mason, R. and Murdoch, A. (eds.) *New Perspectives on the Politics and Culture of Early Modern Scotland* (Edinburgh, 1981)

Flinn, M. W. (ed.) *Scottish Population History from the Seventeenth Century to the 1930s* (Cambridge, 1977)

Fox, R. C. 'The burghs of Scotland, 1327, 1601, 1670', *Area*, 13 (1981)

Gibb, A. *Glasgow: the Making of a City* (Beckenham, 1983)

Gilbert, J. M. (ed.) *Flower of the Forest: Selkirk, a new History* (Galashiels, 1985)

Gordon, G. and Dicks, B. (eds.) *Scottish Urban History* (Aberdeen, 1983)

Grant, I. F. *The Social and Economic Development of Scotland before 1603* (Edinburgh, 1930)

Houston, J. M. 'The Scottish burgh', *Town Planning Rev.*, 25 (1954), 114–27

Innes, C. *Ancient Laws and Customs of the Burghs of Scotland*, 2 vols. (SBRS, 1868–9)

Keith, T. 'Trading privileges of the royal burghs of Scotland', *English Hist. Rev.*, 28 (1913), 545–71, 678–90

Kellett, J. R. 'Glasgow', in *Historic Towns*, vol. i, ed. I. Lobel (1969), 1–13

Kennedy, W. *Annals of Aberdeen from the Reign of King William the Lion to the End of the Year 1818* (Aberdeen, 1818)

Lee, M. *Government by Pen: Scotland under James VI and I* (Chicago, 1980)

Lynch, M. *Edinburgh and the Reformation* (Edinburgh, 1981)

—— 'The Scottish early modern burgh', *History Today*, 35 (Feb., 1985), 10–15

—— 'Scottish Calvinism, 1559–1638', in *International Calvinism, 1541–1715*, ed. M. Prestwich (Oxford, 1985), 225–55

—— 'Whatever happened to the medieval burgh? Some guidelines for sixteenth- and seventeenth-century historians', *Scottish Econ. & Social Hist.*, 4 (1984), 1–17

Lythe, S. G. E. *The Economy of Scotland in its European Setting, 1550–1625* (Edinburgh, 1960)

—— *Life and Labour in Dundee from the Reformation to the Civil War* (Abertay Hist. Soc., 1958)

—— and Butt, J. *An Economic History of Scotland, 1100–1939* (Glasgow, 1975)

Mackenzie, W. M. *The Scottish Burghs* (Edinburgh, 1949)

Maclennan, B. 'The Reformation in the burgh of Aberdeen', *Northern Scotland*, 2 (1974), 119–44

McNeill, P. and Nicholson, R. (eds.) *An Historical Atlas of Scotland, c.400 – c.1600* (St Andrews, 1975)

Makey, W. H. *The Church of the Covenant, 1637–1651: Revolution and Social Change in Scotland* (Edinburgh, 1979)

Marshall, G. *Presbyteries and Profits: Calvinism and the Development of Capitalism in Scotland, 1560–1707* (Oxford, 1980)

Marwick, J. D. *Edinburgh Guilds and Crafts. A Sketch of the History of Burgess-ship, Guild Brotherhood and Membership of Crafts in the City* (SBRS, 1909)

Mathew, D. *Scotland under Charles I* (1955)

Maxwell, A. *The History of Old Dundee* (Edinburgh and Dundee, 1884)

—— *Old Dundee, Eccliastical, Burghal and Social, prior to the Reformation* (Edinburgh and Dundee, 1891)

Mitchison, R. *Lordship to Patronage: Scotland 1603–1745* (1983)

—— 'The making of the old Scottish poor law', *Past and Present*, 63 (1974), 58–93

Morris, D. B. *The Development of Burghal Administration in Scotland* (Edinburgh, 1917)

—— *The Stirling Merchant Guild and Life of John Cowane* (Stirling, 1919)

Murray, A. 'The customs accounts of Dumfries and Kirkcudbright, 1560–1660', *Trans. Dumf. & Galloway Nat. Hist. & Antiq. Soc.*, 42 (1965), 114–32

Murray, D. *Early Burgh Organization in Scotland, as illustrated in the History of Glasgow and some neighbouring Burghs*, 2 vols. (Glasgow, 1924–32)

Pagan, T. *The Convention of Royal Burghs of Scotland* (Glasgow, 1926)

Pryde, G. S. *The Burghs of Scotland: a Critical List* (Oxford, 1965)

—— (ed.) *The Court Book of Kirkintilloch, 1658–1694* (SHS, 1963)

—— 'The burgh courts and allied jurisdictions', *Stair Society*, 25 (1958), 384–94

Rait, R. S. *The Parliaments of Scotland* (Glasgow, 1924)

Reid, W. S. *Skipper from Leith: the History of Robert Barton of Over-Barnton* (Philadelphia, 1962)

Renwick, R. *Peebles during the Reign of Queen Mary* (Peebles, 1903)

—— and Lindsay, J. *History of Glasgow*, 2 vols. (1921)

Roberts, F. and MacPhail, I. M. M. (eds.) *Dumbarton Common Good Accounts, 1614–1660* (Dumbarton, 1972)

Rogers, C. *Social Life in Scotland from Early to Recent Times*, 3 vols. (Edinburgh 1884–6)

Roll of Eminent Burgesses of Dundee, 1513–1886, ed. A. H. Millar (Dundee, 1887)

Rooseboom, M. P. *The Scottish Staple in the Netherlands: an Account of the Trade Relations between Scotland and the Low Countries from 1292 till 1676* (The Hague, 1910)

Sanderson, M. H. B. 'The Edinburgh merchants in society, 1570–1603: the evidence of their testaments' in *The Renaissance and Reformation in Scotland*, ed. I. B. Cowan and D. Shaw (Edinburgh, 1983), 183–99

Scott, W. R. *The Constitution and Finance of English, Scottish and Irish Joint-Stock Companies to 1720*, 3 vols. (Cambridge, 1910–12)

—— 'Scottish industrial undertakings before the Union', *SHR*, 1 (1904), 407–15

Scottish Burgh Records Society Miscellany (Glasgow, 1881)

Scottish Burgh Survey (Univ. of Glasgow) — individual reports on over forty burghs

The Shore Work Accounts of Aberdeen, 1596–1670, ed. L. B. Taylor (Aberdeen, 1972)

Skene, A. *Memorialls for the Government of Royall Burghs in Scotland* (Aberdeen, 1685)

—— *A Succinct Survey of the Famous City of Aberdeen* (Aberdeen, 1685)

Smith, J. S. (ed.) *New Light on Medieval Aberdeen* (Aberdeen, 1985)

Smout, T. C. *A History of the Scottish People, 1560–1830* (1969)

—— *Scottish Trade on the Eve of Union, 1660–1707* (Edinburgh, 1963)

—— 'Coping with plague in sixteenth and seventeenth century Scotland', *Scotia*, 2 (1978), 19–33

—— 'The development and enterprise of Glasgow, 1556–1707', *Scot. J. of Pol. Economy*, 7 (1960), 194–212

—— 'The Glasgow merchant community in the seventeenth century', *SHR*, 47 (1968), 53–71

Stell, G. 'Scottish burgh houses, 1560–1707', in *Town Houses and Structures in Medieval Scotland*, ed. A. T. Simpson and S. Stevenson (Scot. Burgh Survey, Glasgow, 1980)

Stevenson, D. *The Scottish Revolution, 1637–1644* (Newton Abbot, 1973)

—— 'The financing of the cause of the Covenants, 1638–51', *SHR*, 51 (1972), 89–123

Warden, A. J. *The Burgh Laws of Dundee* (1872)

Watson, C. B. B. 'List of owners of property in Edinburgh, 1635', *Bk. of Old Edinburgh Club*, 13 (1924), 93–145

Whatley, C. A. *That Important and Necessary Article: The Salt Industry and its Trade in Fife and Tayside, c.1570–1850* (Abertay Hist. Soc., 1984)

Whitehand, J. W. R. and Alauddin, K. 'The town plans of Scotland: some preliminary considerations', *Scot. Geog. Mag.*, 85 (1969), 109–21

Whittington, G. and Whyte, I. D. (eds.) *An Historical Geography of Scotland* (1983)

Whyte, I. D. *Agriculture and Society in Seventeenth-Century Scotland* (Edinburgh, 1979)

—— 'The growth of periodic market centres in Scotland, 1600–1707', *Scot. Geog. Mag.*, 95 (1979), 13–25

Wood, M. 'Edinburgh poll tax returns', *Bk. of Old Edinburgh Club*, 25 (1945), 90–126

—— 'Survey of the development of Edinburgh', *Bk. of Old Edinburgh Club*, 34 (1974), 23–56

Wormald, J. *Court, Kirk and Community: Scotland 1470–1625* (1981)

—— *Lords and Men in Scotland: Bonds of Manrent, 1442–1603* (Edinburgh, 1985)

Unpublished Theses

Anderson, A. H. 'The Burgh of the Canongate and its Court' (Edinburgh Univ. Ph.D., 1949)

Bennett, H. M. 'The Origins and Development of the Hand-Knitting Industry in Scotland' (Edinburgh Univ. Ph.D., 1982)

Brown, J. 'The Social, Political and Economic Influences of the Edinburgh Merchant Elite, 1600–38' (Edinburgh Univ. Ph.D., 1985)

Coutts, W. 'Social and Economic History of the Commissariot of Dumfries from 1600 to 1665 as disclosed by the Register of Testaments' (Edinburgh Univ. M. Litt., 1982)

di Folco, J. 'Aspects of Seventeenth-Century Social Life in Central and North Fife' (St. Andrews M.Phil., 1975)

Dodd, W. A. 'The Medieval Town Plan at Dumfries' (Edinburgh Univ. M.Phil., 1978)

Ferguson, J. A. 'A Comparative Study of Urban Society in Edinburgh [Canongate], London and Dublin in the Late Seventeenth Century' (St Andrews Ph.D., 1981)

Flett, I. 'The Conflict of Reformation and Democracy in the Geneva of Scotland [Dundee], 1443–1610' (St Andrews M.Phil., 1981)

Fox, R. C. 'The Morphological, Social and Functional Development of the Royal Burgh of Stirling, 1124–1881' (Strathclyde Univ. Ph.D., 1978)

Guy, I. 'The Scottish Export Trade 1460–1599, from the Exchequer Rolls' (St Andrews M.Phil., 1982)

McMillan, J. 'A Study of the Edinburgh Burgess Community and its Economic Activities, 1600–1680' (Edinburgh Univ. Ph.D., 1984)

MacNiven, D. 'Merchant and Trader in Early Seventeenth-Century Aberdeen' (Aberdeen Univ. M.Litt., 1977)

Pryde, G.S. 'Scottish Burgh Finances prior to 1707' (St Andrews Ph.D., 1928)

Shepherd, W. S. 'The Politics and Society of Glasgow, 1648–74' (Glasgow Univ. Ph.D., 1978)

Smith, L. M. 'Scotland and Cromwell: a Study in Early Modern Government' (Oxford Univ. D.Phil., 1979)

Stevenson, A. W. K. 'Trade between Scotland and the Low Countries in the Later Middle Ages' (Aberdeen Univ. Ph.D., 1982)

Torrie, E. P. D. 'The Gild of Dunfermline in the Fifteenth Century' (Edinburgh Univ. Ph.D., 1984)

Verschuur, M. B. 'Perth and the Reformation: Society and Reform, 1540–1560' (Glasgow Univ. Ph.D., 1985)

White, A. 'Religion, Politics and Society in Aberdeen, 1543–1593' (Edinburgh Univ. Ph.D., 1985)

Index

Abercrombie, Richard 114
Aberdeen 2, 19, 45, 181, 221,
223
  and country 11–12, 13, 19,
      23, 25, 34n73, 83–4,
      161, 166n90, 228
  and crown 59–60, 66–8, 71,
      81, 98, 101n76, 108–9
  and Reformation 12, 19, 55,
      62, 75n3, 86–99
  and Scottish Revolution 167,
      172, 182, 184
    resistance to 178–80, 185,
      186
  church 28, 88–9, 92
    patronage 88–9, 94–9
      passim
  crafts 13, 82, 97–8
    piety 88–9
    political agitation 10, 12,
      14, 26, 67, 97
    specialisation 237
  economic problems 7–8, 12
  elite 11–12, 82–3, 86, 90,
      98–9
  government 12, 14, 55, 82–3,
      90–2, 98–9
    noble patronage 12, 19,
      21–2, 62, 65, 76n22,
      83–6, 93–4, 105
    see also Huntly, earls of
  intellectual contacts 81, 87
  kirk session 86, 96, 98–9
  lawyers 14, 27
  merchant guild 15, 27,
      32n48–9, 67, 82
  merchants 11–12, 13, 16,
      126–7, 129, 141
    specialisation 11, 128
  occupational structure 11–12,
      13, 15, 17, 31n34, 127,
      224–32 *passim*, 237
  plague 182
  Protestant minority 75n3, 87,
      91–2, 96, 98–9
    regional centre 11, 17, 236,
      238, 239
    tax assessments 4–6, 17,
      72–3
    trade 7–8, 12, 81, 126–7,
      128, 226
      fluctuations 7–8, 180–1,
      187
    university 81, 88, 95
    violence 59, 84, 111
    wealth distribution 234–5,
      236
Aboyne 225, 230, 235
Aboyne, James Gordon, 2nd
    Lord 186
agricultural prices 152
agriculture 23, 148–50, 161,
    228
Albany, John, duke of 40
Amsterdam 128, 130, 131, 193
Angus, William Douglas, 10th
    earl 118
Annan 103
Anstruther 194, 225, 230, 238
apprentices 15–16, 25, 163, 207
Argyll, Archibald Campbell, 1st
    marquis 172
Argyll, Colin Campbell, 6th earl
    21
Armstrong, Thomas 157
Arnot, James 139
Arran, James Hamilton, 1st
    earl, duke of Châtelherault
    42–3, 59–60, 62, 84–6
Arran, James Stewart, earl of
    56–8, 63, 104, 113
Atholl, John Stewart, 5th earl 63
Ayr 5, 78n58, 110, 116
  and Scottish Revolution 178,
    186

Baillie, Robert 7
Banff 178, 180–1, 186

250

wealth distribution 38,
210–14, 234–6
see also apprentices, industry,
occupational structure,
urban specialisation and
individual towns
Crail 12, 32n39, 116, 178, 194
Crawford, David Lindsay, 11th
earl 111
and Aberdeen 22
and Dundee 56–8, 63, 110
and Forfar 110
Crawford, David Lindsay,
master 113
Crawford, William Lindsay,
18th earl 222
credit 3, 6–8, 18, 24, 30n19,
125, 154, 161–2
Crombie, John 119
Cromwell, Oliver 7, 210
crown 3
and burghs 19, 27, 55–75,
103
authoritarianism 58, 69–71,
74–5
economic regulation of burghs
73–4
see also privy council
financial demands 17, 69–73
see also taxation
interference in burgh
government 14, 17, 18,
21, 22, 40–3, 56–64,
71, 98, 101n76, 104,
107–8, 109, 174–6, 178
Croydie, Robert 158
Cullen, Alexander 107
Culross 139
Cumbria 158
Cupar 44, 111
and Scottish Revolution 178
crown interference 56–8
noble patronage 57

Dalkeith 223
occupational structure 224–40
passim
wealth distribution 234–5
Danzig 135
trade 129–34 *passim*, 193

David I 210, 202
David II 72
Deer 225, 230, 235
Denholm, John 184
Derby 157
de Rohan, Henri, duc 197–8
Dick, Alexander 87
Dick, Francis 135, 136
Dick, Sir William, of Braid 7,
16, 187, 212
business interests 24, 133,
136–7, 139, 140, 141,
209–10
Dieppe 128, 133, 137, 158, 159,
193
factors 135–6, 155, 160
domestic servants 222, 227
Donaldson, Adam 117–18
Dort 129
Dougal, John 137
Dougal, Michael 155, 156
Drummond, John 184
Dumbarton 5, 111
and Scottish Revolution 178,
187
Dumfries 15, 34n71, 78n58,
111, 147–63, 221
and crown 58, 63, 64
and hinterland 33, 34n73,
148–50, 159–60, 161
and Scottish Revolution
181–2
craftsmen 148, 150, 161–2,
163
merchant guild 148, 151, 161,
162
merchants 148–63 *passim*
noble patronage 103–4
trade 150–1, 154–8, 160–1,
226
wealth distribution 158, 163
see also merchants, partnerships
Dunbar 118, 139
Dundee 9, 21, 87, 119
and crown 58, 62, 63, 64, 69,
70
and Scottish Revolution 172,
181
craft agitation 10
merchants 23, 34n73

252

farming 148–50, 154, 159
rural investment 12, 23–4,
    34n73, 83–4, 138–9,
    161, 166n90
see also hinterland, satellite
    towns, suburbs
building 18, 27, 161, 200,
    202, 204–5, 214
control 204–5
rents 206–7, 209, 222
church 2, 8
and Reformation 94–9,
    101n76
finances 17, 205
patronage 88–9, 95–6
urban parish 28, 205
community of burgh 14,
    37–8, 84, 86, 89–90, 131
ceremony 38, 97
changing 16–17, 27–8, 48,
    51–2
see also kinship
courts 22, 27, 47, 49, 51, 91,
    92
and feuds 116–17, 119–20
and rival jurisdictions
    66–7, 75n58–9
commissariot 147
justice of peace 16, 33n52
economic regulation 14–15,
    26, 29, 72–5, 78n59,
    131, 168, 170
economy 4–13 *passim*
see craftsmen, industry,
    merchants,
    occupational structure
    and individual towns
elites 11–12, 13–14, 37–8,
    43, 81–3, 126–41 *passim*,
    163, 208–10, 219
see also merchant guild,
    oligarchy
gentry presence 9, 111,
    113–14, 119, 217n25,
    222, 223
government 11, 13–14, 16,
    27–8, 37, 40–4, 51,
    82–3, 90–2, 98–9,
    214–15
gentrification 22, 51, 64–5

oligarchy 13–14, 16, 37,
    51, 86, 90, 214–15
variations 13–14, 61
see also crown interference,
    noble patronage
inland 226
manufacturing 12–13, 38,
    139–40, 227–8, 239–41
see also industry,
    manufactories
noble patronage 12, 19–23,
    39–44, 48, 51, 56–9,
    64, 76n19, 81–6, 88,
    103–8
limitations 62
rival claims 39–43, 57–8,
    59, 109
occupational structure 3,
    12–13, 25, 38, 208–15,
    219–42
classifications 221–2, 229
sources 219, 221
ports 11, 12, 194, 226–7,
    233, 240, 241
see also Bo'ness, Leith
regional centres 5, 9, 11–12,
    23, 111, 226, 236, 238,
    239
seats of sheriffdoms 20, 223
social mobility 13–16, 18, 28,
    33n49, 82
social structure 8–17,
    passim
reshaping 25, 27–9, 74
variations 8–12, 61
topography 27, 84, 192–3,
    197–205
urban specialisation 11–12,
    128–9, 150, 151, 220–1,
    226–41 *passim*
see also industry, merchants
wealth distribution 9, 11, 38,
    127, 158, 206–14, 234–6
trade
coastal 11, 12, 194
inland 5, 11–12, 151, 154,
    195, 226
overseas 2–3, 4, 81, 126–38
    passim, 193–5
customs revenue 71–2